從一開始就是第一
全世界日銷80萬瓶
THE FIRST AND THE BEST
800,000 BOTTLES ENJOYED
WORLDWIDE EVERY DAY

No.

李錦記
香 HONG 港 KONG
LEE KUM KEE

www.angliss.com.hk

With a passion for food,

ANGLISS PEOPLE MAKE THE DIFFERENCE

Angliss Greater China is an integrated foodservice company providing more than 2,000 quality food products including meat, seafood, poultry, dairy, pastry, groceries, vegetables and gourmet fine foods to over 3,000 customers in the Greater China region.

With a team of 650 professionals and specialist operations in pastry (PastryGlobal), imported fine foods (Gourmet Cuisine) and groceries (Him Kee), Angliss Greater China is also well equipped with a 6000-tonne cold room with processing facilities, a fleet of 60 trucks to provide reliable and regular just-in-time delivery, state-of-the-art food processing equipment and test kitchens on-site to deliver value-added foods according to customer needs.

MICHELIN GUIDE

HONG KONG MACAU 2012

RESTAURANTS & HOTELS

米芝蓮指南
香港 / 澳門 2012
餐廳及酒店

DEAR READER

We are delighted to present the 2012 edition of the MICHELIN Guide Hong Kong Macau.

The success of our guide has had quite an impact. The quality of the restaurants in Hong Kong and Macau is constantly improving and our teams have updated the selection in order to fully reflect the richness and diversity of the two cities.

As part of our meticulous and highly confidential evaluation process, Michelin inspectors have spent the year conducting anonymous visits to Hong Kong and Macau restaurants and hotels.

The Michelin inspectors are the eyes and ears of our customers and thus their anonymity is key to ensuring they receive the same treatment as any other guest.

You will see that Michelin Stars are not our only awards – look out too for the Bib Gourmands ⊛. These are restaurants where one can enjoy a carefully prepared but simpler style of cooking for under $300. We first pointed out restaurants that provided quality meals at reasonable prices in the 1950s; this award became known as the red "R" in the '70s, before becoming the Bib Gourmand in the '90s. Quality and price remain the twin considerations and we are delighted to recommend so many good value establishments in Hong Kong and Macau, covering many different types of cuisine.

All the restaurants within this guide have been chosen first and foremost for the quality of their cooking. You'll find comprehensive information on over 200 dining establishments within these pages, ranging from noodle shops to internationally renowned restaurants. The diverse and varied selection bears testament to the rich and buoyant dining scene in Hong Kong and Macau, which now enjoy a worldwide reputation for the breadth and quality of their restaurants.

As well as restaurants, our team of independent inspectors has also chosen over 50 hotels. From the small and intimate to the grand and luxurious, these hotels underline Hong Kong and Macau's reputations for the quality of their accommodation, which can rival that of any city in the world. Adopting the same selection criteria and system of classification as in all our guides, these hotels are also listed in order of their level of comfort.

This guide is renewed and revised each year and we are committed to providing the most up to date information to ensure the success of your dining experience. This is why only this year's edition of the guide to Hong Kong and Macau is worthy of your complete trust.

We are always very interested to hear what you, our readers, think. Your opinions and suggestions matter greatly to us and help shape the guide, so please do get in touch.
Email us at michelinguide.hongkong-macau@cn.michelin.com

We wish you the very best in your Hong Kong and Macau hotel and dining experiences.

Bon appétit!

親愛的讀者

很高興向你宣佈：《米芝蓮指南 香港 澳門》2012年版隆重登場！

本指南取得的成功，為飲食界帶來了頗大的影響。 香港及澳門地區餐廳質素的不斷提升，我們的團隊盡一切努力地搜羅資訊，令指南內各式各樣的餐廳均經過精挑細選及更新，務求能充份表現兩個城市多姿多彩的美食佳餚。

米芝蓮評審員到訪香港及澳門的餐廳和酒店時不會透露身份，因此評選過程一絲不苟而且高度保密。 他們充當顧客的耳目，保持神秘身份能確保與任何其他顧客都享受相同遇待。

你會發現除了獲得米芝蓮星級評分的餐廳之外，我們也有「米芝蓮車胎人美食」（Bib Gourmand）的推介榜「☺」。 這些餐廳的烹調風格雖然簡單，但過程絕不馬虎，並以不高於 $300 的價錢便可享用。始於 1950 年代，我們就開創先河，推介以實惠價錢提供優質美食的餐廳；這些推介在 70 年代以紅 "R" 標示，並在 90 年代演變為「米芝蓮車胎人美食」（Bib Gourmand）。 我們依然以質素和價錢為考慮因素，並十分高興為大家推介香港和澳門多家價廉物美、涵蓋各種美食的餐廳。

米芝蓮指南介紹的餐廳都以高質素的廚藝掛帥，從小小的麵家到享譽全球的餐廳，我們為你帶來超過200間食肆最全面的資料。 港澳兩地的餐廳一向以質優和種類繁多而聞名，本指南內各式各樣的餐廳均經過精挑細選，能充份表現兩個城市多姿多彩的美食佳餚。

除了餐廳外，我們的獨立評審員亦選出了超過50家酒店。 這些酒店由小型親切到富麗堂皇兼收並蓄，彰顯香港和澳門兩地卓越住宿質素的美譽，能夠媲美全球任何城市。 稟承我們各大指南的挑選原則和分類系統，這些酒店以其舒適程度來順序排列。

本指南每年更新修訂，致力提供最新資訊，讓你的覓食旅程更美滿。 故此，是年版的香港及澳門指南絕對值得你的百分百信任。

我們樂意聆聽所有讀者的想法，包括你。 你的意見和提議對我們來説意義重大，並能協助我們把指南做得更好。 請經電郵與我們聯絡：

michelinguide.hongkong-macau@cn.michelin.com

祝你在香港和澳門擁有精彩、愉快的住宿和美食體驗！

Bon appétit!

THE MICHELIN GUIDE'S COMMITMENTS

"This volume was created at the turn of the century and will last at least as long".

This foreword to the very first edition of the MICHELIN guide, written in 1900, has become famous over the years and the guide has lived up to the prediction. It is read across the world and the key to its popularity is the consistency of its commitment to its readers, which is based on the following promises.

Anonymous inspections:

Our inspectors make regular and anonymous visits to restaurants and hotels to gauge the quality of products and services offered to an ordinary customer. They settle their own bill and may then introduce themselves and ask for more information about the establishment. Our readers' comments are also a valuable source of information, which we can then follow up with another visit of our own.

Independence:

Our choice of establishments is a completely independent one, made for the benefit of our readers alone. The decisions to be taken are discussed around the table by the inspectors and the editor. Inclusion in the guide is completely free of charge.

Selection and choice:

Our guide offers a selection of the best restaurants and hotels. This is only possible because all the inspectors rigorously apply the same methods.

Annual updates:

All the practical information, the classifications and awards are revised and updated every single year to give the most reliable information possible.

Consistency:

The criteria for the classifications are the same in every country covered by the MICHELIN guide.

...And our aim:

To do everything possible to make travel, holidays and eating out a pleasure, as part of Michelin's ongoing commitment to improving travel and mobility.

承諾

「這冊書於世紀交替時創辦，亦將繼續傳承下去。」

這是 1900 年米芝蓮首冊指南的前言，多年來享負盛名，並如預期般一直傳承下去。 指南在世界各地均大受歡迎，關鍵在其秉承一貫宗旨，履行對讀者的承諾。

匿名評審：

我們的評審員以匿名方式定期到訪餐廳和酒店，以一般顧客的身份對其產品和服務質素作出評估。 評審員自行結賬後，有時可能會介紹自己，並詢問更多關於餐廳的資料。 讀者的評語和推薦也是寶貴的資訊來源，我們隨後會根據讀者的推薦親身到訪。

獨立性：

餐廳的挑選完全是基於我們獨立的決定，純以讀者的利益為依歸。 經評審員和編輯一同討論後才作出決定，被指南收錄的餐廳完全不會被收取任何費用。

選擇：

全賴所有評審員都使用相同的嚴謹方法，指南才能提供一系列的最佳餐廳和酒店。

每年更新：

所有實用資訊、分類及評級每年都會修訂和更新，務求為讀者提供最可靠的資料。

一致性：

米芝蓮指南涉及的每個國家都用相同的分類準則。

…至於我們的目標：

盡全力令旅遊、放假及外出用膳成為一大樂事，實踐米芝蓮一貫優化旅遊和外出的承諾。

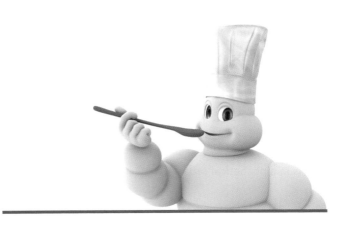

CONTENTS

目錄

THE MICHELIN GUIDE
OVER THE YEARS

Today the MICHELIN Guide and its famous red cover are known around the world. But who really knows the story behind this «travellers' bible» that has served people in many countries for many years? After winning over Europe and the United States, Bibendum – «The Michelin Man» – is now in Asia, and will relate the fantastic adventure that started in France, a long time ago...

The first steps

Everything began one fine day in 1900, when André and Édouard Michelin published a guide to be offered free of charge to motorists. It included information to help these pioneers (barely 3,500 automobiles were on the road) to travel around France: garages, town plans, sights to see, lodgings and restaurants, and so forth. The guide was an instant success and became the indispensable companion of all drivers and travellers, bar none.

On the strength of this success and driven on by the development of the motor car, *the Manufacture française* extended the scope of «the little book

with the Ared cover» to other European countries beginning in 1904, and a few years later (1908) published an adaptation of the *Guide France* in English.

A star is born

As of 1920, the guide was no longer free, but marketed for sale. Little by little, the practical information gave way to a wider selection of hotels and restaurants. The mysterious, daunting «Michelin inspector» was not in the picture at first. Rather, it was touring clubs and readers that contributed to the discerning selection of establishments.

The goal of officially identifying places «where one dines well» was materialized in 1926 by the *Étoile de Bonne Table* – the first Michelin star – soon to be followed by two and three-star establishments (1931 for the provinces and 1933 for Paris). The guide thus clearly focused on gastronomy and the quest for good restaurants became its real driving force.

In step with the times

During the Second World War, the guide did not appear. The post-war edition of 1945 did not use star ratings, which were applied again as of 1951, when conditions were more settled. Ever more successful, the guide was to cover all of Western Europe as of the 1960s. In 1982, *Main Cities of Europe* was published in English, marking Michelin's decidedly European dimension.

100 years young...

2000 was a winning year for Michelin: the guide celebrated its 100th anniversary and The Michelin Man was voted best corporate logo of the century!

More dynamic than ever, the «little red guide» took on new challenges and set off for the United States. The MICHELIN guide New York not only lived up to expectations, but the first edition was awarded the prize for «Best Restaurant Guide in the World».

The newest challenge: discovering the best restaurants in Asia. In autumn 2007, MICHELIN Tokyo guide was published with a great response. Tokyo is well known as one of the world's famous capitals of fine cuisine.

Twenty countries covered in Europe, three guides to US cities, one guide to Hong Kong and Macau and three guides to Japan (Kyoto Osaka Kobe Nara, Tokyo Yokohama Shonan and Bonnes Petites Tables) : in the third millennium, the MICHELIN guide confirms its international credentials. Just a glint in the eyes of the founders more than a century ago, The Michelin Man is now an international star to be proud of, carrying the Michelin tradition into the 21st century.

米芝蓮指南的歷史

今時今日，米芝蓮享譽國際，它的紅色封面家傳戶曉。多年來，這本「旅遊聖經」為很多國家的人提供寶貴資訊，但又有多少人知道它背後的故事呢？

The Michelin Man「米芝蓮車胎人」，在歐洲和美國駐足後，繼而來臨亞洲，將會延續當年在法國展開的探險旅程⋯

旅程的開始

1900 年晴朗的一天，André 和 Édouard Michelin 出版了一本指南，免費贈予駕車人士。當時法國只有約 3,500 部汽車行駛。指南涵蓋環遊法國的資訊：車房位置、城市地圖、觀光景點、住宿、餐廳等等。指南的出版取得空前成功，成為所有駕駛者和旅客的必需品。

適逢指南的空前成功和當時汽車業的迅速發展，米芝蓮公司便乘勝追擊，於 1904 年把這本「紅色指南」帶到其他歐洲國家。1908 年，這本「法國指南」更開始以英文出版。

星的誕生

自 1920 年起，指南開始在市面上發售，不再是免費贈閱。除了實用資訊外，指南日漸覆蓋更多酒店及餐廳資料。

在神秘的米芝蓮評審員出現之前，餐飲推介與選擇的訊息都是來自旅遊俱樂部和讀者。

直至 1926 年，米芝蓮首次引入星級評分制度，得到一星（*Étoile de Bonne Table*）的餐廳為最為美味的餐廳；其後，各省份和巴黎更分別於 1931 年和 1933 年實行二星及三星評分。此後指南便集中評選美食，致力搜羅一流餐廳的資訊。

歐洲之旅

指南業務蒸蒸日上，直至 1939 年戰爭爆發，一切運作暫停。1945 年業務回復正常，從 1950 年起，新一代指南陸續面世：由 1952 年的西班牙到 1994 年的瑞士指南，期間更於不同的歐洲國家出版。1982 年，米芝蓮出版歐洲主要城市指南（*Main Cities of Europe guide*），確立其歐洲主導地位。

長青一百歲

2000年是米芝蓮的勝利年，不但是指南出版的百週年紀念，The Michelin Man「米芝蓮車胎人」更獲選為世紀最佳公司標誌！這本「紅色小指南」比以往更顯積極，不斷迎接新挑戰，並進軍美國市場。紐約指南非但不負眾望，更於初版被譽為「世界上最佳餐廳指南」。 其後，三藩市指南相繼出版，而今年則可見證第一本芝加哥指南的誕生。

我們最新的挑戰是：搜尋全亞洲最頂尖的餐廳。東京是享負盛名的世界美食之都，2007年秋季，米芝蓮東京指南隆重面世，並得到極佳的回響。

踏入二十一世紀，米芝蓮指南已涵蓋多個國家，包括歐洲二十個國家的指南、三個美國城市的指南、香港暨澳門指南、三本日本指南（京都/大阪/神户/奈良、東京/橫濱/湘南和Bonnes Petites Tables），其國際地位實在毋庸置疑。 一個多世紀前，始創人的一絲靈感造就了The Michelin Man「米芝蓮車胎人」的誕生。 今天，「米芝蓮車胎人」是令人引以為榮的國際巨星，引領米芝蓮於二十一世紀與時並進。

HOW TO USE
THIS RESTAURANT GUIDE
如何使用餐廳指南

Map number / coordinates
地圖號碼 / 座標

New entry in the guide
新增推介

Cuisine type
菜式種類

Name of restaurant
餐廳名稱

Stars for good food
美食星級

✿ to ✿✿✿

Bib Gourmand
(Inspectors' favourite
for good value)
(評審員的推介榜)
😊

Restaurant classification
according to comfort
餐廳 — 以舒適程度分類

🍜	Simple shop
	簡單的食店
✗	Quite comfortable
	舒適
✗✗	Comfortable
	頗舒適
✗✗✗	Very comfortable
	十分舒適
✗✗✗✗	Top class comfort
	高級舒適
✗✗✗✗✗	Luxury
	豪華

Particularly pleasant if in red
紅色代表上佳

Noodles/麵食   ● MAP/地圖 12/B-2

Sun Sin NEW
新仙清湯腩咖喱專門店

😊

🍜 💲 ✗🍴

Never mind directions – just follow your nose and those enticing beef aromas will lead you to this small noodle shop in Yau Ma Tei's busiest street. Sun Sin is famous for its well-priced beef brisket in a clear soup and for the curry with its secret recipe. The owner buys high quality beef each morning from a local supplier and it's then cooked for hours. As she sells over three hundred portions each day, don't be surprised when it's all gone.

就算不辨方向，只要跟著你的鼻子，誘人的牛腩香氣就會把你帶到這家位於油麻地最繁忙地段的小麵店。新仙以價廉物美的清湯腩和秘製咖喱聞名。店主每天早上向本地肉商購入高質素的牛腩，並耗時數小時烹煮，每天賣出超過 300 碗，還隨時售罄。

■ ADDRESS/地址
TEL. 2332 6872
37 Portland Street,
Yau Ma Tei, Kowloon
九龍油麻地砵蘭街37號

■ OPENING HOURS, LAST ORDER
營業時間，最後點菜時間
11:30-01:00

■ PRICE/價錢
à la carte/點菜 $ 25-90

248

Cantonese/粵菜   MAP/地圖 22/D-3

Man Wah
文華廳

❀

≤ 🖘 ⟷14 ◐🍴 🍇

Man Wah exudes a luxuriously intimate yet traditional feel. Tables just off the entrance may have the better views, but everyone can appreciate the décor: brass lanterns hang from the wood ceiling and the room is framed by an ornate screen. The Peking duck is a classic, as is the stir-fried lobster with egg white and scallop mousse. Equally good is pork neck with Kuei Hua flavoured pear, and steamed garoupa with ginger, crabmeat and egg white.

文華廳散發著一種傳統高貴典雅的氣質。雖然近門口的餐桌享有較佳的景觀，但所有食客都可以欣賞這裡的裝潢：木天花板吊著黃銅燈籠，及周邊的華麗屏幕。這裡的北京片皮鴨及海棠龍蝦是名副其實的經典美食，桂花梨黑醋脆豬肉及酥薑珊瑚蒸星斑球亦不遑多讓。

■ ADDRESS/地址
TEL. 2825 4003
25F, Mandarin Oriental Hotel,
5 Connaught Road, Central
中環干諾道中5號文華東方酒店25樓
www.mandarinoriental.com/hongkong

■ OPENING HOURS, LAST ORDER
營業時間・最後點菜時間
Lunch/午膳 12:00-14:30 (L.O.)
Dinner/晚膳 18:30-22:30 (L.O.)

■ PRICE/價錢
Lunch/午膳   set/套餐 $468-888
         à la carte/點菜 $ 320-1,100
Dinner/晚膳 set/套餐 $588-988
         à la carte/點菜 $ 320-1,100

200

ⓢ	Cash only 只收現金
👤	Wheelchair access 輪椅適用
🏠	Terrace dining 陽台用餐
≤	With a view 有景觀
🖘	Valet parking 代客泊車
🅿	Car park 停車場
⟷25	Private room with maximum capacity 私人房間及容納人數
🚃	Counter 櫃檯式
◐🍴	Reservations required 需訂座
⊘🍴	Reservations not accepted 不可訂座
🍇	Interesting wine list 供應優良的酒類

HOW TO USE
THIS HOTEL GUIDE
如何使用酒店指南

Map number / coordinates
地圖號碼 / 座標

New entry in the guide
新增推介

Name of hotel
酒店名稱

Hotel classification according to comfort
酒店 — 根據舒適程度分類

MAP/地圖　15/D-1

Icon
唯港薈

NEW

🏠 Quite comfortable
頗舒適

🏠🏠 Comfortable
舒適

🏠🏠🏠 Very comfortable
十分舒適

🏠🏠🏠🏠 Top class comfort
高級舒適

🏠🏠🏠🏠🏠 Luxury
豪華

Particularly pleasant if in red
紅色代表上佳

A team of celebrated designers, including Rocco Yim Sir Terence Conran and William Lim, were brought together to create this most chic of hotels, which is owned and run by the Hong Kong Polytechnic University. The hotel's style credentials are obvious, from the sweeping modern staircase and the 'vertical garden' to the coolly contemporary bedrooms with floor to ceiling windows. The students provide enthusiastic and courteous service.

342

RESTAURANTS/ 餐廳

Recommended/推薦		Also/其他
Above & Beyond/ 天外天	XxX	Green
		The Market

匯聚著名設計師，包括嚴迅奇、泰倫斯·康藍爵士（Sir Terence Conran）和林偉而等，攜手打造出這間由香港理工大學營運、最新最潮的酒店。她的設計風格，由令人驚嘆的現代化樓梯和垂直花園，到設計型格時尚、內有全幅落地玻璃窗的客房，都極其鮮明。酒店的服務由學生負責，十分殷勤有禮。

■ ADDRESS/地址
TEL. 3400 1000
FAX. 3400 1001
17 Science Museum Road,
East Tsim Sha Tsui
九龍尖東科學館道17號
www.hotel-icon.com

■ ROOMS AND SUITES/客房及套房
Rooms/客房 ＝236
Suites/套房 ＝26
■ PRICE/價錢
� $2,200-4,100
♥♥ $2,200-4,100
Suites/套房 $3,000-5,100

343

Restaurant information
餐廳資料

Hotel symbols
酒店標誌

♿	Wheelchair access	輪椅適用
◁	With a view	有景觀
🅿♂	Valet parking	代客泊車
🅿	Car park	室外停車場
🚗	Garage	室內停車場
⇗	Non smoking bedrooms	非吸煙臥室
🏃	Conference rooms	會議室
⋟ ⊠	Outdoor/Indoor Swimming pool	室外 / 室內游泳池
Spa	Spa	水療
⅃	Exercise room	健身室
⊜⊜⊟	Casino	娛樂場

YOU ALREADY KNOW THE MICHELIN GUIDE, NOW FIND OUT ABOUT THE MICHELIN GROUP

The Michelin Adventure

It all started with rubber balls! This was the product made by a small company based in Clermont-Ferrand that André and Edouard Michelin inherited, back in 1880. The brothers quickly saw the potential for a new means of transport and their first success was the invention of detachable pneumatic tyres for bicycles. However, the automobile was to provide the greatest scope for their creative talents. Throughout the 20th century, Michelin never ceased developing and creating ever more reliable and high-performance tyres, not only for vehicles ranging from trucks to F1 but also for underground transit systems and aeroplanes.

From early on, Michelin provided its customers with tools and services to facilitate mobility and make travelling a more pleasurable and more frequent experience. As early as 1900, the Michelin Guide supplied motorists with a host of useful information related to vehicle maintenance, accommodation and restaurants, and was to become a benchmark for good food. At the same time, the Travel Information Bureau offered travellers personalised tips and itineraries.

The publication of the first collection of roadmaps, in 1910, was an instant hit! In 1926, the first regional guide to France was published, devoted to the principal sites of Brittany, and before long each region of France had its own Green Guide. The collection was later extended to more far-flung destinations, including New York in 1968 and Taiwan in 2011.

In the 21st century, with the growth of digital technology, the challenge for Michelin maps and guides is to continue to develop alongside the company's tyre activities. Now, as before, Michelin is committed to improving the mobility of travellers.

MICHELIN TODAY

WORLD NUMBER ONE TYRE MANUFACTURER
- 70 production sites in 18 countries
- 111,000 employees from all cultures and on every continent
- 6,000 people employed in research and development

Moving
for a world

Moving forward means developing tyres with better road grip and shorter braking distances, whatever the state of the road.

CORRECT TYRE PRESSURE

RIGHT PRESSURE

- Safety
- Longevity
- Optimum fuel consumption

-0,5 bar

- Durability reduced by 20% (– 8,000 km)

-1 bar

- Risk of blowouts
- Increased fuel consumption
- Longer braking distances on wet surfaces

forward together
where mobility is safer

It also involves helping motorists take care of their safety and their tyres. To do so, Michelin organises "Fill Up With Air" campaigns all over the world to remind us that correct tyre pressure is vital.

WEAR

DETECTING TYRE WEAR

The legal minimum depth of tyre tread is 1.6mm.

Tyre manufacturers equip their tyres with tread wear indicators, which are small blocks of rubber moulded into the base of the main grooves at a depth of 1.6mm.

Tyres are the only point of contact between vehicle and road.

The photo below shows the actual contact zone.

NEW TYRE

WORN TYRE
(1,6 mm tread)

If the tread depth is less than 1.6mm, tyres are considered to be worn and dangerous on wet surfaces.

Moving forward
means sustainable mobility

By 2050, Michelin aims to cut the quantity of raw materials used in its tyre manufacturing process by half and to have developed renewable energy in its facilities. The design of MICHELIN tyres has already saved billions of litres of fuel and, by extension, billions of tonnes of CO2.

Similarly, Michelin prints its maps and guides on paper produced from sustainably managed forests and is diversifying its publishing media by offering digital solutions to make travelling easier, more fuel efficient and more enjoyable!

The group's whole-hearted commitment to eco-design on a daily basis is demonstrated by ISO 14001 certification.

Like you, Michelin is committed to preserving our planet.

Chat with Bibendum

Go to
www.michelin.com/corporate/fr
Find out more about Michelin's
history and the latest news.

QUIZ

Michelin develops tyres for all types of vehicles. See if you can match the right tyre with the right vehicle…

Solution : A-6 / B-4 / C-2 / D-1 / E-3 / F-7 / G-5

你對米芝蓮指南已經耳熟能詳
現在齊來認識一下米芝蓮集團

米芝蓮的探險歷程

一切從橡膠開始！早在1880年，由米芝蓮兄弟安德烈(André)和愛德華(Edouard)繼承的小型企業，是一家位於法國克萊蒙費朗(Clermont-Ferrand)，以橡膠產品為主的公司。這兩兄弟很快就意識到新型運輸方式的發展潛力，而他們第一個事業的高峰，正是創造出供腳踏車使用的可拆除充氣式輪胎。然而，汽車才是提供他們能夠充份發揮創意的領域。

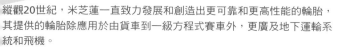

縱觀20世紀，米芝蓮一直致力發展和創造出更可靠和更高性能的輪胎，其提供的輪胎除應用於由貨車到一級方程式賽車外，更廣及地下運輸系統和飛機。

自早期起，米芝蓮已為顧客提供實用的工具和服務，以促進流動性，讓旅遊成為更愉快和更頻密的體驗。早於1900年，米芝蓮指南已為駕駛者提供大量實用性的資訊，內容涵蓋車輛維修、住宿和餐廳等，並成為尋找美食的基準。同時，有關旅遊資訊部門亦為旅客提供個人化的旅遊心得和行程安排。

1910年，米芝蓮出版了第一套公路地圖集，得到空前成功。1926，第一本法國地區指南的推出，專門介紹布列塔尼(Brittany)的主要旅遊點；此後不久，米芝蓮更為法國各地區出版了專屬的綠色指南(Green Guide)。這個系列後來更擴展其版圖，發展至更遠的地區，包括1968年的紐約版和2011年的台灣版。

時至21世紀，面對數碼科技發展一日千里，米芝蓮地圖和指南的挑戰，是要與集團輪胎業務同步發展。一如既往，米芝蓮致力於為提升旅客的移動性而努力不懈。

米芝蓮集團的現況

全球第一輪胎製造商
- 18個國家70個生產基地
- 來自世界各地擁有不同文化背景的111,000名員工
- 6,000名參與研究和開發的人員

共同為世界更安

共同努力的目標,意味著要生產出有更好
抓地性能和更短剎車距離的輪胎,並無懼
任何路面情況。

適當輪胎氣壓

適當胎壓

安全
耐用
最佳耗油量

- 0.5 巴

輪胎壽命減少20%

(- 8,000公里)

- 1 巴

有爆胎危機

增加耗油量

在濕滑地面的剎車
距離增長

全的移動性而努力

米芝蓮更致力於協助駕駛者關注他們自身和輪胎的安全,於全球推廣與正確胎壓相關的活動,不斷提醒駕駛者輪胎保養的重要性。

磨損

留意輪胎磨損情況

輪胎法定的胎紋深度最少要有1.6毫米。輪胎製造商都會在其輪胎上刻有輪胎磨耗標誌,那是模製於主槽紋中的一小塊橡膠,其深度正是1.6毫米。

輪胎是車輛與路面之間的唯一接觸點。

下面的圖片顯示出實際的接觸區域。

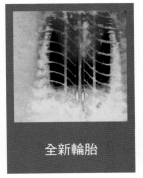

全新輪胎

磨損輪胎
(1.6 毫米胎紋)

如胎紋深度少於1.6毫米,該輪胎則被視為過度磨損,在濕滑路面使用十分危險。

向前邁進，即可持續發展的移動性

創新與環境

在2050之前，米芝蓮的目標是將其用於製造輪胎的原材料數量減半，並開發可再生能源。米芝蓮輪胎的設計，已成功節省數以十億公升的燃料，並減少排放由此產生的數以十億噸計二氧化碳。

同樣，米芝蓮所印製的地圖和指南，均採用可持續發展式管理林木而來的紙張，並致力令其出版媒體之多元化，提供數碼化的方案，令旅遊更容易、燃料使用更有效率和更多樂趣。

集團時刻全力投入符合環保的設計，所獲得的ISO14001的認證，可謂實至名歸。

米芝蓮跟你攜手同心，一齊為保護我們的地球而努力。

的欲與米芝蓮車胎人(Bibendum)

分享更多米芝蓮的歷史和最新消息。

瀏覽：http://www.michelin.com.hk

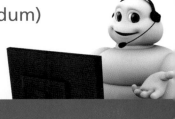

小測試

米芝蓮生產各種類型的交通工具輪胎，
看看你能否為不同的交通工具和輪胎作出配對⋯

HONG KONG
香港

RESTAURANTS
餐廳

STARRED RESTAURANTS

Within this selection, we have highlighted a number of restaurants for their particularly good cooking. When awarding one, two or three Michelin Stars there are a number of factors we consider: the quality and compatibility of the ingredients, the technical skill and flair that goes into their preparation, the clarity and combination of flavours, the value for money and above all, the taste. Equally important is the ability to produce excellent cooking not once but time and time again. Our inspectors make as many visits as necessary, so that you can be sure of the quality and consistency.

A two or three star restaurant has to offer something very special that separates it from the rest. Three stars – our highest award – are given to the very best.

Cuisines in any style of restaurant and of any nationality are eligible for a star. The decoration, service and comfort levels have no bearing on the award.

星級餐廳

在這系列的選擇裡，我們特意指出菜式上佳的餐廳。 給予一、二或三粒米芝蓮星時，我們考慮到以下因素：材料的質素和相容性、烹調技巧和特色、氣味濃度和組合、價錢是否相宜，以及味道。同樣重要的是能夠持續提供美食。 我們的評審員會因應需要而多次到訪，所以讀者可肯定食物品質和一致性。

二或三星餐廳必有獨特之處，比其他餐廳更出眾。最高評級 -三星- 只會給予最好的餐廳。

不論餐廳的風格如何，供應哪個國家的菜式，都可獲星級。 餐廳陳設、服務及舒適程度亦不會影響評級。

Exceptional cuisine, worth a special journey.
出類拔萃的菜餚，值得專程到訪。

One always eats here extremely well, sometimes superbly. Distinctive dishes are precisely executed, using superlative ingredients.

食客可在這裡享用美味的菜餚，有時令人更讚不絕口。獨特的菜式以最高級的材料精密地烹調。

Caprice		XxXX	French 法式	85
L'Atelier de Joël Robuchon	🍃	XX	French contemporary 時尚法式	169
Lung King Heen 龍景軒		XxxX	Cantonese 粵菜	194
8½ Otto e Mezzo - Bombana	🍃	XxX	Italian 意式	221

Excellent cuisine, worth a detour.
傑出美食，值得繞道前往。

Skilfully and carefully crafted dishes of outstanding quality.

有技巧地精心烹調菜餚，品質優秀。

Amber		XxxX	French contemporary 時尚法式	74
Bo Innovation	🍃	XxX	Fusion 多國菜	80
Celebrity Cuisine 名人坊		XX	Cantonese 粵菜	87
Lei Garden (Mong Kok) 利苑酒家 (旺角)	🍃	XX	Cantonese 粵菜	177
Ming Court 明閣		XxxX	Cantonese 粵菜	205
Pierre		XxxX	French contemporary 時尚法式	226
Shang Palace 香宮	🍃	XxX	Cantonese 粵菜	236
Spoon by Alain Ducasse	🍃	XxxX	French 法式	242
Sun Tung Lok 新同樂		XxX	Chinese 中式	249
Yè Shanghai (Kowloon) 夜上海 (九龍)	🍃	XxX	Shanghainese 上海菜	301

NEW : New entry in the guide/ 新增推介

🍃 : Restaurant promoted to a Bib Gourmand or Star/ 評級有所晉升的餐廳

A very good restaurant in its category.
同類別中出眾的餐廳。

A place offering cuisine prepared to a consistently high standard.
持續高水準菜式的地方。

DISCOVERING
THE SECRETS
OF THE BEST CHEFS
S NOT SO DIFFICULT.
JUST TAKE A SEAT
AT THEIR TABLE.

THE FINE DINING WATERS

BIB GOURMAND

This symbol indicates our inspectors' favourites for good value. These restaurants offer quality cooking for $ 300 or less (price of a 3 course meal excluding drinks).

這標誌表示評審員認為價錢合理而美味的餐廳。300 元或以下便可享用優質美食（三道菜式的價錢，不包括飲料）。

Bombay Dreams		XX	Indian 印度菜	81
Chan Kan Kee Chiu Chow 陳勤記鹵鵝飯店	NEW	X	Chiu Chow 潮洲菜	90
Chuen Cheung Kui (Causeway Bay) 泉章居（銅鑼灣）		X	Hakkanese 客家菜	96
Chuen Cheung Kui (Mong Kok) 泉章居（旺角）		X	Hakkanese 客家菜	97
Crystal Jade La Mian Xiao Long Bao (Kowloon Bay) 翡翠拉麵小籠包（九龍灣）		X	Chinese 中式	100
Crystal Jade La Mian Xiao Long Bao (TST) 翡翠拉麵小籠包（尖沙咀）		X	Chinese 中式	101
Crystal Jade La Mian Xiao Long Bao (Wan Chai) 翡翠拉麵小籠包（灣仔）		X	Chinese 中式	102
Da Ping Huo 大平伙		X	Sichuan 川菜	105
Dong Lai Shun 東來順		XX	Chinese 中式	111
Dragon Inn 容龍	⤴	XX	Seafood 海鮮	113

NEW : New entry in the guide/ 新增推介

⤴ : Restaurant promoted to a Bib Gourmand or Star/ 評級有所晉升的餐廳

RESTAURANTS BY AREA
餐廳 — 以地區分類

Hong Kong Island/香港島

Admiralty/金鐘

Café Gray Deluxe		XX	European contemporary 時尚歐陸式	83
Domani		XX	Italian 意式	110
Golden Leaf 金葉庭		XxX	Cantonese 粵菜	134
Lobster Bar and Grill 龍蝦吧		XX	Seafood 海鮮	189
Nicholini's 意寧谷		XxxX	Italian contemporary 時尚意式	211
Petrus 珀翠	✿	XXXX	French 法式	225
Summer Palace 夏宮	✿	XxX	Cantonese 粵菜	246
Thai Basil		X	Thai 泰式	264
Yè Shanghai (Admiralty) 夜上海（金鐘）		XxX	Shanghainese 上海菜	300

Causeway Bay/銅鑼灣

Chuen Cheung Kui (Causeway Bay) 泉章居（銅鑼灣）	⊕	X	Hakkanese 客家菜	96
Din Tai Fung (Causeway Bay) 鼎泰豐（銅鑼灣）		X	Shanghainese 上海菜	108
Fan Tang 飯堂		XxX	Chinese 中式	118
Farm House 農圃		XX	Cantonese 粵菜	119
Forum 富臨	✿	XX	Cantonese 粵菜	124
Fu Sing (Causeway Bay) 富聲（銅鑼灣）	⊕	XxX	Cantonese 粵菜	128
Hainan Shaoye (Causeway Bay) 海南少爺（銅鑼灣） NEW		X	Singaporean 星加坡菜	140
Hakka Yé Yé (Causeway Bay) 客家爺爺（銅鑼灣） NEW		X	Hakkanese 客家菜	141

NEW : New entry in the guide/ 新增推介
⁹⁵ : Restaurant promoted to a Bib Gourmand or Star/ 評級有所晉升的餐廳

Central/中環

| Le 188° | | | ✕✕✕ | European contemporary 時尚歐陸式 | 182 |
| Yuè 粵 | NEW | ✿ | ✕✕ | Cantonese 粵菜 | 302 |

Quarry Bay/鰂魚涌

Noodle Concepts
| 麵創坊 | NEW | | ✕ | Noodles 麵食 | 213 |
| Tulsi 羅勒 | NEW | ☺ | ✕ | Indian 印度菜 | 284 |

Sai Wan Ho/西灣河

Hin Ho Curry (Sai Wan Ho)
| 恆河咖喱屋（西灣河） | | ☺ | 🍴 | Indian 印度菜 | 146 |

Sai Ying Pun/西營盤

Ba Yi 巴依 NEW ✕ Xinjiang 新疆菜 76

Shau Kei Wan/筲箕灣

Hin Ho Curry (Shau Kei Wan)
| 恆河咖喱屋（筲箕灣） | | ✿ | 🍴 | Indian 印度菜 | 147 |
| On Lee 安利 | | | 🍴 | Noodles 麵食 | 219 |

Sheung Wan/上環

Chan Kan Kee Chiu Chow
| 陳勤記鹵鵝飯店 | NEW | ☺ | ✕ | Chiu Chow 潮洲菜 | 90 |
| Lin Heung Kui 蓮香居 | | ☺ | 🍴 | Cantonese 粵菜 | 185 |

Sang Kee Congee & Noodles (Sheung Wan)
| 生記清湯牛腩麵家（上環） | | | 🍴 | Noodles and Congee 粥麵 | 231 |

Sun Yuen Hing Kee
新園興記		☺	🍴	Cantonese Roast Meats 燒味	250
Tim's Kitchen 桃花源小廚		✿	✕✕✕	Cantonese 粵菜	276
Trattoria Doppio Zero NEW			✕	Italian 意式	280
Wagyu Kaiseki Den		✿	✕✕	Japanese 日式	286

Tai Koo Shing/太古城

Grand Cuisine Shanghai Kitchen
| 君頤上海小廚 | NEW | | ✕ | Shanghainese 上海菜 | 137 |

Peking Garden (Tai Koo Shing)
| 北京樓（太古城） | | | ✕✕✕ | Pekingese 京菜 | 224 |

Tin Hau/天后

Wan Chai/灣仔

Cheung Sha Wan/長沙灣

Hung Hom/紅磡

Jordan/佐敦

Kowloon Bay/九龍灣

Crystal Jade La Mian Xiao Long Bao (Kowloon Bay)
翡翠拉麵小籠包 (九龍灣)　ⓐ　X　　Chinese 中式　　　　　　100

Lei Garden (Kowloon Bay)
利苑酒家 (九龍灣)　❀　XX　　Cantonese 粵菜　　　　　　175

Shanghai Xiao Nan Guo (Kowloon Bay)
上海小南國 (九龍灣)　🐷　ⓐ　XX　Shanghainese 上海菜　　　235

Siu Shun Village Cuisine
肇順名匯河鮮專門店　　　　X　　Shun Tak 順德菜　　　　　　240

Tasty (Kowloon Bay)
正斗粥麵專家 (九龍灣)　ⓐ　X　　Noodles and Congee 粥麵　263

Kwun Tong/觀塘

Dragon King (Kwun Tong)
龍皇 (觀塘)　　　NEW　　XX　　Cantonese 粵菜　　　　　　114

Lei Garden (Kwun Tong)
利苑酒家 (觀塘)　　　　XX　　Cantonese 粵菜　　　　　　176

Shanghai Wing Wah
上海榮華川菜館　　NEW　🍜　　Chinese 中式　　　　　　　234

Mong Kok/旺角

Chuen Cheung Kui (Mong Kok)
泉章居 (旺角)　　　ⓐ　X　　Hakkanese 客家菜　　　　　　97

Fung Shing (Mong Kok)
鳳城 (旺角)　　　　　X　　Cantonese 粵菜　　　　　　　127

Good Hope Noodles
好旺角麵家　🐷　　ⓐ　🍜　Noodles and Congee 粥麵　　136

Lei Garden (Mong Kok)
利苑酒家 (旺角)　🐷　❀❀　XX　Cantonese 粵菜　　　　　177

Malaysia Port Klang Cuisine
馬拉盞星馬美食　　　　🍜　　Malaysian 馬拉菜　　　　　198

Ming Court 明閣　　　❀❀　XXX　Cantonese 粵菜　　　　　205

One Dim Sum 一點心　　❀　🍜　Dim Sum 點心　　　　　　217

Tim Ho Wan (Mong Kok)
添好運 (旺角)　　　❀　🍜　Dim Sum 點心　　　　　　274

Tokoro　　　　　　XX　Japanese 日式　　　　　　　278

Wing Hap Lung 永合隆　ⓐ　🍜　Cantonese Roast Meats 燒味　289

Prince Edward/太子

Lan Yuen Chee Koon 蘭苑饍館 NEW ⊛ 🍴	Cantonese 粵菜			168
Superior Rice Roll Pro Shop 第一腸粉專賣店 NEW ⊛ 🍴	Dim Sum 點心			251

San Po Kong/新蒲崗

Tak Lung 得龍 ⊛ 🍴	Cantonese 粵菜			257

Sham Shui Po/深水埗

Lau Sum Kee (Fuk Wing Street) 劉森記麵家 (福榮街) 🥢 ⊛ 🍴	Noodles and Congee 粥麵			170
Tam's Yunnan Noodles (Sham Shui Po) 譚仔雲南米線 (深水埗) ⊛ 🍴	Noodles 麵食			258
Thai Chiu 泰潮 ⊛ 🍴	Thai 泰式			265
Tim Ho Wan (Sham Shui Po) 添好運 (深水埗) ✿ 🍴	Dim Sum 點心			275
Yung Kee Siu Choi Wong 容記小菜王 🍴	Chinese 中式			305

Tsim Sha Tsui/尖沙咀

Above & Beyond 天外天 NEW ✗✗✗	Cantonese 粵菜			70
Ah Yat Harbour View 阿一海景飯店 NEW ✿ ✗✗✗	Cantonese 粵菜			72
Al Molo NEW ✗✗	Italian 意式			73
Angelini ✗✗✗	Italian 意式			75
BLT Steak ✗	Steakhouse 扒房			79
Celestial Court 天寶閣 ✗✗	Cantonese 粵菜			88
Chesa 瑞樵閣 ✗✗	Swiss 瑞士菜			92
Crystal Jade La Mian Xiao Long Bao (TST) 翡翠拉麵小籠包 (尖沙咀) ⊛ ✗	Chinese 中式			101
Cuisine Cuisine at The Mira 國金軒 (The Mira) ✿ ✗✗✗	Cantonese 粵菜			103
Din Tai Fung (Tsim Sha Tsui) 鼎泰豐 (尖沙咀) ✿ ✗	Shanghainese 上海菜			109
Dong Lai Shun 東來順 ⊛ ✗✗	Chinese 中式			111

Red Seasons (Lam Tei)					
季季紅 (藍地)		⊛	✗	Cantonese 粵菜	228
Tai Wing Wah 大榮華		⊛	✗	Cantonese 粵菜	255
Yue Kee 裕記	♨	⊛	✗	Cantonese 粵菜	303

RESTAURANTS BY CUISINE TYPE
餐廳 — 以菜式分類

Cantonese/粵菜

NEW : New entry in the guide/ 新增推介
❀ : Restaurant promoted to a Bib Gourmand or Star/ 評級有所晉升的餐廳

Yung Kee 鏞記			XX	Central/中環	304

Cantonese Roast Meats/燒味

Joi Hing 再興				Wan Chai/灣仔	161
Keung Kee Meat Shop (Wan Chai) 強記飯店 (灣仔) NEW				Wan Chai/灣仔	163
Sun Yuen Hing Kee 新園興記	🍴			Sheung Wan/上環	250
Wing Hap Lung 永合隆	🍴			Mong Kok/旺角	289

Chinese/中式

Crystal Jade La Mian Xiao Long Bao (Kowloon Bay) 翡翠拉麵小籠包 (九龍灣)	🍴	X		Kowloon Bay/九龍灣	100
Crystal Jade La Mian Xiao Long Bao (TST) 翡翠拉麵小籠包 (尖沙咀)	🍴	X		Tsim Sha Tsui/尖沙咀	101
Crystal Jade La Mian Xiao Long Bao (Wan Chai) 翡翠拉麵小籠包 (灣仔)	🍴	X		Wan Chai/灣仔	102
Dong Lai Shun 東來順	🍴	XX		Tsim Sha Tsui/尖沙咀	111
Fan Tang 飯堂		XXX		Causeway Bay/銅鑼灣	118
Golden Valley 駿景軒	✿	XXX		Happy Valley/跑馬地	135
Kwan Cheuk Heen 君綽軒		XXX		North Point/北角	165
Lei Bistro 利小館		X		Causeway Bay/銅鑼灣	171
Nanhai No.1 南海一號	✿	XX		Tsim Sha Tsui/尖沙咀	208
Shanghai Wing Wah 上海榮華川菜館 NEW				Kwun Tong/觀塘	234
Sun Tung Lok 新同樂	✿✿	XXX		Tsim Sha Tsui/尖沙咀	249
The Chinese Restaurant 凱悅軒		XXX		Tsim Sha Tsui/尖沙咀	268
Wing Lai Yuen 詠藜園 NEW		X		Hung Hom/紅磡	290
Xi Yan Sweets 囍宴 甜‧藝	🐝	🍴 X		Wan Chai/灣仔	295
Yung Kee Siu Choi Wong 容記小菜王				Sham Shui Po/深水埗	305

Chiu Chow/潮洲菜

Chan Kan Kee Chiu Chow 陳勤記鹵鵝飯店 NEW	🍴	X		Sheung Wan/上環	90
Chiu Chow Garden (Tsuen Wan) 潮江春 (荃灣)		XX		West New Territories/新界西部	95
Hung's Delicacies 阿鴻小吃	✿			North Point/北角	155

Congee/粥品

Delicious Congee 和味生滾粥店		Jordan/佐敦	106
Trusty Congee King 靠得住		Wan Chai/灣仔	281

Dim Sum/點心

Dim Sum 譽滿坊		Happy Valley/跑馬地	107
One Dim Sum 一點心		Mong Kok/旺角	217
Superior Rice Roll Pro Shop 第一腸粉專賣店 NEW		Prince Edward/太子	251
Tim Ho Wan (Mong Kok) 添好運 (旺角)		Mong Kok/旺角	274
Tim Ho Wan (Sham Shui Po) 添好運 (深水埗)		Sham Shui Po/深水埗	275

Dumplings/餃子

Dumpling Yuan (Central) 餃子園 (中環)		Central/中環	115
Wang Fu 王府		Central/中環	287

European/歐陸式

Hugo's 希戈		Tsim Sha Tsui/尖沙咀	153

European contemporary/時尚歐陸式

Café Gray Deluxe		Admiralty/金鐘	83
Felix NEW		Tsim Sha Tsui/尖沙咀	120
Gold by Harlan Goldstein NEW		Central/中環	132
Le 188°		North Point/北角	182
Madam Sixty Ate NEW		Wan Chai/灣仔	195
Mandarin Grill + Bar 文華扒房+酒吧		Central/中環	199

French/法式

Agnès b. Le Pain Grillé (Central)		Central/中環	71
Bettys Kitschen NEW		Central/中環	77
Bistronomique NEW		Kennedy Town/堅尼地城	78
Brass' NEW		Central/中環	82
Caprice		Central/中環	85

Gaddi's 吉地士		XXXXX	Tsim Sha Tsui/尖沙咀	130
La Marmite	NEW	⊕ X	Central/中環	167
On Lot 10		X	Central/中環	220
Petrus 珀翠		✿ XXXXX	Admiralty/金鐘	225
Spoon by Alain Ducasse	😋	✿✿ XXX	Tsim Sha Tsui/尖沙咀	242
The Press Room		X	Central/中環	271

French contemporary/時尚法式

Amber		✿✿ XXX	Central/中環	74
Cépage		✿ XXX	Wan Chai/灣仔	89
L'Atelier de Joël Robuchon	😋 ✿✿✿ XX		Central/中環	169
Mirror	NEW	✿ XXX	Wan Chai/灣仔	206
Pierre		✿✿ XXXX	Central/中環	226
St. George	😋	✿ XXX	Tsim Sha Tsui/尖沙咀	245
Whisk		XX	Tsim Sha Tsui/尖沙咀	288

Fusion/多國菜

Bo Innovation	😋	✿✿ XXX	Wan Chai/灣仔	80

Hakkanese/客家菜

Chuen Cheung Kui (Causeway Bay) 泉章居 (銅鑼灣)	⊕	X	Causeway Bay/銅鑼灣	96
Chuen Cheung Kui (Mong Kok) 泉章居 (旺角)	⊕	X	Mong Kok/旺角	97
Hakka Yé Yé (Causeway Bay) 客家爺爺 (銅鑼灣)	NEW	X	Causeway Bay/銅鑼灣	141
Hakka Yé Yé (Central) 客家爺爺 (中環)		X	Central/中環	142

Hang Zhou/杭州菜

Hong Zhou 杭州酒家	✿	XX	Wan Chai/灣仔	151

Hunanese/湖南菜

Hunan Garden (Causeway Bay) 洞庭樓 (銅鑼灣)		XXX	Causeway Bay/銅鑼灣	154

Noodles and Congee/粥麵

Pekingese/京菜

Portuguese/葡式

Seafood/海鮮

Chuen Kee Seafood 全記海鮮菜館		✗	East New Territories/新界東部	98
Dot Cod	NEW	✗✗	Central/中環	112
Dragon Inn 容龍	♨ ⊕	✗✗	West New Territories/新界西部	113
Hing Kee 避風塘興記		✗	Tsim Sha Tsui/尖沙咀	145
Lobster Bar and Grill 龍蝦吧		✗✗	Admiralty/金鐘	189

Shanghainese/上海菜

Din Tai Fung (Causeway Bay) 鼎泰豐 (銅鑼灣)		✗	Causeway Bay/銅鑼灣	108
Din Tai Fung (Tsim Sha Tsui) 鼎泰豐 (尖沙咀)	✿	✗	Tsim Sha Tsui/尖沙咀	109
Grand Cuisine Shanghai Kitchen 君頤上海小廚 NEW		✗	Tai Koo Shing/太古城	137
Liu Yuan Pavilion 留園雅敘		✗✗	Wan Chai/灣仔	187
Shanghai Garden 紫玉蘭		✗✗	Central/中環	233
Shanghai Xiao Nan Guo (Kowloon Bay) 上海小南國 (九龍灣) ♨ ⊕		✗✗	Kowloon Bay/九龍灣	235
Snow Garden (Causeway Bay) 雪園 (銅鑼灣)		✗✗	Causeway Bay/銅鑼灣	241
Yè Shanghai (Admiralty) 夜上海 (金鐘)		✗✗✗	Admiralty/金鐘	300
Yè Shanghai (Kowloon) 夜上海 (九龍) ♨	✿✿	✗✗✗	Tsim Sha Tsui/尖沙咀	301

Shun Tak/順德菜

Siu Shun Village Cuisine 肇順名匯河鮮專門店		✗	Kowloon Bay/九龍灣	240

Sichuan/川菜

Chilli Fagara 麻辣燙	✿	✗	Central/中環	94
Da Ping Huo 大平伙	⊕	✗	Central/中環	105
Mask of Sichuen & Beijing 面譜京川料理 NEW ⊕		✗	Tsim Sha Tsui/尖沙咀	201
Yellow Door Kitchen 黃色門廚房		✗	Central/中環	299

Singaporean/星加坡菜

Hainan Shaoye (Causeway Bay)
海南少爺（銅鑼灣） NEW ✗ Causeway Bay/銅鑼灣 140

Spanish/西班牙菜

Fandango	NEW		✗✗	Tsim Sha Tsui/尖沙咀	117
Fofo by el Willy		⊛	✗	Central/中環	121
Mesa 15	NEW	⊛	✗	Central/中環	204
Olé	NEW		✗✗	Central/中環	216
Uno Más			✗	Wan Chai/灣仔	285

Steakhouse/扒房

BLT Steak ✗ Tsim Sha Tsui/尖沙咀 79

Grand Hyatt Steakhouse
NEW ✗✗✗ Wan Chai/灣仔 138

Steik World Meats ✗✗ Tsim Sha Tsui/尖沙咀 244

The Bostonian
美岸海鮮廳 NEW ✗✗ Tsim Sha Tsui/尖沙咀 266

The Steak House ✗✗✗ Tsim Sha Tsui/尖沙咀 273

Wooloomooloo Steakhouse (Wan Chai)
✗✗ Wan Chai/灣仔 292

Swiss/瑞士菜

Chesa 瑞樵閣 ✗✗ Tsim Sha Tsui/尖沙咀 92

Thai/泰式

Lil' Siam NEW ✗ Central/中環 183

May's Sawaddee Thailand
旺泰特食 NEW ⊛ East New Territories/新界東部 202

Thai Basil ✗ Admiralty/金鐘 264

Thai Chiu 泰潮 ⊛ Sham Shui Po/深水埗 265

Vietnamese/越南菜

Café Hué
華順越南餐廳 NEW North Point/北角 84

Lo Chiu (Jordan) 老趙（佐敦） Jordan/佐敦 190

Lo Chiu (Tsim Sha Tsui)
老趙（尖沙咀） Tsim Sha Tsui/尖沙咀 191

RESTAURANTS WITH A VIEW
有景觀的餐廳

NEW : New entry in the guide/ 新增推介

㌘ : Restaurant promoted to a Bib Gourmand or Star/ 評級有所晉升的餐廳

PARTICULARLY PLEASANT RESTAURANTS
上佳的餐廳

NEW : New entry in the guide/ 新增推介
⤳ : Restaurant promoted to a Bib Gourmand or Star/ 評級有所晉升的餐廳

Above & Beyond NEW
天外天

Designed by Sir Terence Conran, the restaurant of the Hotel Icon (partly run by the education sector and staffed by keen students) is unsurprisingly contemporary and boasts a chic lounge and bar and stunning harbour views. What is unexpected is that this Western-style restaurant serves authentic Cantonese cuisine – dishes like smoked pigeon with Oolong tea leaves, and braised tofu with morels and Chinese mushrooms stand out.

由泰倫斯・康藍爵士（Sir Terence Conran）設計的唯港薈中菜廳（由大學教育部門營運，部分員工為充滿熱誠的學生），其貫徹如一的時尚格調，配以型格的酒吧大廳和醉人的維港景致，叫人讚嘆不已。令人意外的是，一間裝潢這般西式的餐廳，提供的卻是傳統粵菜，如凍頂烏龍茶燻鴿、野生羊肚菌炆腐皮等，都做得十分出色。

■ ADDRESS/地址
TEL. 3400 1318
28F, Hotel Icon, 17 Science Museum Road, East Tsim Sha Tsui, Kowloon
九龍尖東科學館道17號唯港薈28樓
www.aboveandbeyond.com.hk

■ OPENING HOURS, LAST ORDER
　營業時間，最後點菜時間
Lunch/午膳　11:00-15:00 (L.O.)
Dinner/晚膳　18:00-23:00 (L.O.)

■ PRICE/價錢
Lunch/午膳　set/套餐　　　$ 120-150
　　　　　　à la carte/點菜 $ 250-1,300
Dinner/晚膳　à la carte/點菜 $ 250-1,300

Agnès b. Le Pain Grillé (Central)

🍴14 ☎🍴 🐝

Located within the celebrated fashion store, Agnès b. and decorated to resemble a private, if luxurious, French country home from the 19C. It's divided into three rooms: Paris, Antibes, and Lyon; each with its own character and personality. Chic it most certainly is, to match its elegant clientele. Not surprisingly, the menu is French, but with plenty of contemporary touches. The impressive wine list features over 80 champagnes.

餐廳位於Agnès b.時裝店內，裝潢模仿十九世紀私人奢華法國田園家居。餐廳分為三個空間：Paris、Antibes和Lyon；每個都具有獨特個性風格。餐廳的時尚風格毋庸置疑，配合其高貴客源。菜單一如所料，是極具現代風格的法國菜。酒牌上更有超過80種香檳可供選擇。

■ ADDRESS/地址
TEL. 2805 0798
Shop 3096-3097, Podium Level 3,
IFC Mall, 8 Finance Street, Central
中環金融街8號國際金融中心商場3樓
3096-3097號舖
www.agnesb-lepaingrille.com

■ OPENING HOURS, LAST ORDER
　營業時間，最後點菜時間
Lunch/午膳　12:00-15:00 (L.O.)
Dinner/晚膳　19:00-22:30 (L.O.)

■ PRICE/價錢
Lunch/午膳　set/套餐　　　$238-328
　　　　　　à la carte/點菜 $450-1,000
Dinner/晚膳　à la carte/點菜 $450-1,000

Ah Yat Harbour View NEW
阿一海景飯店

As with his other restaurant, The Forum, you cannot fail to notice the large photo of owner-chef Yeung Koon Yat in the lobby. The sight of this celebrated chef should prompt you to order his famous dish – Ah Yat abalone – but don't ignore the other specialities, such as Ah Yat fried rice in a clay pot and stewed oxtail in red wine. The contemporary dining room has great views and there are four terrific private rooms.

這家飯店跟富臨飯店的相似之處，莫過於食客必定在飯店大堂看到老闆兼名廚楊貫一的大照。名廚的肖像往往促使他們點其招牌菜式阿一鮑魚大快朵頤。其他馳名菜式如阿一炒飯及紅酒燴牛尾亦不可錯過。飯店裝潢時尚，坐擁優美景觀，並設有四間廂房。

■ ADDRESS/地址
TEL. 2328 0983
29F, iSquare, 63 Nathan Road,
Tsim Sha Tsui, Kowloon
九龍尖沙咀彌敦道63號iSquare 29樓

■ OPENING HOURS, LAST ORDER
營業時間，最後點菜時間
Lunch/午膳 12:00-14:30 (L.O.)
Dinner/晚膳 18:00-22:30 (L.O.)

■ PRICE/價錢
Lunch/午膳　set/套餐　　　　$ 170-220
　　　　　à la carte/點菜 $ 250-12,000
Dinner/晚膳　à la carte/點菜 $ 250-12,000

Al Molo　NEW

Modern Italian cuisine by way of New York was brought to Ocean Terminal by celebrated chef Michael White in 2011. This eye-catching restaurant covers an area of 7,000ft² and is divided into three distinct dining sections: there's a relaxed spot in front of the pizza ovens; a comfortable middle room with a lively open kitchen and a waterfront terrace overlooking the harbour. Standouts include home-made pasta, polipo and osso buco.

星級名廚Michael White於2011年將時尚紐約式意大利佳餚引進香港海運大廈。這間矚目的餐廳佔地7,000平方呎，共分為三大區域：薄餅烤爐前方的雅座；設置開放式廚房的中庭及傲視壯麗維港景觀的臨海露台。馳名菜式包括：自製意大利麵，烤八爪魚(polipo)及烤牛膝(osso buco)。

■ ADDRESS/地址

TEL. 2730 7900

Shop G63, GF, Ocean Terminal, Harbour City, Tsim Sha Tsui, Kowloon
九龍尖沙咀海運大廈海港城地下G63號舖
www.diningconcepts.com.hk

■ OPENING HOURS, LAST ORDER
營業時間，最後點菜時間
12:00-23:00

■ PRICE/價錢

Lunch/午膳	set/套餐	$138-228
	à la carte/點菜	$330-1,350
Dinner/晚膳	à la carte/點菜	$330-1,350

Amber

❀ ❀   XXXX

    ♿   ☞   🍽20   🕐🍴

The hanging ceiling sculpture, which features over 3,500 copper tubes, is the most striking element of Adam Tihany's bold restaurant design. Service is detailed and courteous without ever being stuffy or starchy. But it is the adventurous and creative French cuisine, using superb ingredients, which attracts diners to these plush surroundings. The sommeliers can be relied upon for sound recommendations from the comprehensive wine list.

從天花懸垂下來，以超過3,500條銅管做成的雕像，是Adam Tihany 前衛餐廳設計的最觸目元素。服務禮貌週到而不會令客人有咄咄逼人、吃不消的感覺。不過，採用優質材料烹調，大膽而富創意的法國菜才是真正將客人吸引到這豪華的環境。你可信任品酒師的可靠建議，從齊全的酒單挑選合適的選擇。

■ ADDRESS/地址

TEL. 2132 0066

7F, The Landmark Mandarin Oriental Hotel, 15 Queen's Road, Central
中環皇后大道中15號置地文華東方酒店7樓
www.mandarinoriental.com/landmark

■ ANNUAL AND WEEKLY CLOSING
   休息日期
Closed Sunday dinner
週日晚膳休息

■ OPENING HOURS, LAST ORDER
   營業時間，最後點菜時間
Lunch/午膳 12:00-14:30 (L.O.)
Dinner/晚膳 18:30-22:30 (L.O.)

■ PRICE/價錢

Lunch/午膳	set/套餐	$ 518-748
	à la carte/點菜	$ 900-2,000
Dinner/晚膳	set/套餐	$ 1,288-1,588
	à la carte/點菜	$ 900-2,000

Angelini

While other regions are represented, it is the cooking of Northern Italy that gets the upper hand at this stylish Italian restaurant at the Shangri-la hotel. Specialities on the extensive and varied menu include linguine with clams, mussels and red mullet roe, and grilled whole Mediterranean sea bass. The wine list includes an interesting range of regional Italian wines. A window seat is a must as the views are spectacular.

這家別具型格的意大利餐廳設於九龍香格里拉酒店，提供來自意大利各地區的佳餚，但最具代表性的還是來自意大利北部的美食。在琳瑯滿目的菜式之中，特別推介鮮蜆伴青口紅鰹魚子扁麵，還有香烤地中海全鱸魚。這裡更提供一系列別具韻味的意大利佳釀。靠窗的座位能飽覽壯麗景觀。

■ ADDRESS/地址

TEL. 2733 8750

Mezzanine Level, Kowloon Shangri-La Hotel, 64 Mody Road, East Tsim Sha Tsui, Kowloon
九龍尖東麼地道64號
九龍香格里拉酒店閣樓
www.shangri-la.com

■ OPENING HOURS, LAST ORDER
　營業時間，最後點菜時間
Lunch/午膳 12:00-15:00 (L.O.)
Dinner/晚膳 18:30-22:30 (L.O.)

■ PRICE/價錢
Lunch/午膳　à la carte/點菜 $400-1,000
Dinner/晚膳　à la carte/點菜 $400-1,000

Ba Yi NEW
巴依

It may be a little out of the way, but lamb lovers will be glad they made the effort to find this Xinjiang restaurant. The interior is suitably rustic, with the room dominated by a huge map of the silk route. Most of the meats are imported from Xinjiang and the special lamb dishes include dumplings, roast leg and mutton skewers. Well-organised parties should consider pre-ordering (four days in advance) the roasted whole lamb.

也許位置有點偏僻，但喜愛羊肉的食家一定無悔尋找這家新疆餐廳。舉目所見，是一幅巨型絲綢之路的路線地圖，裝潢別具鄉土氣息。其大部分肉類均由新疆入口，羊肉特式菜包括餃子、烤羊腿和羊肉串燒等。計劃周詳者，可考慮預訂他們的烤全羊(四天前預訂)。

■ ADDRESS/地址
TEL. 2484 9981
43 Water Street, Sai Ying Pun
西營盤水街43號

■ ANNUAL AND WEEKLY CLOSING
休息日期
Closed 2 weeks Lunar New Year
農曆新年休息兩星期

■ OPENING HOURS, LAST ORDER
營業時間，最後點菜時間
Lunch/午膳　12:00-15:00 L.O.14:30
Dinner/晚膳　18:00-23:00 L.O.22:30

■ PRICE/價錢
Lunch/午膳　à la carte/點菜 $ 30-100
Dinner/晚膳　à la carte/點菜 $ 100-380

Bettys Kitschen   NEW

Alan Yau made his name as a restaurateur par excellence in London with such hits as Hakkasan and Yauatcha. In 2011 he came to Hong Kong, his place of birth, to open this elegant and contemporary French restaurant. Southern France exerts an influence on the menu and there are a number of Basque dishes, such as Txangurro spider crab gratin, alongside more traditional offering like Dover sole meunière. Breakfast and afternoon tea are also served.

丘德威先生是倫敦的飲食界名人，於當地開設了Hakkasan和Yauatcha等備受歡迎的餐廳。2011年，他回歸出生地香港，開設此華麗又富現代感的法國餐廳。這裡的菜式融合了法國南部風情，並提供相當的巴斯克美食，如Txangurro烤蜘蛛蟹，以及傳統菜式如香煎龍脷魚等(Dover sole meunière)。早餐和下午茶餐在此亦有供應。

■ ADDRESS/地址
TEL. 2979 2100
Shop 2075, Podium Level 2, IFC Mall, 8 Finance Street, Central
中環金融街8號國際金融中心商場2樓2075號舖
www.bettys.com.hk

■ OPENING HOURS, LAST ORDER
營業時間，最後點菜時間
Lunch/午膳　11:45-16:00 (L.O.)
Dinner/晚膳　18:00-22:00 (L.O.)

■ PRICE/價錢
Lunch/午膳　à la carte/點菜 $ 300-620
Dinner/晚膳　à la carte/點菜 $ 400-800

Bistronomique　NEW

For their next act, the owners of On Lot 10 ventured out to a residential area not overburdened with restaurants and opened a similarly relaxed if slighter larger bistro, but with the same focus on French cuisine. At lunch a reasonably priced set menu is on offer; for dinner dishes are more elaborate in nature and more expensive. The cooking shows genuine respect for French traditions, whether in the tête de cochon or the skate wing Grenobloise.

這家以法國菜為主的餐廳與On Lot 10 一脈相承，設於未有開滿食肆的住宅區，地方較大但感覺同樣閒適。午市提供價格合理的套餐，晚市菜式則較豐富，價錢亦較高。這裡的美食如豬頭肉（tête de cochon）和牛油煎魔鬼魚翼（skate wing Grenobloise），均表現出其忠於法國傳統的特色。

■ ADDRESS/地址
TEL. 2818 8266
1B Davis Street, Kennedy Town
堅尼地城爹核士街1B號舖

■ ANNUAL AND WEEKLY CLOSING
　　休息日期
Closed Monday
週一休息

■ OPENING HOURS, LAST ORDER
　　營業時間，最後點菜時間
Lunch/午膳　12:00-14:30 (L.O.)
Dinner/晚膳　18:30-22:00 (L.O.)

■ PRICE/價錢
Lunch/午膳　set/套餐　　　$ 128
Dinner/晚膳　à la carte/點菜 $ 350-425

BLT Steak

In this instance those initials stand for Bistro Laurent Tourondel, a New York celebrity chef. His restaurant specialises in prime beef from the US and Australia, all USDA certified and naturally aged. Choose your cut – perhaps a Porterhouse or a rib-eye – a sauce and sides. There are a few lighter options for those intimidated by a 16oz New York strip. Its terrace overlooking the Star Ferry quay and Victoria Harbour is a 'prime' spot.

BLT 取紐約名廚 (Bistro) Laurent Tourondel之名，餐廳以來自美國及澳洲頂級牛排為主，全部通過美國農產部認證，自然生長。你可選擇喜歡食用的部份，從大脊骨牛排到肉眼排任君選擇，並配上自選醬汁及配菜。你亦可選擇較輕盈的16oz紐約無骨西冷扒。其平台花園是「搶手」熱點，可觀賞天星碼頭及維多利亞港景致。

■ ADDRESS/地址
TEL. 2730 3508
Shop G62, GF, Ocean Terminal,
Harbour City, Tsim Sha Tsui, Kowloon
九龍尖沙咀海運大廈海港城地下G62號舖
www.diningconcepts.com.hk

■ OPENING HOURS, LAST ORDER
營業時間，最後點菜時間
12:00-23:00 (L.O.)

■ PRICE/價錢
Lunch/午膳　set/套餐　　　　$ 168
　　　　　　à la carte/點菜　$ 380-770
Dinner/晚膳　à la carte/點菜　$ 380-770

Bo Innovation

Having the open kitchen enjoy a raised position in front of the dining room is entirely fitting as there's a strong theatrical element to owner-chef Alvin Leung's highly imaginative and innovative cooking. The origins behind each tantalising creation are fully explained and it's clear that this is not creativity for its own sake but a modern interpretation of traditional Chinese flavours; no greater example is the 'molecular xiao long bao'.

於食客用膳區的前方較高地方設置開放式廚房，此格局正好配合餐廳老闆兼廚師梁經倫的強烈表演慾及創新煮意。侍應會給客人介紹每道菜的材料和做法。梁經倫熱衷為傳統食譜全新演繹，務求為食客帶來嶄新的感受，其分子料理小籠包便是絕佳例子。

■ ADDRESS/地址

TEL. 2850 8371
2F, J Residence, 18 Ship Street, Wan Chai
灣仔船街18號嘉薈軒2樓
www.boinnovation.com

■ ANNUAL AND WEEKLY CLOSING
　　休息日期
Closed 3 days Lunar New Year, Sunday
and lunch Saturday and Public Holidays
農曆新年3天、週日、週六及公眾假期午
膳休息

■ OPENING HOURS, LAST ORDER
　　營業時間，最後點菜時間
Lunch/午膳 12:00-14:00 (L.O.)
Dinner/晚膳 19:00-22:00 (L.O.)

■ PRICE/價錢
Lunch/午膳 set/套餐　　$228-750
Dinner/晚膳 set/套餐　　$780-1,680

Bombay Dreams

Although most regions of India are represented, the kitchen's strengths lie with dishes from more northerly parts of the country. Lunch sees a well-stocked buffet; at dinner you can experience dishes like spicy prawns with garlic and mustard or spring lamb marinated in yoghurt and spices. The authentic cooking and appealing prices mean that booking is recommended. The pleasantly contemporary room allows for interesting views into the kitchen.

這裡提供印度大部份地區的菜式，當中最擅長為印度北部地區之佳餚。午市提供豐富的自助餐，晚市則可一嚐蒜香芥末辣味大蝦，或乳酪香草滷羔羊等美食。食物以正宗方法烹調，而且價錢相宜，建議預先訂座；這裡用餐環境舒適又富現代氣息，並可一窺廚房的工作情況，饒富趣味。

■ ADDRESS/地址

TEL. 2971 0001
4F, 75-77 Wyndham Street, Central
中環雲咸街75-77號4樓
www.diningconcepts.com.hk

■ OPENING HOURS, LAST ORDER
    營業時間，最後點菜時間
Lunch/午膳   12:00-15:00 (L.O.)
Dinner/晚膳   18:00-23:30 (L.O.)

■ PRICE/價錢
Lunch/午膳   set/套餐 $ 118
            à la carte/點菜 $ 250-400
Dinner/晚膳   à la carte/點菜 $ 250-400

Brass'   NEW

 12

They are busy people, the toilers of Central, so their choice of lunch destination is often governed by time. This French brasserie responded by cleverly setting out its lunchtime starters and desserts on a buffet. Dinner here, however, is an altogether different experience: the atmosphere is less hectic and the kitchen more ambitious, offering imaginative dishes such as poached lobster salad in a curry-coco vinaigrette with quinoa tabouleh.

中環區的上班一族，都少不免營營役役，午膳選擇亦要顧及時間的分配。此法國餐廳的聰明之處，就是以自助形式提供午市的頭盤和甜品。不過，一踏入晚市，這裡的餐飲體驗截然不同：氣氛格外輕鬆，廚師則會花費更多心思，炮製出充滿想像力的菜式，如焓龍蝦沙律伴咖喱及椰汁醬汁，再配以藜麥沙律(quinoa tabouleh)。

■ ADDRESS/地址

TEL. 2899 2216

2F, Nexxus Building,
77 Des Voeux Road, Central
中環德輔道中77號盈置大廈2樓

■ ANNUAL AND WEEKLY CLOSING
　　休息日期
Closed 5 days Lunar New Year and
Sunday
農曆新年5天及週日休息

■ OPENING HOURS, LAST ORDER
　　營業時間，最後點菜時間
Lunch/午膳 11:30-14:30 (L.O.)
Dinner/晚膳 19:00-22:00 (L.O.)

■ PRICE/價錢
Lunch/午膳　set/套餐　　　　$ 198-288
Dinner/晚膳　à la carte/點菜 $ 440-700

Café Gray Deluxe

Café Gray Deluxe is a suitably cool restaurant to have on the 49th floor of the fashionable Upper House hotel. There's a terrific, lively bar – homage perhaps to Gary Kunz's New York background – the views are spectacular and the service fluent and good-looking. The kitchen adds its own twists to mostly European dishes with the likes of pasta fiore with tomato and lemon thyme, steak tartar with gaufrettes and ketjap, and chocolate rum toast.

型格餐廳Café Gray Deluxe，位處時尚的奕居酒店49樓。內裏充滿活力的酒吧，彷彿是要向主廚Gary Kunz的紐約背景致敬。用餐的同時可欣賞維港的超凡景致，服務亦極為周到。餐廳菜式以歐陸佳餚為主，並加入獨有的變化，如意大利粉配番茄及檸檬百里香、牛肉他配窩夫脆餅及甜醬油，以及朱古力冧酒多士。

■ ADDRESS/地址

TEL. 3968 1106
49F, The Upper House Hotel,
Pacific Place, 88 Queensway,
Admiralty
香港金鐘道88號太古廣場奕居49樓
www.cafegrayhk.com

■ OPENING HOURS, LAST ORDER
營業時間，最後點菜時間
Lunch/午膳 12:00-14:30 (L.O.)
Dinner/晚膳 18:00-22:30 (L.O.)

■ PRICE/價錢

Lunch/午膳	set/套餐	$355
	à la carte/點菜	$430-670
Dinner/晚膳	set/套餐	$675
	à la carte/點菜	$480-740

Café Hué NEW
華順越南餐廳

The Vietnamese owner-chef sells around 250 bowls of her raw beef noodle soup every day and is just one reason why her simple, hidden-away shop is always busy. Other popular Vietnamese favourites include country soup vermicelli and steamed pork roll. The environment is basic but clean and the atmosphere never less than lively; prices are also pretty competitive. The private room can accommodate up to twenty guests.

這家隱藏於街中一角的越南餐廳，東主身兼主廚之職，每天賣出約二百五十碗生牛肉河粉，足見這小店其門如市。其他備受歡迎的越南菜式尚有漁村湯檬曉和蒸豬肉粉卷等。餐廳環境簡樸而整潔又充滿生氣，價格也十分實惠；其貴賓房可容納多達二十名食客。

■ ADDRESS/地址
TEL. 2512 8323
GF, Echo Tower, 61 Fort Street, North Point
北角堡壘街61號寶峰閣地下

■ OPENING HOURS, LAST ORDER
營業時間，最後點菜時間
11:00-22:30 (L.O.)

■ PRICE/價錢

Lunch/午膳	set/套餐	$ 30-40
	à la carte/點菜	$ 30-150
Dinner/晚膳	à la carte/點菜	$ 30-150

Caprice

❀ ❀ ❀   ✗✗✗✗✗

♿ ⇐ ☞♪ **P** 🟣12 🕾🍽 Ω

Dominating the glamorous room is the large, raised, open kitchen which is framed by a jewelled canopy. From here, the sizeable brigade of chefs produce highly accomplished French dishes such as langoustine ravioli with sweetbreads, and Normandy sole with Iberico ham. Be sure to sample the impressive selection of cheeses. Add in wonderful harbour views and meticulous, charming service and you have a true destination restaurant.

處身璀璨華麗的用餐大堂，以水晶珠簾圍繞著的大型開放式廚房最為矚目。在這裡，陣容鼎盛的廚師團隊精心炮製出各款法國佳餚，如螯龍蝦牛核雲吞，以及諾曼第龍脷伴伊比利亞火腿等；這裡出色的特選芝士系列令人一試難忘。迷人的維港景緻與及一絲不苟的服務，更增添這餐廳的非凡魅力。

■ ADDRESS/地址

TEL. 3196 8860
6F, Four Seasons Hotel, 8 Finance Street, Central
中環金融街8號四季酒店平臺6樓
www.fourseasons.com/hongkong

■ OPENING HOURS, LAST ORDER
營業時間，最後點菜時間
Lunch/午膳 12:00-14:30 (L.O.)
Dinner/晚膳 18:00-22:30 (L.O.)

■ PRICE/價錢
Lunch/午膳   set/套餐 $480
      à la carte/點菜 $850-1,500
Dinner/晚膳 set/套餐 $980
      à la carte/點菜 $850-1,500

Casa Lisboa

Caldo verde, stuffed crab, seafood stews, suckling pig and a reassuringly large selection of bacalhau recipes are just some of the highlights of an appealing menu which sees subtle Macanese influences added to Portuguese dishes. It may be on the 8th floor of the LKF Tower but this cosy room is brightly decorated in a traditional Portuguese style with blue and white azulejos. The national flag is also reflected in the colours of the waitresses' aprons.

傳統葡國腸薯蓉翠蔬湯、葡式釀蟹蓋、海鮮雜燴、葡式烤乳豬及多姿多采的馬介休菜式系列，不過是這吸引人的餐牌上部分重點部分，令它的葡國菜流露出絲絲澳門色彩。雖然位於蘭桂坊 LKF Tower 8樓，但明亮鮮艷的裝潢，以傳統葡萄牙風格配上藍白瓷磚畫（azulejos），給人溫暖而舒適的感覺。侍應圍裙的顏色亦採用葡萄牙國旗顏色。

■ ADDRESS/地址

TEL. 2905 1168

8F, LKF Tower, 55 D'Aguilar Street, Central
中環德己立街55號LKF Tower 8樓
www.ad-caterers.com

■ ANNUAL AND WEEKLY CLOSING
　　休息日期
Closed 4 days Lunar New Year and Sunday
農曆新年4天及週日休息

■ OPENING HOURS, LAST ORDER
　　營業時間，最後點菜時間
Lunch/午膳 12:00-15:00 L.O.14:30
Dinner/晚膳 18:30-24:00 L.O.23:00

■ PRICE/價錢
Lunch/午膳　set/套餐　　　　$148
　　　　　　à la carte/點菜 $270-500
Dinner/晚膳　à la carte/點菜 $300-530

Celebrity Cuisine
名人坊

❀ ❀ ✖✖

🍱20 ☎🍴

With only six tables and many regulars, booking ahead is vital at this very discreet but colourful restaurant concealed within the Lan Kwai Fong hotel. The Cantonese menu may be quite short but there are usually plenty of specials; highlights of the delicate, sophisticated cuisine include whole superior abalone in oyster sauce; deep-fried crab claw stuffed with minced shrimp and, one of the chef's own creations, 'bird's nest in chicken wing'.

這家隱藏在蘭桂坊酒店內的餐廳，看似不甚出眾但別具吸引力，加上只有六張檯而常客眾多，故此提早預約至關重要。這裡的廣東菜餐牌頗為精簡，但提供大量特選菜式，精美菜餚推介有全隻蠔油頂級鮑魚、百花釀蟹鉗，以及主廚自創菜式「燕窩釀雞翼」。

■ ADDRESS/地址
TEL. 3650 0066
1F, Lan Kwai Fong Hotel,
3 Kau U Fong, Central
中環九如坊3號蘭桂坊酒店1樓

■ ANNUAL AND WEEKLY CLOSING
　休息日期
Closed 3 days Lunar New Year
農曆新年3天

■ OPENING HOURS, LAST ORDER
　營業時間，最後點菜時間
Lunch/午膳 12:00-15:00 (L.O.)
Dinner/晚膳 18:00-23:00 (L.O.)

■ PRICE/價錢
Lunch/午膳　set/套餐　　　　$ 168-188
　　　　　à la carte/點菜 $ 250-800
Dinner/晚膳　à la carte/點菜 $ 250-800

Celestial Court
天寶閣

♿ ☞ 🔲100 📞🍴

Red and green tones, silks and wood adorn this spacious, traditional dining room within the Sheraton Hotel. Despite its size, scores of regulars mean that queuing for a table is sometimes required. A large selection of Cantonese and Chinese specialities include braised bean-curd sheet rolls filled with mushrooms and assorted vegetables, steamed boneless chicken with Yunnan ham and assorted seasonal creations. Service comes courtesy of an experienced team.

紅與綠的色調、絲綢與木材裝飾著喜來登酒店內這寬敞、傳統的中菜廳。眾多的常客令這間面積不小的中菜廳偶然也需要排隊輪候。餐牌選擇甚多，包括許多廣東和其他中國地方的佳餚，如鴛鴦素千層、金華玉樹雞和時令菜式。禮貌週到的服務團隊經驗十分豐富。

■ ADDRESS/地址
TEL. 2369 1111
2F, Sheraton Hotel, 20 Nathan Road, Tsim Sha Tsui, Kowloon
九龍尖沙咀彌敦道20號喜來登酒店2樓
www.sheraton.com/hongkong

■ OPENING HOURS, LAST ORDER
營業時間，最後點菜時間
Lunch/午膳 11:30-15:00 (L.O.)
Dinner/晚膳 18:00-23:00 (L.O.)

■ PRICE/價錢
Lunch/午膳   set/套餐 $238
            à la carte/點菜 $350-900
Dinner/晚膳 set/套餐 $588
            à la carte/點菜 $350-900

Cépage

♿ 🕰20

From the same stable as Les Amis in Singapore come these three floors of stylish design, offering the chic diner sophistication but also a relaxed atmosphere. The cuisine is contemporary French but with Asian touches and uses fine ingredients. Look out for langoustine 'dim sum style', grilled amadai with vin jaune sauce followed by dark chocolate soufflé. The wine list, with over 2,000 bottles, is one of the most impressive in Hong Kong.

Cépage 跟新加坡的Les Amis一脈相承，其三層型格設計，為追求品味的食家帶來高雅又輕鬆的用餐環境。餐廳提供當代法國菜，並揉合亞洲特式，採用優質食材。推介「點心風格小龍蝦」、「香烤甘鯛魚伴法式黃酒汁」，還有「黑朱古力梳乎厘」。餐廳更有超過2,000款葡萄酒以供選擇，堪稱城中數一數二。

■ ADDRESS/地址
TEL. 2861 3130
23 Wing Fung Street, Wan Chai
灣仔永豐街23號
www.lesamis.com.sg

■ ANNUAL AND WEEKLY CLOSING
休息日期
Closed 4 days Lunar New Year
農曆新年4天

■ OPENING HOURS, LAST ORDER
營業時間，最後點菜時間
Lunch/午膳 12:00-14:30 L.O.14:00
Dinner/晚膳 19:00-22:30 L.O.22:15

■ PRICE/價錢
Lunch/午膳 set/套餐 $370-580
            à la carte/點菜 $600-1,200
Dinner/晚膳 set/套餐 $680-1,580
            à la carte/點菜 $600-1,200

Chan Kan Kee Chiu Chow
陳勤記鹵鵝飯店

Ms Chan's grandfather set up this family business in 1948 in Sheung Wan; it moved to its current location in 1994 and was completely refurbished in 2010, when the kitchen was also expanded. Chiu Chow goose, cooked in a secret family recipe, remains the main event here, but there are other Chiu Chow specialities on offer such as deep-fried crabmeat ball, baby oyster congee, and double-boiled pig's lung and almond soup.

陳小姐的祖父於1948年在上環開創此家族生意，1994年遷至現址，及後於2010年大規模翻新，廚房規模亦加以擴充。家傳秘方炮製的潮州鹵鵝仍然是招牌菜，另外還提供其他潮州特色美食，如潮州炸蟹棗、潮州蠔仔泡粥和杏汁燉白肺湯等。

■ ADDRESS/地址
TEL. 2858 0033
11 Queen's Road West, Sheung Wan
上環皇后大道西11號

■ ANNUAL AND WEEKLY CLOSING
　休息日期
Closed 3 days Lunar New Year
農曆新年3天

■ OPENING HOURS, LAST ORDER
　營業時間，最後點菜時間
11:00-21:45 (L.O.)

■ PRICE/價錢
Lunch/午膳　set/套餐　　　　　$ 40-90
　　　　　　à la carte/點菜　$ 75-420
Dinner/晚膳　à la carte/點菜　$ 75-420

Che's
車氏粵菜軒

35

This unremarkable-looking little restaurant is popular with the local businessmen who come here in their droves for speedy service of the house speciality - crispy pork buns. But there are a few other reasons to visit: the dim sum at lunch, the extensive menu of classic dishes like crispy chicken or crab and dry scallop soup with bitter melon, simpler offerings such as congee or braised claypot dishes and the blueberry pudding with which to end.

這家小餐館可能並不起眼,但其實在本地商界人士間卻享負盛名,對其馳名脆皮叉燒包趨之若鶩。除此之外,還有午市點心、簡單而美味的粥品及煲仔菜,選擇豐富的經典名菜如脆皮炸子鷄或蟹肉瑤柱涼瓜羹,最後加一道藍桑子布甸便是個完美結束。服務快速且有效率,午餐時分往往座無虛席。

■ ADDRESS/地址
TEL. 2528 1123
4F, The Broadway,
54-62 Lockhart Road, Wan Chai
灣仔駱克道54-62號博匯大廈4樓

■ OPENING HOURS, LAST ORDER
營業時間,最後點菜時間
Lunch/午膳 11:30-15:00 L.O.14:15
Dinner/晚膳 18:00-22:15 (L.O.)

■ PRICE/價錢
Lunch/午膳　à la carte/點菜 $160-750
Dinner/晚膳　à la carte/點菜 $160-750

Chesa
瑞樵閣

For over forty years, the cuisine of Switzerland has found a charming niche here. An imposing wood door leads you into an intimate Swiss-style chalet with wooden objects left, right and centre. Traditional Swiss dishes sit alongside the cheese specialities: fondue Vaudoise (traditional fondue) or raclette du Valais (hot melted cheese with potatoes, pickled onions and gherkins). For dessert: chocolate fondue or Swiss chocolate mousse.

瑞士美食在香港穩佔一席位超過四十年。壯觀的木門帶領你到親切的瑞士農舍，裡面四處都有木製的裝飾。傳統瑞士菜式與特選芝士系列互相輝映：沃州芝士火鍋（傳統芝士火鍋）或瓦萊州烤芝士（熱熔的芝士配馬鈴薯、醃洋蔥及青瓜）。至於甜品，巧克力火鍋或瑞士巧克力慕絲是兩大必吃！

■ ADDRESS/地址

TEL. 2315 3169

1F, The Peninsula Hotel, Salisbury Road, Tsim Sha Tsui, Kowloon

九龍尖沙咀梳士巴利道半島酒店1樓

www.peninsula.com

■ OPENING HOURS, LAST ORDER
營業時間，最後點菜時間
Lunch/午膳 12:00-14:30 (L.O.)
Dinner/晚膳 18:30-22:30 (L.O.)

■ PRICE/價錢

Lunch/午膳	set/套餐	$280
	à la carte/點菜	$500-700
Dinner/晚膳	à la carte/點菜	$500-700

Cheung Kee
祥記飯店

Things almost seem to spill out onto the colourful street at this compact establishment that's divided into two small rooms. It's been going since 1948 and has quite a substantial local following, so it's best to book ahead. The good value menu features honest and earthy dishes that include Sahn Dong roasted chicken and braised pork knuckle, all served by their long-standing team. But it's the Peking duck that remains the must-have dish.

自1948年創業以來，這家老店擁有大量忠實食客，兩個餐室內經常座無虛席，每每熱鬧得幾乎把人客擠出五光十色的街道之上。如欲前往用餐，最好先行預約。這裏的菜式樸實地道，價錢合理，服務團隊更是經驗老到。推介菜式包括山東燒雞及紅燒元蹄，北京填鴨更是非吃不可的招牌菜。注意別吃太飽，留點胃口嚐嚐高力豆沙！

■ ADDRESS/地址

TEL. 2529 0707
1F, 75 Lockhart Road, Wan Chai
灣仔駱克道75號1樓

■ OPENING HOURS, LAST ORDER
　營業時間，最後點菜時間
Lunch/午膳　12:00-14:30 (L.O.)
Dinner/晚膳　18:00-22:30 (L.O.)

■ PRICE/價錢
Lunch/午膳　à la carte/點菜　$170-280
Dinner/晚膳　à la carte/點菜　$170-280

Chilli Fagara
麻辣燙

Chillies are a passion here! The window's filled with them, as well as orange flames, which act as a forewarning! Rich red walls create an intimate atmosphere. The heat is turned up as you progress from mild 'natural' dishes through to the likes of red hot chilli prawn – which is only for the very brave. Caramelized banana and chrysanthemum tea cool things down at the end. A sweet ambience prevails as the small team ensures all runs smoothly.

這裡充滿辣椒的激情！窗口充滿著辣椒，而橙色的火焰就像是預警！濃艷的紅牆營造親切的氣氛，當你從溫和的「普通」菜式吃到辣椒蝦之類的菜餚時，便會渾身發熱！當然，只有夠膽的人才會一嚐後者。最後可用拔絲香蕉及菊花茶涼快下來。為數不多的員工，和諧的團隊合作，令餐廳運作順暢，更顯溫馨。

■ ADDRESS/地址
TEL. 2893 3330
Shop E, GF, 51A Graham Street,
SoHo, Central
中環店蘇豪嘉咸街51A地下E舖
www.chillifagara.com

■ ANNUAL AND WEEKLY CLOSING
  休息日期
Closed 8 days Lunar New Year
農曆新年8天

■ OPENING HOURS, LAST ORDER
  營業時間，最後點菜時間
Lunch/午膳 11:30-14:00 (L.O.)
Sat. & Sun./週六、日午膳 12:00-14:00 (L.O.)
Dinner/晚膳 17:00-23:30 L.O.23:00

■ PRICE/價錢
Lunch/午膳   set/套餐 $78
Dinner/晚膳   à la carte/點菜 $220-400

Chiu Chow Garden (Tsuen Wan)
潮江春（荃灣）

🍴🍴

📷70 📞🍴

You will find this Maxim group restaurant busy during peak hours as it is situated in a shopping centre which is conveniently integrated into Tsuen Wan station. Instead of ordering from the main menu, opt for the little sheets of colourful paper which offer a range of dim sum and small dishes at great prices. Some of the most popular dishes include soyed sliced goose, deep-fried sliced pomfret with salad dip and sautéed kale with salted pork.

你會發現這家美心集團屬下的酒家在繁忙時間擠滿食客，因為她所處的商場直通港鐵荃灣站。與其從餐牌點菜，倒不如在不同顏色的點心紙上選擇經濟美味的點心和小食。部分受歡迎菜式包括澄海鹵水鵝片、潮州沙律鯧魚片和潮州鹹肉炒芥蘭。

■ ADDRESS/地址

TEL. 2498 3381

Shop 10-12, 2F, Luk Yeung Galleria, 22-66 Wai Tsuen Road, Tsuen Wan, New Territories
新界荃灣蕙荃路22-66號綠楊坊2樓10-12號舖
www.maxims.com.hk

■ OPENING HOURS, LAST ORDER
營業時間，最後點菜時間
Lunch/午膳 08:00-16:15 (L.O.)
Dinner/晚膳 18:00-23:00 (L.O.)

■ PRICE/價錢
Lunch/午膳 　à la carte/點菜 ＄120-700
Dinner/晚膳 　à la carte/點菜 ＄200-700

Chuen Cheung Kui (Causeway Bay)
泉章居 (銅鑼灣)

This may not be the easiest place to find but customers have been coming here in droves for 30 years. The reason is that it's a family business, based around excellent value Hakkanese cuisine, and they employ chefs from this region to ensure authenticity. Of course there's salt baked chicken, but the stewed pork with preserved vegetables and the tofu are good too. The dining rooms are vast and seat over 400 so the more in your party the better.

位於銅鑼灣廣場的泉章居位置不易找。然而，超過30年來，一直有大量顧客慕名而來，必有其吸引之處。餐館是家族式經營，以超值的客家菜為主，更特地從客家地區聘請主廚，以確保菜式正宗。鹽焗雞是必然之選，而梅菜扣肉和豆腐亦相當美味。餐廳可容納400人以上，是值得大夥人一聚的食店！

■ ADDRESS/地址

TEL. 2577 3833

7-8F, Causeway Bay Plaza I,
489 Hennessy Road, Causeway Bay
銅鑼灣軒尼詩道489號
銅鑼灣廣場第一期7-8樓

■ OPENING HOURS, LAST ORDER
營業時間，最後點菜時間
11:00-23:15 (L.O.)

■ PRICE/價錢
à la carte/點菜 $ 120-250

Chuen Cheung Kui (Mong Kok)
泉章居 (旺角)

Highlights of the menu of this first floor restaurant, which overlooks the street below, are those dishes based largely on traditional Hakkanese recipes, such as chicken baked in salt or stewed pork with preserved vegetables. In the afternoon, the smaller ground floor room is used for the serving of simpler, rice-based dishes. The restaurant has been owned by the same family since the 1960s and relocated to its current location in 2004.

餐館的一樓，可看到街景。精選菜式以傳統客家菜為主，為人樂道的如鹽焗雞和梅菜扣肉。面積較小的地下，在下午時分主要供應烹調較簡單的「碟頭飯」。菜館自1960年代起一直由同一家族經營，直至2004年才遷至現址。

■ ADDRESS/地址
TEL. 2396 0672
Lisa House, 33 Nelson Street, Mong Kok, Kowloon
九龍旺角奶路臣街33號依利大廈

■ ANNUAL AND WEEKLY CLOSING
　休息日期
Closed 4 days Lunar New Year
農曆新年4天

■ OPENING HOURS, LAST ORDER
　營業時間，最後點菜時間
11:00-23:15 (L.O.)

■ PRICE/價錢
à la carte/點菜　　　　　　　$ 100-330

Chuen Kee Seafood
全記海鮮菜館

Two family-run restaurants overlook a pleasant harbour to distant islands; choose the one with the rooftop terrace and the quayside plastic seats. An extraordinary range of seafood is available from adjacent fishmongers: cuttlefish, bivalve, crab and lobster, mollusc, shrimps, prawns... Go to the tank, select your meal, and minutes later it appears in front of you, steamed, poached, or wok fried. Then settle back and watch the boats go by.

這兩家餐廳是家族生意，位置優越，可觀賞海港及離島。天台陽台那一家，以及碼頭邊的塑膠座位備受推介。這裡海鮮種類繁多，包括墨魚、貝殼、蟹、龍蝦、賴尿蝦、大蝦小蝦等等。你可以到魚缸挑選你的海鮮，蒸、燉、炒也好，幾分鐘後便會奉到餐桌上，成為你的食物。然後你便可輕鬆地細賞船艇來來往往。

■ ADDRESS/地址

TEL. 2791 1195
53 Hoi Pong Street, Sai Kung
西貢海傍街53號

■ OPENING HOURS, LAST ORDER
　營業時間，最後點菜時間
11:00-23:00 L.O. 22:30

■ PRICE/價錢
set/套餐　　　　　　$ 174
à la carte/點菜　　　$ 180-380

City Hall Maxim's Palace
大會堂美心皇宮

City Hall not only hosts a concert hall, theatre and exhibition room but also this huge dining room, well known for its dim sum and nicely decorated in a 19C European style. Bookings are not accepted at lunch so be prepared to queue for the traditional but tasty dim sum, to be chosen directly from the carts. At dinner the menu focuses on Cantonese dishes, such as steamed king prawns stuffed with mushrooms, and roasted crispy chicken.

大會堂不只設有音樂廳、劇院和展覽廳，更設有這家以點心聞名的大型酒家。最近這裡重新裝修，以十九世紀歐洲風格示人。午市不設訂座服務，因此，要嘗試這裡傳統、美味，而且可以直接在手推車點菜挑選的點心，恐怕免不了輪候一番。晚市菜牌以廣東菜為主，例如珍菌燴銀龍與脆皮燒雞。

■ ADDRESS/地址
TEL. 2521 1303
2F, Low Block, City Hall, Central
中區大會堂低座2樓
www.maxims.com.hk

■ ANNUAL AND WEEKLY CLOSING
　　休息日期
Closed Lunar New Year
年初一休息

■ OPENING HOURS, LAST ORDER
　　營業時間，最後點菜時間
Lunch/午膳 11:00-15:00 (L.O.)
Dinner/晚膳 17:30-23:30 (L.O.)

■ PRICE/價錢
Lunch/午膳　à la carte/點菜 $150-250
Dinner/晚膳　à la carte/點菜 $200-800

Crystal Jade La Mian Xiao Long Bao (Kowloon Bay)
翡翠拉麵小籠包 (九龍灣)

& ⌷14

This simple shop is slightly smaller than the other establishments in the group, which was founded in Singapore in 1991. The many customers come here largely for their La Mian noodles, which are served in a number of different styles: perhaps with chicken and preserved vegetables or minced meat and mushroom in a spicy sauce. The menu also features a variety of different regional specialities and dim sum is served all day.

集團1991年於新加坡創辦。與其他分店相比,此店顯得略小。許多顧客都是為了這裡多款不同拉麵而來:嫩雞煨麵或者炸醬麵都是不錯的選擇。菜單上亦有各種地道小吃與點心,全日供應。

■ ADDRESS/地址
TEL. 2305 9990
Shop 520, 5F, Telford Plaza II, Kowloon Bay
九龍灣德福廣場第2期5樓520號舖
www.crystaljade.com

■ ANNUAL AND WEEKLY CLOSING
休息日期
Closed 2 days Lunar New Year
農曆新年休息2天

■ OPENING HOURS, LAST ORDER
營業時間,最後點菜時間
11:00-23:00 (L.O.)

■ PRICE/價錢
à la carte/點菜 $ 100-200

Crystal Jade La Mian Xiao Long Bao (TST)
翡翠拉麵小籠包 (尖沙咀)

Could this be Harbour City Mall's most popular eatery? Very probably. It's a modern cafeteria that buzzes all day - if your party is less than four strong, you'll be eating communally with strangers. The food – a mix of Northern Chinese and Sichuan, prepared in a sizzling semi-open kitchen – is very fresh, aromatic and tasty. Signature dishes include steamed pork dumpling with warm soup, or La Mian hand-made noodles with shrimp and cashew nuts.

這裡是海港城裡最受歡迎的食肆嗎？很可能是。這是家整天繁忙的餐廳，如果同行少於四人，你們很可能要和人併桌而坐。食物混合了中國北方菜式和四川菜，在熱烘烘的半開放式廚房烹調，非常新鮮，既香又美味。招牌菜包括上海小籠包、四川擔擔拉麵。

■ ADDRESS/地址
TEL. 2622 2699
Shop 3328, 3F, Gateway Arcade, Harbour City, Canton Road, Tsim Sha Tsui, Kowloon
九龍尖沙咀廣東道海港城
港威商場3樓3328號舖
www.crystaljade.com

■ ANNUAL AND WEEKLY CLOSING
  休息日期
Closed 2 days Lunar New Year
農曆新年休息2天

■ OPENING HOURS, LAST ORDER
  營業時間，最後點菜時間
11:00-23:00 L.O. 22:30

■ PRICE/價錢
à la carte/點菜 $ 100-200

Crystal Jade La Mian Xiao Long Bao (Wan Chai)
翡翠拉麵小籠包 (灣仔)

⬚ 24

Has quickly established a reputation for its Shanghai dumplings and noodles. This modern, slightly retro looking diner, with its plush booths, has light flooding through it. The place positively buzzes with atmosphere and there is a distinct air of satisfaction from its customers. Look out for smoked duck with tea leaves and fried Shanghai rice cake. Being a pre-eminent member of this group, they also specialise in double-boiled soups.

上海小籠包與麵食很快就為餐廳打響名堂。餐廳裝潢在現代中帶點懷舊，設有絲絨卡座，雖然位於三樓依然吸引不少食客。餐廳氣氛熱鬧，從中清楚感受到顧客的滿足。值得一試的有樟茶鴨及上海炒年糕。作為集團的新星，炖湯亦是餐廳的主打。

■ ADDRESS/地址
TEL. 2573 8844
Shop 310, 3F, Tai Yau Plaza, Wan Chai
灣仔大有廣場3樓310號舖
www.crystaljade.com

■ ANNUAL AND WEEKLY CLOSING
　　休息日期
Closed 2 days Lunar New Year
農曆新年休息2天

■ OPENING HOURS, LAST ORDER
　　營業時間，最後點菜時間
11:00-22:30 (L.O.)

■ PRICE/價錢
à la carte/點菜　　　　　　$ 100-200

Cuisine Cuisine at The Mira
國金軒 (The Mira)

When you come across a stylish and contemporary dining room such as this one, located on the 3rd floor of the fashionable Mira hotel, with its eye-catching chandeliers, intimate spaces and modern furniture, you can be fairly certain that the Cantonese food will also come with a few modern twists. Signature dishes include honey-glazed barbecue pork, pan-fried cod fillet with pomelo sauce and rack of lamb with cumin.

位於時尚的The Mira酒店三樓,這家餐廳時髦而充滿現代感,配上引人注目的吊燈、私人空間、摩登家具,你幾乎可以肯定這裡的廣東菜也會加上一些現代變化。招牌菜包括蜜餞叉燒皇、柚子汁燒鱈魚與孜然燒羊架。

■ ADDRESS/地址
TEL. 2315 5222
3F, The Mira Hotel, 118 Nathan Road, Tsim Sha Tsui, Kowloon
九龍尖沙咀彌敦道118號The Mira 3樓
www.cuisinecuisine.hk

■ OPENING HOURS, LAST ORDER
營業時間,最後點菜時間
Lunch/午膳 11:30-14:30 (L.O.)
Dinner/晚膳 18:00-22:30 (L.O.)

■ PRICE/價錢
Lunch/午膳　à la carte/點菜 $ 300-1,350
Dinner/晚膳à la carte/點菜 $ 300-1,350

Cuisine Cuisine (IFC)
國金軒（國際金融中心）

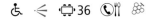

Six huge glass chandeliers hang from the 20ft high ceiling; one entire wall is decorated with 36 Chinese signs denoting the 36 different cooking styles; and floor to ceiling windows take care of the views – Cuisine Cuisine certainly makes the most of the space it occupies in the IFC mall. The roll-call of Cantonese classics includes abalone marinated with Chinese Hua Diao wine, honey-glazed barbecue pork, and braised beef brisket with leek.

在這裡，二十呎高的天花懸掛著六盞巨型柱狀吊燈；其中一面牆壁以三十六個中國文字點綴，代表了三十六種烹調方式；一列落地玻璃窗，讓動人美景飽覽無遺。不過這家位於國際金融中心商場的中菜館，主角仍然是佳餚美食。推介廣東經典菜式包括酒香鮑魚、蜜餞叉燒皇和錦醬青蒜牛腩。

■ ADDRESS/地址
TEL. 2393 3933
Shop 3101, Podium Level 3, IFC Mall, 8 Finance Street, Central
中環金融街8號
國際金融中心商場3樓3101號舖
www.cuisinecuisine.hk

■ OPENING HOURS, LAST ORDER
營業時間，最後點菜時間
Lunch/午膳 12:00-14:30 (L.O.)
Dinner/晚膳 18:00-22:30 (L.O.)

■ PRICE/價錢
Lunch/午膳　set/套餐　　　$ 298-398
　　　　　　à la carte/點菜 $ 200-860
Dinner/晚膳 à la carte/點菜 $ 250-860

Da Ping Huo
大平伙

This charming, hidden restaurant is ideal for those wanting something a little different. It is run by a couple from Sichuan: he is an artist and his wife is a singer. Here she cooks a nightly 12 course menu, using authentic and family-style Sichuan recipes while he welcomes the guests into the modern and elegant restaurant which he created himself. And at the end of the meal, she'll even sing for her customers.

這家獨具魅力卻鮮為人知的餐廳讓追求與眾不同的人士有多一個選擇。餐廳由一對來自四川的夫婦經營：丈夫是藝術家，太太則是歌手。太太負責烹調十二道菜的晚餐，以正宗四川家庭菜譜炮製，丈夫則負責在他親自設計，既現代又優雅的餐廳內招待賓客。酒足飯飽之際，太太甚至會為人客高歌一兩首民謠。

■ ADDRESS/地址
TEL. 2559 1317
LG, Hilltop Plaza, 49 Hollywood Road, Central
中環荷李活道49號鴻豐商業中心地下低層

■ ANNUAL AND WEEKLY CLOSING
　　休息日期
Closed 3 days Lunar New Year, Easter, mid-August, Christmas and Sunday
農曆新年3天、復活節、8月中、聖誕節及週日休息

■ OPENING HOURS, LAST ORDER
　　營業時間，最後點菜時間
Dinner/晚膳 18:30-24:00 L.O.23:30

■ PRICE/價錢
set/套餐 $ 280

Delicious Congee
和味生滾粥店

The regulars have been coming to this simple shop for years because they know good congee. The menu is on the wall and the most popular dish is the congee with fish, whether that's the fish lips, tail or slices of fillet. It can come enriched with beef, pork belly, heart and even frogs' legs too. Other small dishes are also available, such as fish balls, deep-fried fish skin and rice dumplings.

熟客多年來經常來訪這家簡樸小店的原因，是他們都懂得欣賞好粥。餐單貼在牆上，最著名的菜式是魚粥，不管是魚嘴、魚尾或魚片粥都同樣出色。要令粥品更豐富，則可選擇牛肉、豬肚、豬心、還有田雞腿。此外亦提供其他小食，如鯪魚球、炸魚皮和咸肉粽。

■ ADDRESS/地址
TEL. 2783 0935
75 Woosung Street, Jordan, Kowloon
九龍佐敦吳松街75號

■ ANNUAL AND WEEKLY CLOSING
　休息日期
Closed 2 days Lunar New Year
農曆新年休息2天

■ OPENING HOURS, LAST ORDER
　營業時間，最後點菜時間
07:30-03:00

■ PRICE/價錢
à la carte/點菜　　　$ 25-50

Dim Sum
譽滿坊

The charm of old Hong Kong is successfully evoked through vintage billboards, wood panelling, chandeliers and booths. From the wide choice of dim sum, start with steamed dumplings, Leong Har Gao and Siu Mai; popular luxury choices include abalone Siu Mai and Koon Yin Gao, but also worth trying are Loong Har Tong (lobster bisque) and Goon Tong Gao (soup with a giant dumpling). Get here early to beat the loyal Happy Valley followers.

懷舊海報、木製屏風、柱裝掛燈，再加上卡式座位，成功營造出老香港的魅力。這裡提供多種點心任君選擇，可先試燕液蝦餃、竹笙龍蝦餃和燒賣；備受歡迎的矜貴之選有BB鮑燒賣和官燕鮮蝦餃，值得一試的還有竹笙龍蝦湯和灌湯餃。這裡的跑馬地常客眾多，定必要早到才能確保入座。

■ ADDRESS/地址

TEL. 2834 8893
63 Shing Woo Road, Happy Valley
跑馬地成和道63號

■ ANNUAL AND WEEKLY CLOSING
　休息日期
Closed 5 days Lunar New Year
農曆新年休息5天

■ OPENING HOURS, LAST ORDER
　營業時間，最後點菜時間
Lunch/午膳 11:00-16:30 L.O.16:00
Dinner/晚膳 18:00-22:30 L.O.22:00

■ PRICE/價錢
Lunch/午膳　à la carte/點菜 $ 100-250
Dinner/晚膳　à la carte/點菜 $ 100-250

Din Tai Fung (Causeway Bay)
鼎泰豐 (銅鑼灣)

It was inevitable that the success of the Tsim Sha Tsui branch would lead to the opening of another. This more recent addition may be larger but that doesn't mean the queues are any shorter. The menu is a mix of Shanghainese and Taiwanese, with dumplings a highlight; popular dishes are the double-boiled chicken soup and braised beef brisket noodle soup. First-timers will find the instructions on eating the renowned Xiao Lang Bao helpful.

尖沙嘴店的成功，促成了下一間分店的開幕。這間位於銅鑼灣的分店不但更摩登，而且佔地更廣，也同樣備受追捧，很多時仍需要等候入座。菜牌包括上海菜與台灣菜，小籠包更是重點所在。熱賣菜式有原盅雞湯與紅燒牛肉湯麵。飯店更為初次光顧的客人提供進食馳名小籠包的説明以供參考，非常周到。

- ADDRESS/地址
TEL. 3160 8998
Shop 3-9, GF, 68 Yee Woo Street,
Causeway Bay
銅鑼灣怡和街68號地下3-9舖
www.dintaifung.com.hk

- ANNUAL AND WEEKLY CLOSING
  休息日期
Closed 3 days Lunar New Year
農曆新年休息3天

- OPENING HOURS, LAST ORDER
  營業時間，最後點菜時間
11:30-22:00 (L.O.)

- PRICE/價錢
à la carte/點菜 $ 110-280

Din Tai Fung (Tsim Sha Tsui)
鼎泰豐 (尖沙咀)

🎴12

Mr Yang opened up his dumpling shop in Taiwan back in 1958 and focused on delivering service, price and quality; there are now branches in all major Asian cities. Fresh, handmade Shanghai dumplings are their speciality and they are extremely good; the steamed pork ones being especially tasty. Queues are the norm here, but don't worry: a team of 130 smart and efficient staff serve at least 1000 people a day and take it all in their stride.

楊先生在1958年於台灣開辦其第一家小籠包店，特別注重服務、價格及品質；如今，已在所有主要亞洲城市開辦分店。新鮮手包的上海小籠包是餐廳主打，令人食指大動；蒸豬肉餡更是美味。店前總擠滿排隊等候的人，但不用擔心：由130名員工組成精明有效率的服務團隊，每天服務最少一千名客人，令人賓至如歸。

■ ADDRESS/地址

TEL. 2730 6928

Shop 130 & Restaurant C, 3F, Silvercord, 30 Canton Road, Tsim Sha Tsui, Kowloon
九龍尖沙咀廣東道30號
新港中心3樓C130號舖
www.dintaifung.com.hk

■ ANNUAL AND WEEKLY CLOSING
　休息日期
Closed 3 days Lunar New Year
農曆新年休息3天

■ OPENING HOURS, LAST ORDER
　營業時間，最後點菜時間
11:30-22:30 (L.O.)

■ PRICE/價錢
à la carte/點菜　　　　$ 110-280

Domani

Now in partnership with chef Pier Bussetti from Piedmont, the kitchen is responsible for some of the more original Italian cooking found in Hong Kong, with dishes like Earl Grey tea risotto, and hazelnut-crusted lamb with cabbage. The room, within a glass structure offering good views and natural light, is elegantly furnished, with an open kitchen and wave patterned ceiling. The wine list is comprehensive and there is an appealing lunch menu.

現時這家餐廳的合伙人之一是來自皮埃蒙特的廚師Pier Bussetti，他們致力炮制出多款全港最原汁原味的義大利菜，包括伯爵茶意大利飯及榛子脆烤羊排配椰菜。餐室位處太古廣場的玻璃建築當中，提供絕佳景觀及自然光，且經過精緻裝潢，附有開放式廚房及波浪形天花。酒牌提供不少選擇，午市套餐亦相當吸引。

■ ADDRESS/地址

TEL. 2111 1197
Shop 406, Level 4, Pacific Place,
88 Queensway, Admiralty
金鐘金鐘道88號太古廣場4樓406號舖
www.domani.hk

■ OPENING HOURS, LAST ORDER
    營業時間，最後點菜時間
Lunch/午膳 12:00-14:30 (L.O.)
Dinner/晚膳 19:00-22:30 (L.O.)

■ PRICE/價錢

Lunch/午膳	set/套餐	$ 320-350
	à la carte/點菜	$ 400-750
Dinner/晚膳	set/套餐	$ 650-920
	à la carte/點菜	$ 400-750

Dong Lai Shun
東來順

The first Dong Lai Shun was founded in 1903 in Peking, and has been successfully transplanted to the basement of the Royal Garden hotel. Its décor is contemporary with distinct Asian nuances, such as panels and paintings; there's a water feature which creates a relaxing atmosphere. The mix of Beijing and Huaiyang recipes includes hot pot, Peking duck and 'shuan yang rou': paper thin slices of Mongolian black-headed mutton.

於1903年在北京創辦的東來順，其後成功遷移到帝苑酒店地庫層。餐廳的裝修揉合了現代和傳統格調；　鮮明細緻的亞洲特色，從牆板和壁畫便可略窺一二。這裡的人工噴泉更營造了輕鬆的氣氛。食物方面，餐廳的北京和淮陽菜共冶一爐，包括火鍋、北京填鴨，以及「涮羊肉」：採用蒙古黑頭白羊的上乘部分，肉質薄如紙，軟如棉。

■ ADDRESS/地址
TEL. 2733 2020
B2F, The Royal Garden Hotel,
69 Mody Road, East Tsim Sha Tsui,
Kowloon
九龍尖東麼地道69號帝苑酒店地庫2樓
www.rghk.com.hk

■ OPENING HOURS, LAST ORDER
　　營業時間，最後點菜時間
Lunch/午膳 11:30-14:30 (L.O.)
Dinner/晚膳 18:00-22:30 (L.O.)

■ PRICE/價錢

Lunch/午膳	set/套餐	$88-314
	à la carte/點菜	$180-1,300
Dinner/晚膳	set/套餐	$228-314
	à la carte/點菜	$220-1,300

Dot Cod   NEW

🍴 20 ☎️🍽️

A favourite spot for many in Central is this basement restaurant owned by the Hong Kong Cricket Club. The bar gets busy, especially when a match is being shown, but the dining room is a slightly more relaxing spot. It's the seafood that bowls them over here; your waiter will present the daily special on a tray at your table. Fish pie, 'surf and turf' and Blue crab cakes are perennial favourites. Wednesday night is 'Oyster night'.

這家由香港木球會主理、位於地庫的餐廳,是中環一族經常流連之處。內裡的酒吧在有球賽進行期間特別繁忙,用餐區則相對悠閒。海鮮是這裡一大賣點,侍應會把一大盤當日精選海鮮放在餐桌旁供你點選;魚餡餅、海陸大餐和藍蟹餅是全年都大受歡迎的菜式;逢星期三是這裡的生蠔之夜。

■ ADDRESS/地址

TEL. 2810 6988

B4, Prince's Building,
10 Charter Road, Central
中環遮打道10號太子大廈地庫B4
www.dotcod.com

■ ANNUAL AND WEEKLY CLOSING
  休息日期
Closed Public Holidays
公眾假期休息

■ OPENING HOURS, LAST ORDER
  營業時間,最後點菜時間
07:30-22:30 (L.O.)

■ PRICE/價錢
Lunch/午膳   set/套餐 $ 238-288
                à la carte/點菜 $ 325-1,130
Dinner/晚膳 à la carte/點菜 $ 325-1,130

Dragon Inn
容龍

There aren't many in this area who haven't heard of The Dragon Inn as it's been here in one form or another since 1939 and, with such great views to the sea across tropical gardens, it's not surprising. But it's the seafood most come for – some don't even look at the main menu, but just pick dishes from the seafood speciality list. Baked baby lobster with cheese or baked oysters with port are favourites. Ask for a window table when booking.

容龍海鮮酒家的大名在本區幾乎無人不曉。自1939年開業，不少遊人都喜愛到那裏享受一望無際的海景，同時欣賞它的熱帶花園，受歡迎可謂意料中事。但最吸引客人的是這裡的海鮮。有些人根本不翻看主菜牌，而是直接從海鮮單挑選。芝士焗龍蝦與砵酒焗生蠔都是必然之選。預訂時可選擇靠窗座位。

■ ADDRESS/地址

TEL. 2450 6366
Castle Peak Road, Miles 19,
Tuen Mun, New Territories
新界屯門青山19咪

■ ANNUAL AND WEEKLY CLOSING
　休息日期
Closed 2 days Lunar New Year
農曆新年休息2天

■ OPENING HOURS, LAST ORDER
　營業時間，最後點菜時間
11:00-23:00 (L.O.)

■ PRICE/價錢
à la carte/點菜　　　　$ 150-500

Dragon King (Kwun Tong)  NEW
龍皇 (觀塘)

Creative Cantonese dishes largely focusing on seafood are the draw at this contemporary dining room owned by famous local chef Wong Wing Chee. Standout dishes on the large menu include Australian Tiger Jade abalone in a herb sauce, and Mantis prawns steamed in a bamboo basket. The room is dominated by a large fish tank and there are a number of spacious private rooms available. Lunchtimes are particularly busy with local corporate types.

這家富現代感的中菜館，提供以海鮮為主的創新廣東菜式，東主為香港著名廚師黃永幟。在芸芸美食之中，最出眾的有香草焗老虎鮑和清蒸斑馬富貴蝦。這裡的大型魚缸主導了你的視線，同場還有多個寬敞的貴賓房提供。午餐時間其門如市，以本地商務食客為主。

■ ADDRESS/地址

TEL. 2955 0668
2F, Yen Sheng Centre,
64 Hoi Yuen Road, Kwun Tong,
Kowloon
九龍觀塘開源道64號源成中心2樓
www.dragonking.com.hk

■ OPENING HOURS, LAST ORDER
營業時間，最後點菜時間
Lunch/午膳 11:00-15:00 (L.O.)
Dinner/晚膳 18:00-22:30 (L.O.)

■ PRICE/價錢
Lunch/午膳 à la carte/點菜 $200-580
Dinner/晚膳 à la carte/點菜 $200-580

Dumpling Yuan (Central)
餃子園 (中環)

You might wonder why there are only ladies working here – it's because they take their dumplings very seriously and don't consider men to have the required patience or the delicate touch needed to make good dumplings. We recommend the pork with cabbage and the mutton with green onions; but also try bean curd with wild vegetables, and spiced donkey meat with noodles. If it's full here then try their branch across the road.

你也許會奇怪為何這裡只有女性員工，因為此店非常重視他們的餃子，他們不認為男性具備做出色餃子必須的條件—足夠耐性與纖細觸覺。推薦鮮肉白菜餃與北蔥羊肉餃。另外這裡的上海菜也非常出色，特別推介香干馬蘭頭，五香驢肉及炸醬麵。滿座時，可選擇馬路對面的分店。

■ ADDRESS/地址
TEL. 2525 9018
69 Wellington Street, Central
中環威靈頓街69號

■ ANNUAL AND WEEKLY CLOSING
休息日期
Closed 3 days Lunar New Year
農曆新年休息3天

■ OPENING HOURS, LAST ORDER
營業時間，最後點菜時間
11:00-23:00 (L.O.)

■ PRICE/價錢
à la carte/點菜 $ 40-100

Dynasty
滿福樓

Dine in elegant and very spacious surroundings here on the third floor of the Renaissance Harbour View hotel. The flying fairy motif is used to good effect to highlight the Cantonese menu's signature dishes, which are well worth trying: traditional plates of barbecue pork, roast pigeon, and steamed crab claw, along with family-style dishes of boiled rice in clay pots with chicken and salted fish. Desserts are also done particularly well.

滿福樓位處香港萬麗海景酒店三樓，用餐環境高雅寬敞。天外飛仙的主題無處不在，用以點出粵菜菜單中值得一試的招牌菜更為適合：古法叉燒拼盤、燒乳鴿、蒸蟹鉗，還有住家風味的鹹魚雞粒煲仔飯。甜品特別出色。雖然身處酒店三樓，你仍可在幾可亂真的棕櫚樹旁用餐。

■ ADDRESS/地址

TEL. 2584 6971
3F, Renaissance Harbour View Hotel, 1 Harbour Road, Wan Chai
灣仔港灣道1號萬麗海景酒店3樓
www.renaissancehotels.com/HKGHV

■ OPENING HOURS, LAST ORDER
  營業時間，最後點菜時間
Lunch/午膳 12:00-15:00 (L.O.)
Dinner/晚膳 18:30-23:00 (L.O.)

■ PRICE/價錢
set/套餐 $ 300-700
à la carte/點菜 $ 300-700

Fandango   NEW

If ever there was a restaurant ideal for a first date then this it is – for when decoration is as exuberant as this, you're never likely to run out of conversation. Think Castilian hacienda designed by Salvador Dali; and all accompanied by an inimitable live band. The atmosphere is also pretty laid back and the cooking is suitably authentic. Dishes not to be missed are the Iberico ham, the paella and the boquerones.

若要選初次約會的理想勝地，非它莫屬。單是充滿活力的裝潢就讓你話題滔滔不絕。試假想由薩爾瓦多·達利設計的西班牙園莊，配以別出心裁的現場樂隊演奏，懶洋洋的氣氛加上正宗的西班牙菜餚，是一個何等多姿多彩的畫面。黑毛豬火腿、西班牙炒飯和鳳尾魚都不容錯過。

■ ADDRESS/地址

TEL. 2957 8797

9F, The Toy House, 100 Canton Road, Tsim Sha Tsui, Kowloon

九龍尖沙咀廣東道100號彩星集團9樓

■ ANNUAL AND WEEKLY CLOSING
    休息日期

Closed 2 days Lunar New Year

農曆新年休息2天

■ OPENING HOURS, LAST ORDER
    營業時間，最後點菜時間

Lunch/午膳 12:00-14:30 (L.O.)

Dinner/晚膳 18:00-23:00 (L.O.)

■ PRICE/價錢

Lunch/午膳	set/套餐	$88-128
	à la carte/點菜	$280-750
Dinner/晚膳	à la carte/點菜	$280-750

Fan Tang
飯堂

Press the buzzer, the façade slides open and you enter a different world. Seven large and exquisitely laid tables are surrounded by mirrors, fine art and rich drapes; the private dining rooms upstairs are even more opulent. The Chinese cooking uses mostly Cantonese and Sichuan influences but there are also subtle touches of originality. Look out for Sichuan style cucumber and green pepper on preserved duck egg or stewed pig trotters with dried vegetables.

只要你按下門鐘，店門立刻為你而開，帶領你進入一個與別不同的世界。鏡子、藝術品與帷簾圍繞著七張大桌，非常雅致。樓上的貴賓房更為富麗堂皇。這裡的中國菜主要以粵菜與川菜為主，但也帶有原創味道。川式怪味青瓜、尖椒拌皮蛋與菜干炆豬手都值得一試。

■ ADDRESS/地址
TEL. 2890 3339
93-95 Leighton Road, Causeway Bay
銅鑼灣禮頓道93-95號

■ ANNUAL AND WEEKLY CLOSING
　　休息日期
Closed 3 days Lunar New Year
農曆新年休息3天

■ OPENING HOURS, LAST ORDER
　　營業時間，最後點菜時間
Lunch/午膳 12:00-15:00 L.O.14:30
Dinner/晚膳 18:30-23:00 L.O. 22:00

■ PRICE/價錢
Lunch/午膳 à la carte/點菜 $250-750
Dinner/晚膳 à la carte/點菜 $300-750

Farm House
農圃

Set in a sleek business building, this contemporary dining room has private rooms leading off it as well as an eye-catching aquarium running the entire length of one wall. A highlight of the Cantonese menu is the deep-fried chicken wing with stuffed glutinous rice, while other specialities include the steamed minced pork with preserved duck egg and squid, and steamed egg white with seafood. Many of the ingredients are also available to buy.

這家裝潢富現代感的飯店位處線條流麗的商業大廈中，一進門便可見數間貴賓房和一個伸延整道牆的巨型水族箱，非常引人注目。農圃的粵菜選用特級新鮮材料炮製而成，著名菜式有古法釀雞翼、咸蛋土魷蒸肉餅和「是但」也就是海鮮蒸蛋。飯店亦出售一些難於家中烹調的食物如鮑魚及海參。

■ ADDRESS/地址

TEL. 2881 1331
1F, 8 Sunning Road, Causeway Bay
銅鑼灣新寧道8號1樓
www.farmhouse.com.hk

■ OPENING HOURS, LAST ORDER
營業時間，最後點菜時間
Lunch/午膳 11:00-15:00 L.O. 14:45
Dinner/晚膳 18:00-24:00 L.O. 23:00

■ PRICE/價錢
Lunch/午膳	set/套餐	$268
	à la carte/點菜	$200-900
Dinner/晚膳	set/套餐	$298-1,280
	à la carte/點菜	$200-900

Felix　NEW

The unmistakeable hand of designer Philippe Starck has been at work here at the top of The Peninsula and his striking restaurant has a certain ethereal quality. The kitchen matches the surroundings by using modern techniques and influences to create inventive, delicate dishes. Competing with the theatrical design are some of the best views you'll find in any restaurant in the world; be sure to have a drink first in the suitably chic bar.

著名設計師Philippe Starck匠心獨運，讓半島酒店的頂樓餐廳盡顯不凡。廚房配合整體環境，運用現代技巧和趨勢，創作新穎精緻的佳餚。全球只有少數餐廳能與之匹敵的醉人景色，與舞台般的室內設計完美配合，千萬別錯過先到時尚的酒吧淺酌一杯。

■ ADDRESS/地址
TEL. 2315 3188
28F, The Peninsula Hotel, Salisbury Road, Tsim Sha Tsui, Kowloon
九龍尖沙咀梳士巴利道半島酒店28樓
www.peninsula.com

■ OPENING HOURS, LAST ORDER
營業時間，最後點菜時間
Dinner/晚膳　18:00-22:30 (L.O.)

■ PRICE/價錢
à la carte/點菜　　　$600-800

Fofo by el Willy

Fofo means 'chubby' and, judging by the look on the faces of the plump pig and penguin figures dotted around the room, therein lies contentment. For those eating here, three of the authentic Spanish dishes for each person, plus a little rice, should bring equal joy. The appealing tapas range from the popular suckling pig, which is slow-roasted overnight, to fried croquettes of Iberian ham and fried gambas with garlic and chilli.

Fofo是「圓胖」的意思。從餐館內的小豬與企鵝裝飾臉上滿足的表情看來，我們不難理解餐廳名字的意思。不過對在此用餐的食客而言，每人來三道傳統西班牙菜，再加點飯，那份快樂亦相去不遠。讓人垂涎三尺的西班牙小菜，從大受歡迎以慢火通宵烤製的脆皮乳豬，到脆炸伊比利亞火腿丸子和蒜椒炸蝦等，應有盡有。

■ ADDRESS/地址
TEL. 2900 2009
20F, M88 2-8 Wellington Street, Central
中環威靈頓街2-8號M88 20樓
www.fofo.hk

■ ANNUAL AND WEEKLY CLOSING
   休息日期
Closed 3 days Lunar New Year, Public Holiday lunch and Sunday
農曆新年3天、公眾假期午膳及週日休息

■ OPENING HOURS, LAST ORDER
   營業時間，最後點菜時間
Lunch/午膳 12:00-14:30 (L.O.)
Dinner/晚膳 18:00-22:30 (L.O.)

■ PRICE/價錢
Lunch/午膳   set/套餐 $ 188
              à la carte/點菜 $ 230-400
Dinner/晚膳   à la carte/點菜 $ 230-400

Fook Lam Moon (Kowloon)
福臨門 (九龍)

This Kowloon branch may have fewer corporate customers than the one in Wan Chai but it shares the same principles: fresh, seasonal ingredients treated with the utmost care. The result is that this refined Cantonese cooking has been attracting a loyal following since the restaurant opened in 1972. Specialities include aged abalone braised in stock with oyster sauce, baked crab shell with onions, and braised bird's nest in bamboo.

與灣仔店相比，光顧九龍分店的商務人士可能較少，但兩店都秉承同一宗旨：以新鮮、時令材料精心炮製。這種優良的粵菜烹調方法備受美食愛好者的欣賞，難怪自1972年開業迄今吸引不少忠實捧場客。不防試一試特別推薦的蠔皇原隻乾鮑和釀焗鮮蟹蓋，以及官燕釀竹笙卷。

■ ADDRESS/地址

TEL. 2366 0286

53-59 Kimberley Road,
Tsim Sha Tsui, Kowloon
九龍尖沙咀金巴利道53-59號
www.fooklammoon-grp.com

■ ANNUAL AND WEEKLY CLOSING
　休息日期
Closed 2 days Lunar New Year
農曆新年休息2天

■ OPENING HOURS, LAST ORDER
　營業時間，最後點菜時間
Lunch/午膳 11:30-14:30 (L.O.)
Dinner/晚膳 18:00-22:30 (L.O.)

■ PRICE/價錢
à la carte/點菜 $ 370-2,000

Fook Lam Moon (Wan Chai)
福臨門（灣仔）

♿ ☞ 🍴150 ☎

Run with considerable passion by the third generation of the same family, Fook Lam Moon is one of the best known restaurants around and attracts many regulars. Decoration of the two large dining rooms is based around a colour scheme of gold, silver and bronze which seems appropriate as there are so many luxury items on the menu. The respect for the ingredients is palpable and signature dishes include baked stuff crab shell and roast suckling pig.

「福臨門」意指「好運來到你家門」，現由創業家族的第三代用心經營，是城中最享負盛名的酒家之一，深受一眾食家愛戴。店內的兩個大堂以金、銀、銅色系裝潢，映襯著菜單上的珍饈百味。食材明顯經過精心處理，招牌菜包括釀焗鮮蟹蓋與大紅片皮乳豬。

■ ADDRESS/地址

TEL. 2866 0663
35-45 Johnston Road, Wan Chai
灣仔莊士敦道35-45號
www.fooklammoon-grp.com

■ ANNUAL AND WEEKLY CLOSING
　休息日期
Closed 2 days Lunar New Year
農曆新年休息2天

■ OPENING HOURS, LAST ORDER
　營業時間，最後點菜時間
Lunch/午膳 11:30-14:30 (L.O.)
Dinner/晚膳 18:00-22:30 (L.O.)

■ PRICE/價錢
Lunch/午膳　à la carte/點菜 $ 300-1,000
Dinner/晚膳　à la carte/點菜 $ 400-1,000

Forum
富臨

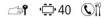

You cannot fail to notice the pictures of owner-chef Yeung Koon Yat. For over thirty years he's been attracting everyone from world leaders to locals to his Forum restaurant, thanks largely to his celebrated speciality: abalone. His fried bird's nest is noteworthy too but it is for the abalone cooked in a clay pot that many come. The restaurant is spread over three floors, with seating for around 150.

你肯定會留意到世界御廚楊貫一的照片。三十多年來，光顧他的客人從世界領導人到本地食客包羅萬有，這大概應歸功於他的拿手名菜：阿一鮑魚。大部分客人都為其砂鍋鮑魚慕名而來，而皇冠燕盞及紅燒翅也相當不俗。飯店佔地三層，可容納約一百五十人。

■ ADDRESS/地址
TEL. 2891 2555
485 Lockhart Road, Causeway Bay
銅鑼灣駱克道485號

■ OPENING HOURS, LAST ORDER
　　營業時間，最後點菜時間
Lunch/午膳　11:00-14:30 (L.O.)
Dinner/晚膳　18:00-22:30 (L.O.)

■ PRICE/價錢
Lunch/午膳　à la carte/點菜　$320-1,500
Dinner/晚膳　set/套餐　　　$1,500-2,800
　　　　　　à la carte/點菜　$420-1,500

Fu Ho (Tsim Sha Tsui)
富豪 (尖沙咀)

Diners have been coming to this Cantonese restaurant on a hidden floor of the Miramar shopping centre for over a decade, thanks to its authentic cooking. Among the specialities that appeal to these scores of regulars are braised superior dried fish maw, bird's nest with almond cream and fried rice 'Ah Yung'. A comprehensive refurbishment in 2011 gave the restaurant a new contemporary look that is elegant yet also comfortable and relaxing.

這家粵菜酒家憑著正宗的烹調打響名堂，即使位於美麗華商場不太起眼的一層，十多年來依然吸引無數饕客。招牌菜有超特厚花膠、杏汁官燕、阿翁炒飯。酒家於2011年重新裝修後，不但時尚優雅，更帶來舒適和悠閒的感覺。

■ ADDRESS/地址

TEL. 2736 2228
4F, Miramar Shopping Centre,
132 Nathan Road, Tsim Sha Tsui,
Kowloon
九龍尖沙咀彌敦道132號美麗華商場4樓

■ OPENING HOURS, LAST ORDER
營業時間，最後點菜時間
11:00-24:00 L.O.22:30

■ PRICE/價錢
Lunch/午膳　set/套餐　　$420-560
　　　　　　à la carte/點菜　$250-2,500
Dinner/晚膳　à la carte/點菜　$250-2,500

Fung Lum
楓林小館

 40

Located opposite Tai Wai station and known for its striking façade, this is the original Fung Lum; the famed replica in Los Angeles was a hit in the 1980s. The recipes remain untarnished to this day, with the seafood being highly recommended, particularly the baked shrimps with salt and lobster and the baked crab with black beans. Regulars believe the pigeon is a must. If ordering several dishes, ask for them to be paced accordingly.

位於大圍火車站對面的楓林小館正面的設計讓人印象深刻；這是原汁原味的楓林；洛杉磯著名的複製品在一九八零年代曾一度讓人瘋靡。今天菜單依然毫不遜色，尤其推薦海鮮，如鹽焗蝦及豉汁焗蟹。常客相信不能缺少一道乳鴿。如果點了好幾道菜，可交由店員編排次序。

■ ADDRESS/地址
TEL. 2692 1175
45-47 Tsuen Nam Road, Tai Wai,
Sha Tin, New Territories
新界沙田大圍村南道45-47號

■ ANNUAL AND WEEKLY CLOSING
　休息日期
Closed 4 days Lunar New Year
農曆新年休息4天

■ OPENING HOURS, LAST ORDER
　營業時間，最後點菜時間
Lunch/午膳 11:00-15:00 (L.O.)
Dinner/晚膳 18:00-22:30 L.O. 22:00

■ PRICE/價錢
à la carte/點菜　　　　　$ 150-500

Fung Shing (Mong Kok)
鳳城 (旺角)

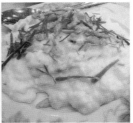

It is the region of Shun Tak that the owner-chef looks to for inspiration for his tasty Cantonese cooking. Look out for dishes such as stir-fried milk with white eggs and crab meat. This family business has been going since 1954, having initially been based in Causeway Bay; their story, together with some recipes, has been published in a book. Divided into two simple rooms, the restaurant is always busy, so it's well worth booking in advance.

主廚兼老闆從順德菜中尋找烹調美味廣東菜的靈感。大良炒鮮奶值得一試。這個家族生意始於1954年，初期位於銅鑼灣。他們的故事與部分食譜已輯錄成書出版。酒家分為兩個大廳。由於這裡客似雲來，建議預早訂座。

■ ADDRESS/地址

TEL. 2381 5261
1-2F, 749 Nathan Road,
Mong Kok, Kowloon
九龍旺角彌敦道749號1-2樓

■ ANNUAL AND WEEKLY CLOSING
　休息日期
Closed 4 days Lunar New Year
農曆新年休息4天

■ OPENING HOURS, LAST ORDER
　營業時間，最後點菜時間
Lunch/午膳　09:00-15:00 (L.O.)
Dinner/晚膳　18:00-22:30 (L.O.)

■ PRICE/價錢
Lunch/午膳　à la carte/點菜　$ 140-350
Dinner/晚膳　à la carte/點菜　$ 180-350

Fu Sing (Causeway Bay)
富聲 (銅鑼灣)

With its contemporary interior, attentive service and accessible
location, it is little wonder that this large second Fu Sing
restaurant has proved so successful. The dim sum selection
is comprehensive and the prices are suitably appealing to
allow for much over-ordering. Specialities include steamed
crab in Chinese wine and soy sauce chicken in Fu Sing style,
but we also recommend the fish soup or the garoupa with
preserved vegetables.

富現代感的裝潢，細心的服務，加上地點方便，難怪這間富聲第二分
店會如此成功。點心選擇豐富，價錢合理，客人總忍不住多點幾道
菜！招牌菜包括富聲花雕蒸蟹和鮑汁豉油雞。我們亦欣賞這裡的魚湯
及甜菜三蔥炒斑球。

■ ADDRESS/地址

TEL. 2504 4228
1F, 68 Yee Wo Street, Causeway Bay
銅鑼灣怡和街68號1樓

■ OPENING HOURS, LAST ORDER
營業時間，最後點菜時間
Lunch/午膳 11:00-15:00 L.O.14:30
Dinner/晚膳 18:00-23:00 L.O.22:30

■ PRICE/價錢
Lunch/午膳　à la carte/點菜 $ 160-600
Dinner/晚膳　à la carte/點菜 $ 200-600

Fu Sing (Wan Chai)
富聲 (灣仔)

🍽 200 📞🍴

The lift in this stylish building brings you out directly into a plush, spacious restaurant but head up to the third floor dining room which is more modern and comes with a glass roof. The service is attentive while the cooking, with its broad repertoire of Cantonese dishes, is undertaken with equal care. Among the recommendations are black pepper and pig bone soup, soy sauce chicken in Fu Sing style and steamed crab in Chinese wine.

富聲位處時尚大樓之中，其升降機可帶你直達這富麗堂皇、佔地寬廣的酒家，三樓餐室更富現代感並設有玻璃天花。餐廳服務非常周到，選擇繁多的一系列粵菜，全屬精心炮製之作。推介菜式包括胡椒豬骨湯、富聲鮑汁豉油雞及花雕蒸蟹。

■ ADDRESS/地址
TEL. 2893 0881
1F, 353 Lockhart Road,
Sunshine Plaza, Wan Chai
灣仔駱克道353號三湘大廈1樓

■ ANNUAL AND WEEKLY CLOSING
　休息日期
Closed 2 days Lunar New Year
農曆新年休息2天

■ OPENING HOURS, LAST ORDER
　營業時間，最後點菜時間
Lunch/午膳 11:00-15:00 (L.O.)
Dinner/晚膳 18:00-23:00 (L.O.)

■ PRICE/價錢
Lunch/午膳 à la carte/點菜 $ 160-600
Dinner/晚膳 à la carte/點菜 $ 200-600

Gaddi's
吉地士

Gaddi's is something of an institution in the city. A private lift whisks you to this 'fine dining' legend which first opened its doors in 1953. Live music and old-style British formality accompany the classical French cuisine. If you want to make an evening of it you should try the tasting menu. Gaddi's harks back to a bygone age where the act of dining is taken very seriously and, as such, gentlemen are required to wear a jacket.

吉地士可說是城內有名的食府。私人電梯迅速把你把帶到這個超過五十年的優質餐飲傳奇之地。現場音樂和古老英國禮節配襯著經典法國菜。如果想享受美好的晚餐，便要品嚐吉地士的tasting menu。餐廳保留著一種昔日的典雅，餐飲的真正意義得以尊重。男士們，謹記帶上一件西裝外套。

■ ADDRESS/地址

TEL. 2315 3171
1F, The Peninsula Hotel,
Salisbury Road, Tsim Sha Tsui,
Kowloon
九龍尖沙咀梳士巴利道半島酒店1樓
www.peninsula.com

■ OPENING HOURS, LAST ORDER
　　營業時間，最後點菜時間
Lunch/午膳 12:00-14:30 (L.O.)
Dinner/晚膳 19:00-22:30 (L.O.)

■ PRICE/價錢
Lunch/午膳   set/套餐 $ 428
　　　　　　 à la carte/點菜 $ 1,000-1,300
Dinner/晚膳 set/套餐 $ 1,488
　　　　　　 à la carte/點菜 $ 1,000-1,300

Gaylord
爵樂

🍽 24 📞🍴

It's easy to see why Gaylord has been pulling in regulars for 40 years: prices are good, especially those of the lunch buffet, staff are enthusiastic and the à la carte menu offers an appealing mix of dishes. Tender boneless lamb in an onion and red pepper sauce and prawns in aromatic spices are signature dishes. The restaurant is warmly decorated; ask for one of the five booths. A live band plays ghazal music every night from 7.30pm.

不難想到爵樂在將近四十年來為何吸引無數常客：價錢合理，尤其是自助午餐；員工的服務殷勤；「à la carte」餐牌上也提供一系列誘人美食可供搭配。香草羊肉和洋蔥香汁鮮蝦是他們的招牌菜。餐廳裝潢溫馨，設有五個廂座，不妨要求坐到其中一個。每晚7:30更有樂隊現場演奏ghazal音樂。

■ ADDRESS/地址

TEL. 2376 1001
1F, Ashley Centre Building,
23-25 Ashley Road, Tsim Sha Tsui,
Kowloon
九龍尖沙咀亞士厘道23-25號雅士利中心1樓
www.chiram.com.hk

■ OPENING HOURS, LAST ORDER
　營業時間，最後點菜時間
Lunch/午餐　12:00-14:45 L.O.14:30
Dinner/晚膳　18:00-22:45 (L.O.)

■ PRICE/價錢
Lunch/午膳　set/套餐　　　　$52-108
　　　　　　à la carte/點菜 $200-350
Dinner/晚膳　à la carte/點菜 $200-350

Gold by Harlan Goldstein

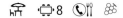

Harlan Goldstein is a restaurateur who doesn't do things by halves. For this, his latest venture, he has sought to recreate the chic, yet relaxed atmosphere of a Manhattan brasserie. To go with the look, the kitchen produces 'modern Western cuisine' which means European ingredients with plenty of Italian thrown in, with dishes such as lobster spaghetti, scallop carpaccio with slow-cooked egg and truffle, and, for dessert, chocolate macaroon.

營辦餐廳經驗深厚的Harlan Goldstein從來貫徹到底。而他這次最新嘗試就是重塑曼哈頓餐館那種時尚又自在的氣氛。表裡如一，菜式主打「現代西式烹調」，以歐洲材料混合大量意大利元素，配搭出龍蝦意粉、以及生帶子薄片配慢煮蛋和松露等精緻菜餚；甜品更有朱古力小圓餅。

■ ADDRESS/地址
TEL. 2869 9986
2F, LFK Tower, 33 Wyndham Street, Central
中環雲咸街33號LFK Tower 2樓
www.gold-dining.com

■ ANNUAL AND WEEKLY CLOSING
　休息日期
Closed Sunday
週日休息

■ OPENING HOURS, LAST ORDER
　營業時間，最後點菜時間
Lunch/午膳 12:00-14:30 (L.O.)
Dinner/晚膳 18:30-22:30 (L.O.)

■ PRICE/價錢
Lunch/午膳	set/套餐	$248-780
	à la carte/點菜	$360-800
Dinner/晚膳	set/套餐	$780
	à la carte/點菜	$360-800

Golden Bauhinia
金紫荊

Conveniently located for visitors to the Hong Kong Convention and Exhibition Centre (and not far from the ferry pier either), this large dining room may be monochrome in tone but it is ideally positioned for admiring the Bauhinia sculpture. The two most popular dishes are crispy rice with a scallop ring, and deep-fried prawn coated with mashed squid; but also try deep-fried chicken marinated in tea leaves. Great care is taken with the service.

前往香港會議展覽中心的人士可輕易找到這家餐廳，離碼頭亦是咫尺之遙。偌大的餐廳配色可能較為單一，但欣賞金紫荊雕像則是一流位置。受歡迎的菜式有酸甜脆米金環帶子、龍皇金縷衣及脆皮茶燻雞。服務亦非常細心。

■ ADDRESS/地址
TEL. 2582 7728
Hong Kong Convention and Exhibition Centre, Golden Bauhinia Square, Expo Drive East, Wan Chai
灣仔博覽道金紫荊廣場
香港會議展覽中心地下

■ OPENING HOURS, LAST ORDER
營業時間，最後點菜時間
Lunch/午膳 12:00-14:45 (L.O.)
Dinner/晚膳 18:30-22:45 (L.O.)

■ PRICE/價錢
Lunch/午膳　set/套餐　　　　$ 138
　　　　　　à la carte/點菜 $ 200-700
Dinner/晚膳　à la carte/點菜 $ 200-700

Golden Leaf
金葉庭

The ever popular Golden Leaf is elegantly dressed with panels, sculptured wood, antique art pieces and chandeliers. It is to this cosy oriental environment that customers come to enjoy the chef's recommendations, such as the steamed fresh crab claw with minced ginger and rice wine or the poached chicken with chicken essence. An attractive set lunch menu and an appealing selection of dim sum are also available.

備受歡迎的金葉庭位處港麗酒店五樓，高貴典雅的餐室，以屏風、木雕、古董藝術品及吊燈裝飾。客人都愛身處此舒適且具東方魅力的環境，享受廚師推介的菜式，如蒸薑米酒鮮蟹鉗，或是貴妃雞。此外，午市亦提供套餐及一系列吸引的點心。

■ ADDRESS/地址
TEL. 2521 3838
5F, Conrad Hotel, Pacific Place,
88 Queensway, Admiralty
香港金鐘道88號太古廣場港麗酒店5樓
www.conradhotels.com

■ OPENING HOURS, LAST ORDER
　營業時間，最後點菜時間
Lunch/午膳 11:30-15:00 (L.O.)
Dinner/晚膳 18:00-23:00 (L.O.)

■ PRICE/價錢

Lunch/午膳	set/套餐	$388-528
	à la carte/點菜	$280-600
Dinner/晚膳	set/套餐	$528-628
	à la carte/點菜	$320-1,050

Golden Valley
駿景軒

The Emperor hotel is a regular haunt of many a famous face and avid race-goer at the celebrated course nearby. The hotel's traditional but fresh looking restaurant serves classic Cantonese and Sichuan cuisines but it is also known for its hotpots, which account for around 80% of its business in the winter months. Deep-fried crispy chicken is a must-have dish, while fish simmered with chilli is another of the kitchen's signature dishes.

英皇駿景酒店鄰近快活谷馬場，經常有城中名流及賽馬愛好者在此出入。酒店的中菜廳具有傳統中式而富新意的裝潢，提供傳統廣東菜和四川菜；其火鍋更備受推崇，於冬季佔業務約八成之多。必試之選有駿景脆皮炸雞，麻辣水煮鮮魚片亦屬其代表作。

■ ADDRESS/地址
TEL. 2961 3330
1F, The Emperor Hotel, 1 Wang Tak Street, Happy Valley
跑馬地宏德街1號英皇駿景酒店1樓
www.emperorhotel.com.hk

■ OPENING HOURS, LAST ORDER
　營業時間，最後點菜時間
Lunch/午膳 11:00-15:30 (L.O.)
Dinner/晚膳 18:00-22:30 (L.O.)

■ PRICE/價錢
à la carte/點菜　　　　　$ 200-600

Good Hope Noodles
好旺角麵家

Choosing what you want to eat here is easy, just watch the chefs preparing food in the two tiny kitchens – wontons and noodles in one, congee in the other - as you wait for a table. Whether having the beef, pork knuckles or wonton noodles, you'll find it all very fresh and tasty, which explains its popularity with those locals who have been coming here for years. Two generations of owners keep the place looking clean and bright.

要決定吃什麼非常容易——在等待座位時看看廚師在兩個小廚房裡如何烹調食物吧。無論是牛肉、豬手或雲吞麵，你都可以在這裡嚐到最新鮮、最美味的麵食，這也解釋了為什麼這餐廳多年來如此受常客歡迎。兩代店主致力保持店面清潔明亮。

■ ADDRESS/地址
TEL. 2393 9036
146 Sai Yeung Choi Street,
Mong Kok, Kowloon
九龍旺角西洋菜街146號

■ ANNUAL AND WEEKLY CLOSING
　休息日期
Closed 4 days Lunar New Year
農曆新年休息4天

■ OPENING HOURS, LAST ORDER
　營業時間，最後點菜時間
11:00-03:00 (L.O.)

■ PRICE/價錢
à la carte/點菜　　　　$ 22-70

Grand Cuisine Shanghai Kitchen   NEW
君頤上海小廚

✗

⊡ 14

Come at lunch during the week and you'll not only have to queue outside for a while but will probably also find yourself sharing your table. The reason for the popularity of this bright restaurant is the traditional Shanghainese cooking; you can watch the chefs prepare the dim sum and La Mian noodles in the open kitchen. Try the steamed prawn with egg white and yellow wine, boiled mixed meat with white cabbage, and La Mian with minced meat.

平常前來午餐，不但要排隊等候，甚至可能要與其他食客同枱用餐。如此受歡迎，皆因其傳統的上海菜餚。您可以看見師傅在開放式廚房製作點心和拉麵。芙蓉花彫蒸蝦球、什錦砂窩津白和炸醬拉麵均值得一試。

■ ADDRESS/地址

TEL. 2568 9989
Shop G510-511, Po On Mansion, Taikoo Shing
太古城寶安閣地下G510-511號舖

■ OPENING HOURS, LAST ORDER
營業時間，最後點菜時間
11:00-22:30 (L.O.)

■ PRICE/價錢
à la carte/點菜 $ 110-450

Grand Hyatt Steakhouse   NEW

Like so many steakhouses around the world, this one has a decidedly masculine feel. Accessed via its own elevator, it's divided into three areas; the best spot is the moodily lit bar which has both counter seats and small tables for two by the windows. The prime cuts of beef are sourced from Canada, Nebraska and Japan and the kitchen clearly knows how to cook meat. Be sure to add the chunky chips cooked in duck fat to your order.

就像世界各地的牛扒屋，總是帶著濃濃的陽剛味。以專屬升降機直達，餐廳分為三區，最佳位置要數富情調的酒吧區，設吧枱座位及靠窗的二人桌。選用的特級牛扒來自加拿大、內布拉斯加和日本，廚師深諳烹調肉類的法門。可別忘了為您的主菜點配以鴨油炮製的厚切薯條。

■ ADDRESS/地址

TEL. 2588 7722

1F, Grand Hyatt Hotel,
1 Harbour Road, Wan Chai
灣仔港灣道1號君悅酒店1樓
www.hongkong.grand.hyatt.com

■ ANNUAL AND WEEKLY CLOSING
　休息日期
Closed Sunday
週日休息

■ OPENING HOURS, LAST ORDER
　營業時間，最後點菜時間
Dinner/晚膳 18:00-22:30 (L.O.)

■ PRICE/價錢
à la carte/點菜 $ 460-1,500

Grissini

Looking for a romantic dinner spot with views to match? Then this smart Italian restaurant with its candlelit tables may just fit the bill. The range of authentic dishes comes from the length and breadth of Italy's regions and there's a good balance struck between tradition and innovation. Specialities include osso bucco and baked sea bass; there's also a decent cheese board. And, as the name suggests, the grissini are rather good too.

假如你嚮往在醉人夜景下享受燭光晚餐，這家時尚的餐廳定是必然之選。真材實料的菜式包羅意大利不同地域的專長，兼顧傳統特色和創意。特色菜包括意式牛仔腿、香焗鱸魚及美味芝士拼盤，而作為店名的grissini長條麵包亦別具水準。

■ ADDRESS/地址
TEL. 2584 7722
2F, Grand Hyatt Hotel,
1 Harbour Road, Wan Chai
灣仔港道1號君悅酒店2樓
www.hongkong.grand.hyatt.com

■ ANNUAL AND WEEKLY CLOSING
　　休息日期
Closed Saturday lunch
週六午膳休息

■ OPENING HOURS, LAST ORDER
　　營業時間，最後點菜時間
Lunch/午膳 12:00-14:30 (L.O.)
Dinner/晚膳 19:00-22:30 (L.O.)

■ PRICE/價錢

Lunch/午膳	set/套餐	$345
	à la carte/點菜	$450-900
Dinner/晚膳	set/套餐	$720-815
	à la carte/點菜	$450-900

Hainan Shaoye (Causeway Bay)
海南少爺 (銅鑼灣)

NEW

Singaporean and Malaysian dishes are on offer at this bright, well-kept spot, whose floor-to-ceiling windows provide pleasant views of the yacht club. Highlights are Hainan Chicken Rice and Bak Kut Teh - pork ribs simmered in a concentrated broth of herbs and spices. Try also the homemade black truffle egg tofu with mushrooms, and Mee Goreng. Dishes are appetisingly presented and the prices are reasonable. It's busy at lunchtimes.

這家餐廳窗明几淨,提供星馬菜式,其落地玻璃窗讓遊艇會美景盡收眼底。推介菜式有海南雞飯和肉骨茶(以中藥及香料濃湯燉煮的豬肉排);值得一試的還有自家製黑松露雞蛋豆腐配蘑菇,以及馬來西亞炒麵。這裡的美食賣相令人垂涎,價格亦合理。午餐時間十分繁忙。

■ ADDRESS/地址
TEL. 2111 3166
Shop P311, 3F, World Trade Centre, 280 Gloucester Road, Causeway Bay
銅鑼灣告士打道280號
世貿中心3樓P311號舖

■ ANNUAL AND WEEKLY CLOSING
　 休息日期
Closed Lunar New Year
年初一休息

■ OPENING HOURS, LAST ORDER
　 營業時間,最後點菜時間
Lunch/午膳 11:30-14:30 (L.O.)
Dinner/晚膳 18:00-22:30 (L.O.)

■ PRICE/價錢
Lunch/午膳　set/套餐　　　　　$78-98
　　　　　　à la carte/點菜 $150-230
Dinner/晚膳　à la carte/點菜 $150-230

Hakka Yé Yé (Causeway Bay)
客家爺爺（銅鑼灣）

 30

Following the success of the original in Central, a second branch was opened in a commercial building in one of Causeway Bay's busiest areas. You can expect the same menu, which means a large choice of Hakkanese inspired dishes, such as Yé Yé stuffed tofu, stir-fried egg whites with shrimp, and fish with Hakka rice wine in a clay pot. In contrast to the relatively traditional cooking, the surroundings are decidedly contemporary.

繼中環總店後，客家爺爺於銅鑼灣一幢商業大廈開辦分店。分店同樣提供一系列客家菜以供選擇，包括爺爺釀荳腐煲、芙蓉蝦仁及香芹糟汁炆魚腩等。餐廳裝潢時尚，與其傳統客家菜烹調方式剛好相反。

■ ADDRESS/地址

TEL. 2577 8018

5F, The Goldmark,
502 Hennessy Road, Causeway Bay
銅鑼灣軒尼詩道502號黃金廣場5樓
www.yeyegroup.com

■ OPENING HOURS, LAST ORDER
　　營業時間，最後點菜時間
Lunch/午膳 11:30-15:00 L.O.14:30
Dinner/晚膳 18:00-23:00 L.O.22:30

■ PRICE/價錢
Lunch/午膳　set/套餐　　　$ 45-85
　　　　　　à la carte/點菜 $ 150-280
Dinner/晚膳　à la carte/點菜 $ 150-280

Hakka Yé Yé (Central)
客家爺爺 (中環)

The food of the Hakka people is very much sophisticated peasant cookery, relying largely on pork and chicken. Specialities here include braised pork belly with preserved vegetables and Emperor chicken. The small contemporary room is simply furnished but the charming team go out of their way to explain the distinctive characteristics of their authentic and reasonably-priced regional cuisine.

客家菜的特色是農家菜，大部分食材選用豬肉和雞肉。這裡的推介菜式包括西施梅菜扣肉和霸爺雞。地方小巧裝潢現代精緻，親切友善的員工用獨有方式介紹原汁原味的客家菜，且價錢合理。

■ ADDRESS/地址
TEL. 2537 7060
2F, Parekh House,
63 Wyndham Street, Central
中環雲咸街63號巴力大廈2樓
www.yeyegroup.com

■ ANNUAL AND WEEKLY CLOSING
休息日期
Closed Sunday and Public Holidays
週日及公眾假期休息

■ OPENING HOURS, LAST ORDER
營業時間，最後點菜時間
Lunch/午膳 12:00-14:15 (L.O.)
Dinner/晚膳 18:30-22:15 (L.O.)

■ PRICE/價錢
Lunch/午膳　set/套餐　　$96
　　　　　à la carte/點菜 $160-360
Dinner/晚膳　à la carte/點菜 $160-360

Harbour Grill

The décor here is elegant and comfortable and suits a romantic evening just as well as a more formal business occasion. The international menu shows ambition, placing French classics alongside grilled dishes that could include Wagyu beef, whole Italian sea bass or Welsh lamb rack. Other specialities include scallops seared with pork belly, lobster bisque and dark chocolate cake. An extensive wine list has been well chosen.

這裡的裝潢優雅舒適，既適合浪漫約會，也可用於較正式的商業場合。菜單上來自世界各地的佳餚顯示了餐廳的野心，如將傳統法國菜配合燒烤菜式，包括和牛、全條意大利海鱸或威爾斯羊架。其他招牌菜包括烤帶子配豬腩、龍蝦濃湯與黑巧克力蛋糕。酒單經過精心挑選，選擇甚豐。

■ ADDRESS/地址

TEL. 2996 8433

GF, Harbour Grand Kowloon Hotel,
20 Tak Fung Street, Whampoa Garden,
Hung Hom, Kowloon
九龍紅磡黃埔花園德豐街20號
九龍海逸君綽酒店地下
www.harbour-grand.com

■ OPENING HOURS, LAST ORDER
　營業時間，最後點菜時間
Lunch/午膳 12:00-14:00 (L.O.)
Dinner/晚膳 18:00-22:00 (L.O.)

■ PRICE/價錢
Lunch/午膳　set/套餐　　　　$ 195-280
　　　　　　à la carte/點菜 $ 450-900
Dinner/晚膳　à la carte/點菜 $ 450-900

Hide-Chan　NEW
秀

After Tokyo and New York, it's Hong Kong's turn to discover this Japanese ramen shop. Choose one of three base soups: White Hide, for original, thick pork bone taste; Black Hide for stronger, charred-garlic tasting pork bone and Red Hide, where a special Korean sweet chilli sauce is added. You choose the noodle's texture and topping, such as soft-boiled egg or black fungus. Watch every step of the ramen making process from the counter.

繼東京及紐約後，這家日本拉麵店正式落戶香港。你可以從三種湯底中選擇：白秀拉麵，是原味豬骨濃湯；黑秀拉麵，味道較重的烤蒜味豬骨湯；赤秀拉麵則特別添加了韓式甜辣醬。你更可自選麵質和配料，如溫泉蛋、黑木耳等。如坐在櫃台位置，可看到拉麵烹煮的整個過程。

■ ADDRESS/地址
TEL. 2522 5990
GF, The Loop,
33 Wellington Street, Central
中環威靈頓街33號地下
www.hide-chan.hk

■ OPENING HOURS, LAST ORDER
營業時間，最後點菜時間
11:00-23:00 (L.O.)

■ PRICE/價錢
à la carte/點菜　　　　　$75-120

Hing Kee
避風塘興記

Originating in Causeway Bay two generations ago, the family moved their business to Tsim Sha Tsui, where they've made a name for themselves with their Boat People style cuisine; further testimony comes from the celebrity signatures lining the walls. Elder sister heads the serving team; younger brother takes charge in the kitchen. They are famous for their stir-fry crabs with black beans and chilli, roast duck and rice noodles in soup and congee.

兩代前已於銅鑼灣開業，家族將餐廳移往尖沙嘴，建立了避風塘特色菜的名聲，牆上貼滿明星簽名，更見證此店美味。招牌菜包括避風塘炒蟹、燒鴨湯河及艇仔粥。

■ ADDRESS/地址
TEL. 2722 0022
1F, Bowa House, 180 Nathan Road, Tsim Sha Tsui, Kowloon
九龍尖沙咀彌敦道180號寶華商業大廈1樓

■ ANNUAL AND WEEKLY CLOSING
　　休息日期
Closed 2 days Lunar New Year
農曆新年休息2天

■ OPENING HOURS, LAST ORDER
　　營業時間，最後點菜時間
Dinner/晚膳 18:00-05:00 (L.O.)

■ PRICE/價錢
à la carte/點菜　　　　　$ 300-600

Hin Ho Curry (Sai Wan Ho)
恆河咖喱屋 (西灣河)

The original, found not that far from here, proved so successful that this second branch was opened, back in 1997. The young Indian chef is passionate about his craft and standout dishes from his extensive menu include lamb massala and the tomato beef flank. The two-storey dining rooms are simply decorated with a vintage look seemingly inspired by the 1970s. Service is young and enthusiastic and it fills quickly at lunch so arrive early.

由於離這裡不遠的原店極為成功，因此這家第二分店便在1997年誕生。年輕的印度主廚對他創作的菜式充滿熱誠。豐富的餐牌中特別出色的菜式有瑪沙拉羊肉與蕃茄咖喱牛仔腩。佔地兩層的餐室陳設簡約，散發懷舊氣息，帶來恍如70年代的感覺。這裡的侍應年輕又朝氣勃勃；午餐時間很快就滿座，建議早些前來。

■ ADDRESS/地址
TEL. 2967 8348
90 Shau Kei Wan Road, Sai Wan Ho
西灣河筲箕灣道90號

■ ANNUAL AND WEEKLY CLOSING
   休息日期
Closed 4 days Lunar New Year
農曆新年休息4天

■ OPENING HOURS, LAST ORDER
   營業時間，最後點菜時間
Lunch/午膳 11:00-15:00 L.O.14:30
Dinner/晚膳 18:00-23:00 L.O.22:30

■ PRICE/價錢
Lunch/午膳   set/套餐 $45-68
                 à la carte/點菜 $150-270
Dinner/晚膳 à la carte/點菜 $150-270

Hin Ho Curry (Shau Kei Wan)
恆河咖喱屋 (筲箕灣)

Seeing the tandoor in the front window tells you that you're in for an authentic experience. The chefs are from Nepal and trained in Delhi so the cuisine has a north Indian bias; Gosht Rajala, lamb with nuts and spices, and Jeera Pullao, delicious buttery rice, are popular choices. If you can't decide then the Nawabi Bhojan or 'Royal Fare' menu offers a great selection of classic dishes. The simple décor comes with a hint of Bollywood.

從櫥窗看到印度式烤爐，就知道這裡必能品嚐正宗印度菜。主廚是尼泊爾人，在德里學師，因此這裡的菜式都帶有北印度風味。香草菓仁燴羊肉與香料炒飯，都是受歡迎的菜式。若你覺得難以取捨，「印度帝皇餐」套餐提供多款傳統印度菜，是不錯的選擇。其簡約的裝修陳設，更隱約有寶萊塢的味道。

■ ADDRESS/地址
TEL. 2560 1268
Shop 11, East Way Tower,
59-99 Main Street East, Shau Kei Wan
筲箕灣東大街東威大廈11號舖

■ OPENING HOURS, LAST ORDER
營業時間，最後點菜時間
Lunch/午膳 11:00-15:00 L.O.14:30
Dinner/晚膳 18:00-23:00 L.O.22:30

■ PRICE/價錢
Lunch/午膳　set/套餐　　$45-68
　　　　　　à la carte/點菜 $150-270
Dinner/晚膳　à la carte/點菜 $150-270

Ho Hung Kee
何洪記

Mr Ho's parents started the business in Wan Chai in 1946 and the restaurant's been here, near Times Square, since 1974; so he advisedly calls it the Original Noodle Shop! His wife claims the noodles won her over before she'd even met him. On both sides of the entrance, two little cooking stations entice you in with their aromas. Exceptional shrimp wonton uses a decades-old recipe and you must try congee with fish or fried beef rice noodles.

東主何先生的父母於1946年已在灣仔經營麵食生意。自1974年以來，這家麵店一直座落於現時位置，毗鄰時代廣場。因此，何先生特意稱它為「老店」！何太太憶稱還未與丈夫見上一次面，他的「麵」就已經贏得芳心。店門兩旁的小廚房總是香味四溢，引領食客進內。著名的鮮蝦雲吞以幾十年的祖傳秘方烹調，而這裡的魚粥及干炒牛河亦絕對不容錯過。

■ ADDRESS/地址
TEL. 2577 6558
2 Sharp Street, Causeway Bay
銅鑼灣雲東街2號

■ ANNUAL AND WEEKLY CLOSING
　　休息日期
Closed 3 days Lunar New Year
農曆新年休息3天

■ OPENING HOURS, LAST ORDER
　　營業時間，最後點菜時間
11:30-23:30 (L.O.)

■ PRICE/價錢
à la carte/點菜　　　　　　$ 35-180

Hoi King Heen
海景軒

As if to compensate for its hotel basement location, the restaurant is elegantly decorated with wood panelling and warm colours; the private dining rooms are also particularly charming. The authentic Cantonese cooking draws plenty of regulars from beyond the hotel, thanks to signature dishes such as steamed garoupa rolls with Yunnan ham; steamed crab claw with egg white and the Fortune chicken – which needs to be ordered in advance.

海景軒以暖色系與木鑲板裝潢，格調高雅，彷彿是彌補位置上的不足之處——位於酒店地庫，貴賓房裝潢更特別雅致。出色的正宗廣東烹調，如其中一款招牌菜龍皇白玉卷，吸引許多酒店以外的常客。花雕蛋白蒸鮮蟹鉗、順德富貴雞必須預訂。

■ ADDRESS/地址
TEL. 2731 2883
B2F, Intercontinental Grand Stanford Hotel, 70 Mody Road, East Tsin Sha Tsui, Kowloon
九龍尖東麼地道70號海景嘉福酒店B2樓
www.hongkong.intercontinental.com

■ OPENING HOURS, LAST ORDER
營業時間，最後點菜時間
Lunch/午膳 11:30-14:30 (L.O.)
Dinner/晚膳 18:30-22:30 (L.O.)

■ PRICE/價錢
Lunch/午膳　set/套餐　　　　$ 168-198
　　　　　　à la carte/點菜 $ 260-1,300
Dinner/晚膳　à la carte/點菜 $ 260-1,300

Hoi Yat Heen
海逸軒

This large restaurant has great harbour views and so too do the two private rooms. With live music every night, it serves carefully prepared Cantonese cooking which has been given a contemporary twist. Specialities include oven-baked crab meat with shredded onion on the crab shell; sautéed sliced pork with pear and black vinegar, and steamed egg white and bird's nest with pumpkin broth. The very diligent manager heads up an attentive team.

這家餐廳不論主廳與貴賓房，都能俯瞰美麗的維港景色。每晚有現場音樂演奏，配搭大廚精美菜式，為廣東菜添上一絲現代感。特色菜包括：金牌焗釀蟹蓋、桂花梨黑醋脆柳及金湯芙蓉燴燕窩。勤快的經理帶領著出色的服務團隊，為客人提供賓至如歸的服務。

■ ADDRESS/地址
TEL. 2996 8459
2F, Harbour Grand Kowloon Hotel,
20 Tak Fung Street, Whampoa
Garden, Hung Hom, Kowloon
九龍紅磡德豐街20號九龍海逸君綽酒店
2樓
www.harbour-grand.com

■ OPENING HOURS, LAST ORDER
　營業時間，最後點菜時間
Lunch/午膳　11:30-15:00 (L.O.)
Dinner/晚膳　18:00-23:00 (L.O.)

■ PRICE/價錢
Lunch/午膳　set/套餐　　　　$198-1,688
　　　　　　à la carte/點菜　$300-1,000
Dinner/晚膳　set/套餐　　　　$998-1,688
　　　　　　à la carte/點菜　$300-1,000

Hong Zhou
杭州酒家

The owner-chef has many of his fresh ingredients delivered directly from Hong Zhou every afternoon and you can certainly tell when you bite into those delicious fried river prawns with Longjing tea leaves; the braised pork belly is also worth trying. The chef inherited his obvious passion for food and the delicate cuisine of Hong Zhou from his father (who was also a famous chef in town) and strives to keep his cooking authentic.

餐廳主廚兼老闆堅持每天下午由杭州運來新鮮食材。你不難察覺食材的高質素：嚐嚐鮮美的龍井河蝦仁吧，東坡肉同樣值得一試。廚師從同為城中名廚的父親身上遺傳了對飲食及杭州美食的熱愛，並努力維持正宗烹調方法。

■ ADDRESS/地址

TEL. 2591 1898
1F, Chinachem Johnston Plaza,
178-186 Johnston Road, Wan Chai
灣仔莊士敦道178-186號
華懋莊士敦廣場1樓

■ ANNUAL AND WEEKLY CLOSING
   休息日期
Closed 2 days Lunar New Year
農曆新年休息2天

■ OPENING HOURS, LAST ORDER
   營業時間，最後點菜時間
Lunch/午膳 11:30-14:15 (L.O.)
Dinner/晚膳 17:30-22:15 (L.O.)

■ PRICE/價錢
Lunch/午膳　à la carte/點菜 $ 220-500
Dinner/晚膳　à la carte/點菜 $ 220-500

Ho To Tai
好到底

Divided into two cosy and simple dining areas, with the first floor being the more animated of the two and from where diners can see through into the equally small kitchen. This noodle shop is still run by the Chan family who opened it back in 1949; they also have their own noodle factory a few blocks away. The most popular dishes are the wonton noodles, dried shrimp's roe with noodles and homemade dumplings stuffed with fish skin.

店內分為兩個簡單而舒適的用餐區。兩層當中,以一樓較為熱鬧,食客可看見小小的廚房裡員工忙碌的情形。這家麵店自1949年開業以來一直由陳氏家族經營,他們更在附近自設製麵工場。最受歡迎的菜式有雲吞麵、蝦子撈麵與特製水餃。

■ ADDRESS/地址
TEL. 2476 2495
67 Fau Tsoi Street, Yuen Long,
New Territories
新界元朗阜財街67號

■ ANNUAL AND WEEKLY CLOSING
　休息日期
Closed 10 days Lunar New Year
農曆新年休息10天

■ OPENING HOURS, LAST ORDER
　營業時間,最後點菜時間
08:00-20:00 (L.O.)

■ PRICE/價錢
à la carte/點菜　　　　$ 17-48

Hugo's
希戈

The original Hugo's was founded back in 1969 but this new version remains true to its origins by offering the charms of a bygone age. That means there's everything from suits of armour to silver Christofle trolleys being wheeled around the room. The chef and his team prepares traditional European style cuisine with pronounced French influences. Expect the likes of escargots, lobster bisque, steak au poivre and soufflés.

希戈本店創立於1969年，新店延續其懷舊感覺，忠於原店的氣氛。這意味著店裡的一切——全套的銀鎧甲、Christofle品牌的頭盤餐車，全都原汁原味重現眼前。主廚與他的團隊為客人準備有明顯法國特色的傳統歐洲菜。你可在這裡找到法國焗田螺、龍蝦湯、法式黑胡椒牛柳扒與梳乎厘一類的菜式。

■ ADDRESS/地址
TEL. 2311 1234
4F, Hyatt Regency Tsim Sha Tsui,
18 Hanoi Road, Tsim Sha Tsui, Kowloon
九龍尖沙咀河內道18號凱悅酒店-尖沙咀
4樓
www.hongkong.tsimshatsui.hyatt.com

■ ANNUAL AND WEEKLY CLOSING
　休息日期
Closed lunch Saturday and Sunday
週六、日午膳休息

OPENING HOURS, LAST ORDER
　營業時間，最後點菜時間
Lunch/午膳 12:00-14:30 (L.O.)
Dinner/晚膳 18:30-22:30 (L.O.)

■ PRICE/價錢

Lunch/午膳	set/套餐	$295-395
	à la carte/點菜	$620-1,500
Dinner/晚膳	set/套餐	$828-888
	à la carte/點菜	$620-1,500

Hunan Garden (Causeway Bay)
洞庭樓 (銅鑼灣)

🍽 🍽 🍽

♿ 📺16 ☎🍽

Emerge on the 13th floor and you will be greeted by courteous staff near a channel of running water complete with live fish. This leads into a striking, spacious and contemporary room with bright chandeliers and painted wood panels on the walls. The Hunan-style cooking uses carefully sourced local ingredients and specialities include chicken with yellow wine sauce, braised pork and fish fillets with fried minced bean.

甫踏進十三樓，首先映入眼簾的是那流水淙淙的小魚池，繼續往前走，便進入了奪目時尚的進餐區。璀璨的吊燈點綴着牆身的漆木板，交織成獨特的風格。這裏的湘菜選料皆採用本地新鮮食材，特別推薦有韶山酒醉跳水雞、紅燒肉及豆酥魚。

■ ADDRESS/地址

TEL. 2506 9288
Shop 1302, 13F, Food Forum,
Times Square,1 Matheson Street,
Causeway Bay
銅鑼灣勿地臣街1號時代廣場
食通天13樓1302號舖
www.maxims.com.hk

■ OPENING HOURS, LAST ORDER
營業時間，最後點菜時間
Lunch/午膳 11:30-14:30 (L.O.)
Dinner/晚膳 18:00-23:00 (L.O.)

■ PRICE/價錢
à la carte/點菜 $ 200-700

Hung's Delicacies
阿鴻小吃

The news of Mr Lai's success has spread far and wide so now there's always a queue of people outside either wanting a table or ordering a take-away from his charming wife. In fact so many people are keen to come, he's taken on more chefs to cope and the menu is now also in English! The quality of the Cantonese and Chiu Chow dishes remains high, whether that's the marinated pork belly or the braised assorted vegetables in red tofu sauce.

黎先生的成功廣為人知，現在慕名而來的人客往往要大排長龍——不論是堂食，還是向魅力十足的黎太太購買外賣。為了應付眾多人客，黎先生雇用了更多廚師，菜單更設有英文版！這裡的粵菜與潮州菜仍然保持高水準，鹵水豬腩肉、南乳粗齋都十分出色。

■ ADDRESS/地址

TEL. 2570 1108
Shop 4, GF, Ngan Fai Building,
84-94 Wharf Road, North Point
北角和富道84-94號銀輝大廈地下4號舖

■ ANNUAL AND WEEKLY CLOSING
　　休息日期
Closed 1 week Lunar New Year,
Monday and Tuesday
農曆新年7天, 週一及週二休息

■ OPENING HOURS, LAST ORDER
　　營業時間, 最後點菜時間
13:00-22:00 (L.O.)

■ PRICE/價錢
à la carte/點菜　　　　　　$ 100-150

Inagiku (Tsim Sha Tsui)
稻菊 (尖沙咀)

Inagiku has a strong pedigree: the first was established over a century ago in Japan. Décor is elegant, the Japanese influences a visual pleasure. There are several dining areas: a sushi bar with a fish tank, a tempura counter, a teppanyaki area and a few tables in the centre of the room; there are five separate private rooms, too. The restaurant is renowned for its tempura and teppanyaki. An attractive list of sake is also available.

稻菊來頭殊不簡單，早在百多年前已於日本開業。這裡的裝潢設計典雅高尚，源自日本人對美學的要求，為食客帶來視覺上的享受。餐廳共有幾個用餐區，包括設有魚缸的壽司吧、天婦羅檯、鐵板燒區，以及餐廳中心的幾張餐桌。此外，稻菊還設有五間私人餐室。這裡的天婦羅及鐵板燒享負盛名，而員工亦可為你推介更多菜式。提供一系列清酒名單任君選擇，相當吸引。

■ ADDRESS/地址

TEL. 2733 2933
1F, The Royal Garden Hotel,
69 Mody Road, East Tsim Sha Tsui,
Kowloon
九龍尖東麼地道69號帝苑酒店1樓
www.rghk.com.hk

■ OPENING HOURS, LAST ORDER
   營業時間，最後點菜時間
Lunch/午膳 12:00-14:30 (L.O.)
Dinner/晚膳 18:00-22:30 (L.O.)

■ PRICE/價錢
Lunch/午膳   set/套餐 $ 170-500
              à la carte/點菜 $ 400-1,380
Dinner/晚膳   set/套餐 $ 270-1,200
              à la carte/點菜 $ 400-1,380

Ippudo   NEW
一風堂

🍴7

Ippudo was founded in Fukuoka by the 'ramen king', Shigemi Kawahara; he now has over 60 shops in Japan alone. In 2011 he opened this large, contemporary dining room and staffed it with an enthusiastic young team. Everyone is here for ramen and there are two main choices: Akamaru Shinajior or Shiromaru Motoaji – the former use a pork bone soup base with miso paste and are thicker and stronger in flavour; the latter are the 'classic' ramen.

來自日本福岡的一風堂，是由有拉麵大王之稱的河原成美所創立，僅是日本現已有超過60間分店。在2011年進軍香港，開設了這間大型富現代感的餐廳，員工都是充滿活力的年青人。這裡所有食客都是為拉麵而來，主要有兩種選擇：赤丸新味或白丸元味；前者以豬骨湯為基礎加上麵豉醬，味道濃厚，後者則是經典原味拉麵。

■ ADDRESS/地址

TEL. 2957 8893
Shop 210, 2F, Silvercord,
30 Canton Road, Tsim Sha Tsui
九龍尖沙咀廣東道30號
新港中心2樓210號舖

■ OPENING HOURS, LAST ORDER
  營業時間，最後點菜時間
  11:30-22:00 (L.O.)

■ PRICE/價錢

  à la carte/點菜 $ 68-128

IR 1968 (Causeway Bay)
印尼餐廳1968 (銅鑼灣)

One of Hong Kong's longest standing and best known Indonesian restaurants is run by the sons of the couple who opened it back in 1968. Continuity also comes courtesy of the head chef, who has been here for almost 30 years. Satay is cooked over charcoal and Nasi Goreng, beef rendang, sweet semur sauce ox tongue and black sticky rice with mango dessert are among the highlights. Dim lighting and antique wood carvings help create an intimate atmosphere.

餐廳在1968年開業，是香港其中一家歷史最悠久而最著名的印尼餐廳，現正由創辦人夫婦的兒子經營。主廚已經在這裡工作30年，食物質素絕對有保證。著名菜式包括以炭火燒烤的沙爹串、印尼炒飯、巴東牛肉、炆牛舌還有芒果黑糯米。昏暗的燈光、古董木雕與藤椅，營造親切、輕鬆的氣氛。

■ ADDRESS/地址
TEL. 2577 9981
28 Leighton Road, Causeway Bay
銅鑼灣禮頓道28號
www.ir1968.com

■ OPENING HOURS, LAST ORDER
　營業時間，最後點菜時間
12:00-23:00 (L.O.))

■ PRICE/價錢
Lunch/午膳　set/套餐　　　　$68-88
　　　　　　à la carte/點菜 $180-300
Dinner/晚膳　à la carte/點菜 $180-300

Island Tang
港島廳

This elegant art deco inspired room, with its chandeliers, rich wood panelling and mirrors, is reminiscent of forties Hong Kong; and it should come as no surprise to learn that Sir David Tang is behind it. The menu offers a range of sophisticated and delicious Cantonese dishes, from king prawns with lobster sauce and baked crab meat to terrific Peking duck and many other classics. As befits the surroundings, service is slick and professional.

靈感來自裝飾藝術的高雅房間配有吊燈、厚木鑲板及鏡子，重現四十年代香港的光景；此情此景，發現幕後主腦原是鄧永鏘爵士，面對如斯景致，你應毫不意外毫不意外。菜單上提供一系列獨特美味的廣東菜，從龍蝦醬皇帝蝦、焗蟹肉到出色的北京填鴨及其他不同經典菜色。悉心專業的服務與出色的環境相得益彰。

■ ADDRESS/地址

TEL. 2526 8798
Shop 222, The Galleria,
9 Queen's Road, Central
中環皇后大道中9號嘉軒廣場222號舖
www.islandtang.com

■ ANNUAL AND WEEKLY CLOSING
   休息日期
Closed 3 days Lunar New Year
農曆新年休息3天

■ OPENING HOURS, LAST ORDER
   營業時間，最後點菜時間
Lunch/午膳 12:00-14:30 (L.O.)
Dinner/晚膳 18:00-22:30 (L.O.)

■ PRICE/價錢
Lunch/午膳   set/套餐 $308-408
               à la carte/點菜 $320-800
Dinner/晚膳   à la carte/點菜 $320-800

Jade Garden (Lockhart Road)
翠園 (駱克道)

As busy as the street in which it is located, Jade Garden reopened in 2010 following extensive redecoration and is now contemporary in style and rather elegant. The dim sum, offered from early morning to lunchtime, still draw the crowds. In the evening however, you should take time to enjoy some of the chef's keenly priced Cantonese specials such as vermicelli with abalone or pan-fried tofu with shrimps, mushrooms and vegetables.

翠園的繁盛程度，就好比其所處街道。酒家於2010年經大規模裝修後重開，變得更富時代感，而不失優雅。由大清早到午市服務的點心車，仍一如過往吸引無數食客。而到了傍晚，你就應該花點時間，細意品嚐廚師精選粵菜，如鮑魚粉絲、或香煎豆腐配鮮蝦菇菌翠蔬等。

■ ADDRESS/地址

TEL. 2573 9339

3F, Causeway Bay Plaza II,
463-483 Lockhart Road, Causeway Bay
銅鑼灣駱克道463-483號
銅鑼灣廣場第2期3樓
www.maxims.com.hk

■ OPENING HOURS, LAST ORDER
　營業時間，最後點菜時間
07:00-22:45 (L.O.)

■ PRICE/價錢
Lunch/午膳　à la carte/點菜 $100-270
Dinner/晚膳　à la carte/點菜 $250-500

Joi Hing
再興

The Chow family have had many barbecue shops but this one has been a feature here in Stewart Road since 1975 and is run very capably by the affable Mrs Chow. Her special recipe for the marinade is an integral part of the appeal. Pork, duck and goose are the primary meats, with BBQ pork being highly recommended. There's no menu – just cards stuck on the walls. If barbecue is not your thing then their curry sauce is pretty legendary too.

周氏家族曾擁有多間燒臘店，這家自1975年於史劍域道開業，由和藹可親的周太太主理的燒臘店一直是備受矚目。她的秘製滷汁是此店吸引人的主因。這裡主要供應豬、鴨、鵝，尤以叉燒為佳。食物清單全都張貼在牆上。如果燒臘非你所好，這裡的咖哩也相當值得嘗試。

■ ADDRESS/地址
TEL. 2519 6639
1C Stewart Road, Wan Chai
灣仔史劍域道1號C

■ ANNUAL AND WEEKLY CLOSING
　休息日期
Closed 2 weeks Lunar New Year,
Sunday and Public Holidays
農曆新年兩星期、週日及公眾假期休息

■ OPENING HOURS, LAST ORDER
　營業時間，最後點菜時間
10:00-22:00 (L.O.)

■ PRICE/價錢
à la carte/點菜 $ 25-45

Kau Kee
九記

You'll probably have to line up in the street first to eat here: Kau Kee has been trading since the 1930s and has consequently built up a huge following which includes some well known faces from show business and politics. It's all very basic and you'll have to share your table but the food is delicious. Beef noodles are the speciality; different cuts of meat with a variety of noodles in a tasty broth or spicy sauce. Try the iced milk tea too.

要在九記用膳，你可能要在街上排隊等候：九記自一九三零年代起開始經營，聚集了大量支持者，包括部分政商名人。九記陳設回歸基本，進餐時要和其他人士共用餐桌，但食物極具水準。九記的特色在於其牛肉麵；不同部位的肉塊與美味清湯或辣醬麵的搭配。奶茶亦值得一試。

■ ADDRESS/地址
TEL. N/A
21 Gough Street, Central
中環歌賦街21號

■ ANNUAL AND WEEKLY CLOSING
　休息日期
Closed 10 days Lunar New Year,
Sunday and Public Holidays
農曆新年10天、週日及公眾假期休息

■ OPENING HOURS, LAST ORDER
　營業時間，最後點菜時間
12:30-22:30

■ PRICE/價錢
à la carte/點菜　　　　　$ 27-70

Keung Kee Meat Shop (Wan Chai) NEW
強記飯店 (灣仔)

It's open from early morning until midnight and offers everything from breakfast, sandwiches and seafood to noodles and double boiled soups, but this simple restaurant is best known for the quality of its crispy roast meats, like barbecue pork, goose and suckling pig. It has been here for over twenty years and, although it may be a little modest in its decoration, it is clean and tidy. It also does a brisk trade in takeaways.

這裡由大清早營業至半夜，由早餐、三文治、海鮮，到粉麵和老火湯，色色俱備。但這家簡單飯店最著名的是其高質素的燒味，如叉燒、燒鵝和乳豬等。這裡已有超過二十年歷史，陳設略為簡樸但整潔。他們的外賣生意亦十分繁忙。

■ ADDRESS/地址
TEL. 2574 5991
9-17 Tin Lok Lane, Wan Chai
灣仔天樂里9-17號

■ OPENING HOURS, LAST ORDER
營業時間，最後點菜時間
11:00-23:45 (L.O.)

■ PRICE/價錢
à la carte/點菜 $ 40-60

Kin's Kitchen
留家廚房

🛗12

A lively atmosphere and keen staff aside, the strength here rests firmly with the cooking. The kitchen successfully blends traditional dishes, such as smoked chicken, braised stuffed duck, and pork ribs in a curry sauce, with more innovative choices like stewed fish lips in a duck sauce. The good value menu also offers Pearl River Delta specialities, such as braised goose feet with pomelo skin. Dim sum is not served on Mondays.

這裏以充滿活力的氣氛和熱心的服務招徠客人，然而最大的賣點還是在於其美食。留家廚房成功地兼容傳統菜式，如留家煙燻雞、寶鴨穿蓮(京酥鴨) 、 留家五味骨及較有創意的菜式，如鴨汁魚唇等。價錢相宜的餐單還包括一系列珠江三角洲美食，如古法柚皮鵝掌。餐廳逢星期一不供應點心。

■ ADDRESS/地址

TEL. 2571 0913
9 Tsing Fung Street, Tin Hau
天后清風街9號
www.yellowdoorkitchen.com.hk

■ ANNUAL AND WEEKLY CLOSING
　休息日期
Closed 3 days Lunar New Year
農曆新年休息3天

■ OPENING HOURS, LAST ORDER
　營業時間，最後點菜時間
Lunch/午膳 12:00-15:00 L.O. 14:30
Dinner/晚膳 18:00-23:00 L.O. 22:30

■ PRICE/價錢
Lunch/午膳　set/套餐　　$88-198
　　　　　à la carte/點菜 $160-410
Dinner/晚膳　set/套餐　　$398-598
　　　　　à la carte/點菜 $160-410

Kwan Cheuk Heen
君綽軒

Pleasant harbour views, dark wood panelling, smart table settings and a welcoming atmosphere all contribute to the appeal of this restaurant on the fifth floor of the Harbour Grand hotel. Along with a comprehensive list of teas, expect Cantonese, Sichuan and other regional specialities such as deep-fried pork ribs in hawthorn sauce and pan-fried crab claw coated with shrimp paste, along with an appealing dim sum selection at lunch.

迷人的維港景緻、精心設計的餐桌擺設和令人賓至如歸的氣氛,在在令人對這家位於港島海逸君綽酒店五樓的中菜廳更有好感。這裏提供一系列的中國名茶,菜式亦具特色,包括粵菜和川菜以至其他省份的菜餚,如山楂脆香骨及百花炸釀蟹鉗。午市更有多款點心選擇。

■ ADDRESS/地址
TEL. 2121 2688
5F, Harbour Grand North Point Hotel,
23 Oil Street, North Point
北角油街23號港島海逸君綽酒店5樓
www.harbourgrand.com/hongkong

■ OPENING HOURS, LAST ORDER
營業時間,最後點菜時間
Lunch/午膳 12:00-14:30 (L.O.)
Dinner/晚膳 18:00-24:00 (L.O.)
■ PRICE/價錢
Lunch/午膳　set/套餐　　　$ 258-398
　　　　　à la carte/點菜 $ 200-500
Dinner/晚膳 set/套餐　　　$ 258-398
　　　　　à la carte/點菜 $ 230-500

Kwan Kee Bamboo Noodle
坤記竹昇麵

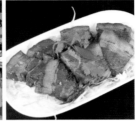

After the success of his family's noodle business in Guangzhou, Mr Lee opened his own place in Hong Kong and named it after his wife's given name. All the noodles here are made using the traditional bamboo method, which may be labour intensive but leaves them tasting great - just try the dried shrimp roe mix with noodles or the braised beef brisket noodles. A glass wall allows you to watch each step of the noodle making process.

在廣州見證了其家人麵食生意的成功後,李先生在香港開設他自己的麵店,並以太太的名字命名。這裏的麵條,全部以極耗人力和時間的竹昇法人手打製,既新鮮又彈牙;試試他們的蝦子撈麵或牛腩麵吧。你可以隔著店內小工房的玻璃,看到麵條製作的全部過程。

■ ADDRESS/地址
TEL. 3484 9126
1 Wing Lung Street,
Cheung Sha Wan, Kowloon
九龍長沙灣永隆街1號

■ ANNUAL AND WEEKLY CLOSING
　休息日期
Closed Lunar New Year
年初一休息

■ OPENING HOURS, LAST ORDER
　營業時間,最後點菜時間
06:00-23:00 (L.O.)

■ PRICE/價錢
à la carte/點菜　　　　$ 19-58

La Marmite NEW

Thanks to La Marmite, homesick émigrés and Francophiles can now come to SoHo to satisfy their cravings. Its large mirrors and old movie posters have helped create the look of a typical French bistro, where the atmosphere is appropriately down-to-earth. The kitchen focuses on producing unfussy classics, from foie gras crème brûlée to thyme-crusted rack of lamb with black olives; and don't miss the tarte Tatin for dessert.

多得La Marmite，思鄉的法男法女和法菜迷只要來到蘇豪區就能大飽口福。巨型鏡子和老電影海報，塑造出典型的法國小酒館風情，連氣氛也是恰到好處的親切。菜式由鵝肝、焦糖布甸到百里香羊架配黑橄欖，絕不賣弄卻全是經典。至於甜品，可別錯過反烤蘋果批。

■ ADDRESS/地址

TEL. 2803 7808
46 Staunton Street, Central
中環士丹頓街46號
www.aqua.com.hk

■ OPENING HOURS, LAST ORDER
　營業時間，最後點菜時間
Lunch/午膳 11:30-15:00 (L.O.)
Dinner/晚膳 18:00-22:30 (L.O.)

■ PRICE/價錢
Lunch/午膳　set/套餐　　　　$118
　　　　　　à la carte/點菜 $300-440
Dinner/晚膳　à la carte/點菜 $300-440

Lan Yuen Chee Koon
蘭苑饎館

The Chan's first place opened back in '84; they moved here in '97 to premises with a proper kitchen and now offer Cantonese claypots, healthy home-style steamed dishes, noodles and deliciously sweet puddings. Fine Chinese furniture is a feature of the small dining room, where Mrs Chan does the cooking and her husband the serving. The set menus at dinner prove particularly popular so be prepared to queue outside.

陳氏的原鋪於1984年開業，並於1997年遷到有正規廚房的現址，為食客提供各種粵式煲仔菜、健康家常蒸煮菜式、麵食和美味的糕點。雅致的中式家具是這家小餐廳的一大特色，陳太在廚房中掌舵，陳先生則負責招呼客人。這裡晚飯時間的套餐特別受歡迎，大有可能需要排隊等候。

■ ADDRESS/地址
TEL. 2381 1369
318 Sai Yeung Choi Street,
Prince Edward, Kowloon
九龍太子西洋菜北街318號

■ ANNUAL AND WEEKLY CLOSING
　　休息日期
Closed 9 days Lunar New Year
農曆新年休息9天

■ OPENING HOURS, LAST ORDER
　　營業時間，最後點菜時間
12:00-22:00 (L.O.)

■ PRICE/價錢
à la carte/點菜　　　　　　$ 60-580

L'Atelier de Joël Robuchon

❀ ❀ ❀   ✗✗

🛖   🍴8   🚋   ☎🍴   🍇

The counter is the place to sit, as you're at the centre of the operation, but if perching on a high chair is not for you, or you require a little more formality, then Le Jardin would be a better choice. The red and black colours marry perfectly and the contemporary French cuisine, which uses prime, seasonal ingredients, produces dishes of exquisite depth, balance and flavour. The superb wine list offers an impressive range of around 3,000 labels.

建議坐在吧檯旁邊，以便觀賞開放式廚房的運作，但若高腳椅非你所好，或者希望爾雅一點，那麼Le Jardin也許更佳。紅色與黑色的配搭與這裡的新派法國菜配合得天衣無縫－－選用上等時令食材，烹調出既有深度又恰到好處的美味佳餚。這裡的酒牌包羅超過3000款佳釀，絕對出色。

■ ADDRESS/地址

TEL. 2166 9000
Shop 401, 4F, The Landmark,
15 Queen's Road, Central
中環皇后大道中15號
置地廣場4樓401號舖
www.robuchon.hk

■ OPENING HOURS, LAST ORDER
  營業時間，最後點菜時間
Lunch/午膳 12:00-14:30 (L.O.)
Dinner/晚膳 18:30-22:30 (L.O.)

■ PRICE/價錢

Lunch/午膳	set/套餐	$398-1,850
	à la carte/點菜	$730-2,150
Dinner/晚膳	set/套餐	$980-1,850
	à la carte/點菜	$730-2,150

Lau Sum Kee (Fuk Wing Street)
劉森記麵家 (福榮街)

This is one noodle shop that is not afraid of the competition. In a street overflowing with noodle shops, Lau Sum Kee (and its sister shop around the corner) are packed with customers buzzing in and out. It is run by the third generation of the family, the noodles are pressed by bamboo and the wontons are freshly made at the shop. Recommendations include wonton noodles, dry prawn roe mix with noodles and pork knuckles mixed with noodles.

這家麵店可謂經得起競爭。在滿佈各家麵店的街上，劉森記麵家（及其轉角位的姐妹店）擠滿來往的食客。此麵店由家族第三代經營，在店內新鮮製造竹昇麵及雲吞。推薦菜式包括雲吞麵、蝦子麵及豬手麵。

■ ADDRESS/地址

TEL. 2386 3583

82 Fuk Wing Street, Sham Shui Po, Kowloon
九龍深水埗福榮街82號

■ ANNUAL AND WEEKLY CLOSING
　休息日期
Closed 3 days Lunar New Year
農曆新年休息3天

■ OPENING HOURS, LAST ORDER
　營業時間，最後點菜時間
12:30-23:30 (L.O.)

■ PRICE/價錢
à la carte/點菜　　　　　$ 24-50

Lei Bistro
利小館

Providing healthy, appealingly priced cooking for everyone is the aim of this very popular restaurant concept from the Lei Garden group. Influences are Northern and Southern Chinese but there are also Cantonese dishes, along with some new creations. Specialities include steamed pork dumpling in Shanghai style, a daily Cantonese style soup, and chilled mango with grapefruit and sago. Despite a capacity of 150, it is still advisable to book.

為所有客人提供健康，大眾化價錢的小菜，正是利苑集團開設這間餐館的概念。菜式來自大江南北，亦有提供新派廣東菜。特式菜包括上海小籠包、粵式老火湯和楊枝金露。雖然餐館可容納150名客人，但亦建議預先訂座。

■ ADDRESS/地址
TEL. 2602 8283
Shop B217-218, Basement 2,
Times Square, 1 Matheson Street,
Causeway Bay
銅鑼灣勿地臣街1號
時代廣場地庫2樓B217-B218號舖
www.leibistro.com

■ OPENING HOURS, LAST ORDER
營業時間，最後點菜時間
11:00-23:00 L.O.22:30

■ PRICE/價錢
à la carte/點菜 $ 110-180

Lei Garden (Causeway Bay)　NEW
利苑酒家 (銅鑼灣)

There appears to be no hindering the proliferation of Lei Garden restaurants – this branch in Times Square opened in 2010. As per usual, Cantonese cuisine is the draw, with many coming specifically for the double-boiled soups, roast pork, fried prawns coated with salted egg yolk or the lunchtime dim sum. It is little wonder that the large dining room and numerous private rooms are often full but the equally vast kitchen copes with aplomb.

利苑酒家的擴展大計似乎從沒休止，此時代廣場分店正是於2010年開幕。廣東菜當然是酒家吸引力所在，一眾食客對其老火湯、蜜汁叉燒、黃金蝦或午間點心趨之若鶩。令人讚嘆的是，偌大的主餐室和多間私人客房經常座無虛席，有相當規模的廚房面對大量食客仍可應付自如。

■ ADDRESS/地址
TEL. 2506 3828
Shop 1003, 10F, Times Square,
1 Matheson Street, Causeway Bay
銅鑼灣勿地臣街1號
時代廣場食通天10樓1003號舖
www.leigarden.com.hk

■ ANNUAL AND WEEKLY CLOSING
　休息日期
Closed 3 days Lunar New Year
農曆新年休息3天

■ OPENING HOURS, LAST ORDER
　營業時間，最後點菜時間
Lunch/午膳　11:30-15:30 L.O.14:30
Dinner/晚膳　18:00-23:30 L.O.22:30

■ PRICE/價錢
Lunch/午膳　à la carte/點菜 $ 180-900
Dinner/晚膳　à la carte/點菜 $ 180-900

Lei Garden (Elements)
利苑酒家（圓方）

♿ ♻ 40 ⏲

The restaurant is located in the blue-tinted 'water' area of this large shopping mall and its décor is more contemporary than some of the other Lei Garden branches. It is composed of a huge dining room, which can be a little noisy when full, and other more intimate rooms. The cooking throughout is reliable Cantonese, with a broad range of interesting seafood preparations as well as some highly unusual double-boiled tonic soups.

這家裝潢華麗優雅的餐館位於巨大的購物商場中的藍色「水」區，比其他利苑分店更有時代感。這裡設有一個巨形的主廳，滿席的時候可能有點吵鬧，亦可選擇其他更能提供私人空間的飯廳。菜色是清一色的廣東菜，但以各種方法烹調的海鮮和與別不同的燉湯，都令這裡顯得分外出色。

■ ADDRESS/地址

TEL. 2196 8133
Shop 2068-70, 2F, Elements,
1 Austin Road West, Kowloon
九龍柯士甸道西1號
圓方2樓2068-70號鋪
www.leigarden.com.hk

■ ANNUAL AND WEEKLY CLOSING
　休息日期
Closed 3 days Lunar New Year
農曆新年休息3天

■ OPENING HOURS, LAST ORDER
　營業時間，最後點菜時間
Lunch/午膳 11:30-14:45 (L.O.)
Dinner/晚膳 18:00-22:45 (L.O.)

■ PRICE/價錢
Lunch/午膳　à la carte/點菜 $ 180-900
Dinner/晚膳　à la carte/點菜 $ 180-900

Lei Garden (IFC)
利苑酒家（國際金融中心）

Forward planning is advisable here – not only when booking but also when selecting certain roast meat dishes and some of their famous double-boiled soups which require advance notice. The extensive menu features specialist seafood dishes and the lunchtime favourites include shrimp and flaky pastries filled with shredded turnip. All this is served up by an efficient team in clean, contemporary surroundings.

到利苑用餐，無論座位，還是食物如燒味或受歡迎的燉湯，提早預約都十分重要。這裡菜式繁多，其中以海鮮炮製的佳餚最具特色，而午市時段的美食首推銀蘿千層酥。格局設計富時代感，潔淨雅致，服務效率亦十分高。

■ ADDRESS/地址
TEL. 2295 0238
Shop 3008-3011, Podium Level 3, IFC Mall, 1 Harbour View Street, Central
中環港景街1號國際金融中心商場
第2期3樓3008-3011號舖
www.leigarden.com.hk

■ ANNUAL AND WEEKLY CLOSING
休息日期
Closed 3 days Lunar New Year
農曆新年休息3天

■ OPENING HOURS, LAST ORDER
營業時間，最後點菜時間
Lunch/午膳 11:30-15:00 (L.O.)
Dinner/晚膳 17:30-22:30 (L.O.)

■ PRICE/價錢
Lunch/午膳 à la carte/點菜 $180-900
Dinner/晚膳 à la carte/點菜 $180-900

Lei Garden (Kowloon Bay)
利苑酒家（九龍灣）

🍽 40　📞🍴

Service is one of the strengths of this Lei Garden, located in a shopping mall near the MTR station. Signature dishes include the 10 different varieties of double-boiled tonic soups (to be ordered in advance), sautéed scallops with macadamia nuts and yellow fungus, and braised boneless spare-ribs with sweet and sour sauce. Those who like to eat lunch early or at pace are rewarded with a discount if they vacate their tables before 12.45pm.

這家利苑分店位於地鐵站附近的商場內，服務周到是她的強項。招牌菜包括10種不同的燉湯（須提前預訂）、米網黃耳夏果炒帶子、宮庭醬烤骨。對於喜歡提早吃午飯或者時間不太足夠可因其下午12:45前離席而獲得折扣優惠。

■ ADDRESS/地址

TEL. 2331 3306
Shop Unit F2, Telford Plaza 1,
33 Wai Yip Street, Kowloon Bay, Kowloon
九龍灣偉業街33號德福廣場F2號鋪
www.leigarden.com.hk

■ ANNUAL AND WEEKLY CLOSING
　　休息日期
Closed 3 days Lunar New Year
農曆新年休息3天

■ OPENING HOURS, LAST ORDER
　　營業時間，最後點菜時間
Lunch/午膳　11:30-15:00 (L.O.)
Dinner/晚膳　18:00-23:00 (L.O.)

■ PRICE/價錢
Lunch/午膳　à la carte/點菜 $ 180-900
Dinner/晚膳　à la carte/點菜 $ 180-900

Lei Garden (Kwun Tong)
利苑酒家 (觀塘)

Avoid the escalators and use the shuttle lift to get to the fifth floor in this confusingly arranged shopping mall. Once there, the set up will seem familiar if you've experienced other Lei Garden branches: dishes are standard Cantonese but are reliably cooked using fresh ingredients. The place is as frantic as the others but has been partitioned into different seating areas by smart trellises. Try not to sit near the entrance as it's noisy.

由於這新建商場的設計混亂且複雜,最好不要使用扶手電梯;升降機可直達5樓。假如你曾光顧利苑的其他分店,你絕不會感到陌生:依然是清一色的廣東菜與可靠的美食及新鮮的材料。當然,這裡同樣擠滿了利苑的忠實擁躉,店內設計簡潔的屏風巧妙地將餐廳分隔成不同的用餐區。入口附近太嘈吵,最好不要選擇那裡的座位。

■ ADDRESS/地址

TEL. 2365 3238
Shop L5-8, Level 5, apm, Millennium City 5,
418 Kwun Tong Road, Kwun Tong
觀塘觀塘道418號創紀之城第5期
apm5樓L5-8號舖
www.leigarden.com.hk

■ ANNUAL AND WEEKLY CLOSING
　　休息日期
Closed 3 days Lunar New Year
農曆新年休息3天

■ OPENING HOURS, LAST ORDER
　　營業時間,最後點菜時間
Lunch/午膳 11:30-15:00 (L.O.)
Dinner/晚膳 18:00-23:30 L.O. 23:00

■ PRICE/價錢
Lunch/午膳　à la carte/點菜 $180-900
Dinner/晚膳　à la carte/點菜 $180-900

Lei Garden (Mong Kok)
利苑酒家 (旺角)

❀ ❀　　　　　　　　　　　　　　　　　　　　　𝄔𝄔

⬚ 30　⊙𝄔

This is the original Lei Garden, which opened back in the 1970s; it's as busy as ever so it's essential to book. The contemporary restaurant is spread over two floors and the upper space has views out onto the busy street. The long and varied Cantonese menu certainly represents good value and includes such excellent seafood recommendations as giant sea whelk sautéed with ginger and scallions, and steamed Alaska king crab with Hua Diao wine.

由於這家長青的餐廳實在太受歡迎，食客必須預先訂座。這家利苑總店開業於1970年代。富時代感的餐廳共分為兩層，樓上可看到旺角繁華的街景。以廣東菜為主的菜單花樣多變令人目不暇給，絕對物有所值，特別推薦薑蔥爆薄殼大響螺及花雕蒸亞拉斯加蟹。

■ ADDRESS/地址
TEL.2392 5184
121 Sai Yee Street,
Mong Kok, Kowloon
九龍旺角洗衣街121
www.leigarden.com.hk

■ ANNUAL AND WEEKLY CLOSING
　休息日期
Closed 3 days Lunar New Year
農曆新年休息3天

■ OPENING HOURS, LAST ORDER
　營業時間，最後點菜時間
Lunch/午膳 11:30-15:00 (L.O.)
Dinner/晚膳 18:00-23:30 (L.O.)

■ PRICE/價錢
Lunch/午膳　à la carte/點菜 $180-900
Dinner/晚膳　à la carte/點菜 $180-900

Lei Garden (North Point)
利苑酒家 (北角)

🛗 16

Tucked away discreetly on the first floor of a residential block, overlooking a pleasant courtyard garden, is this branch of the popular chain. Things here can certainly get quite frenetic as it accommodates up to 200 people. The lengthy Cantonese menu mirrors what's available at other branches, but particular dishes worth noting here are braised prawn with chilli sauce casserole, crispy roasted pork and the famous double-boiled soups.

這家深受歡迎的連鎖酒家分店,隱藏在住宅大廈一樓。從酒家外望是屋苑的翠綠庭園,其寬敞空間可容納多達200人,氣氛往往極為熱鬧。這裡的菜單與其他利苑分店不致相同,特別推薦生中蝦煲,冰燒三層肉和紅酒燜和牛脷。

■ ADDRESS/地址
TEL. 2806 0008
1F, Block 9-10, City Garden,
North Point
北角城市花園9-10座1樓
www.leigarden.com.hk

■ ANNUAL AND WEEKLY CLOSING
休息日期
Closed 3 days Lunar New Year
農曆新年休息3天

■ OPENING HOURS, LAST ORDER
營業時間,最後點菜時間
Lunch/午膳 11:30-15:00 L.O.14:30
Dinner/晚膳 18:00-23:30 L.O.22:30

■ PRICE/價錢
Lunch/午膳 à la carte/點菜 $ 180-900
Dinner/晚膳 à la carte/點菜 $ 180-900

Lei Garden (Sha Tin)
利苑酒家 (沙田)

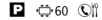

It may have been around town for over 20 years, but refurbishment has kept this Lei Garden feeling fresh. It is located in New Town Plaza Sha Tin, which means that it can get especially busy at weekends when everyone needs refuelling after a day spent shopping. The menu largely follows the theme of others in the group; always ask for the daily special. Pre-ordering the seasonal double-boiled tonic soup is particularly recommended.

這家利苑分店已是二十年的老字號，但經過重新裝潢後，一點也不顯老舊。酒家位於沙田新城市廣場，因此週末購物一整天過後前來小歇一番的茶客更是絡繹不絕。菜單與集團的其他餐廳主題相若；謹記留意是日精選。建議預訂老火湯。

■ ADDRESS/地址
TEL. 2698 9111
6F, Phase I New Town Plaza,
Sha Tin, New Territories
新界沙田新城市廣場第1期6樓
www.leigarden.com.hk

■ ANNUAL AND WEEKLY CLOSING
   休息日期
Closed 3 days Lunar New Year
農曆新年休息3天

■ OPENING HOURS, LAST ORDER
   營業時間，最後點菜時間
Lunch/午膳 11:30-15:00 L.O. 14:45
Dinner/晚膳 18:00-23:30 L.O. 23:00

■ PRICE/價錢
Lunch/午膳   à la carte/點菜 $180-900
Dinner/晚膳 à la carte/點菜 $180-900

Lei Garden (Tsim Sha Tsui)
利苑酒家 (尖沙咀)

The entrance takes you past an intricately carved wooden wall and a series of large fish tanks into a big, bustling, traditional dining room that's brightly lit and comfortable. There's pagoda detailing on the ceiling, bare red-brick walls and an army of staff in attendance. The varied Cantonese menu reiterates what's on offer at the other Lei Gardens. Classic double-boiled soups and steamed fresh sea fish are highly recommended.

先經過入口處雕刻精緻的木質牆飾和一列大魚缸，最後出現在你眼前的是一個燈光明亮，寬敞舒適的餐室；傳統的中式裝潢，天花上築有精美寶塔裝飾，配襯着以紅磚砌成的牆壁。氣氛熱鬧，服務團隊效率超卓。這裡的廣東菜單與其他利苑分店相若。其馳名老火湯及清蒸海上鮮不容錯過。

■ ADDRESS/地址

TEL. 2722 1636
B2F, Houston Centre, 63 Mody Road, East Tsim Sha Tsui, Kowloon
九龍尖東麼地道63號好時中心地庫2樓
www.leigarden.com.hk

■ OPENING HOURS, LAST ORDER
　營業時間，最後點菜時間
Lunch/午膳　11:30-14:45 (L.O.)
Dinner/晚膳　18:00-22:45 (L.O.)

■ PRICE/價錢
Lunch/午膳　à la carte/點菜 $ 180-900
Dinner/晚膳　à la carte/點菜 $ 180-900

Lei Garden (Wan Chai)
利苑酒家 (灣仔)

P   ⊟18   ☏⑪

An inventory of restaurants in Wan Chai wouldn't be complete without a Lei Garden. This branch is quite vast and it enjoys a busy, bustling atmosphere, particularly at lunch. It follows the tried and tested formula evident in its sister restaurants. The extensive menu offers not just luxury ingredients but also less elaborate and classic Cantonese preparations; specialities include Canadian geoduck clams sautéed with ginger or simply fried.

若論灣仔區的出色餐廳，當然少不了利苑的份兒。這家分店驟眼看來有點空洞，但店內充滿忙碌熱鬧的氣氛，午餐時間尤甚。沿用了其他利苑分店的成功菜式，豐富的菜單上不單珍饈百味也有經典粵式小菜。招牌菜有油泡或薑葱爆加拿大象拔蚌。

■ ADDRESS/地址

TEL. 2892 0333

1F, CNT Tower, 338 Hennessy Road, Wan Chai

灣仔軒尼詩道338號北海中心1樓

www.leigarden.com.hk

■ ANNUAL AND WEEKLY CLOSING
　　休息日期

Closed 3 days Lunar New Year

農曆新年休息3天

■ OPENING HOURS, LAST ORDER
　　營業時間，最後點菜時間

Lunch/午膳 11:30-14:45 (L.O.)

Dinner/晚膳 18:00-22:45 (L.O.)

■ PRICE/價錢

Lunch/午膳　à la carte/點菜 $ 180-900

Dinner/晚膳　à la carte/點菜 $ 180-900

Le 188°

Sitting triumphantly on the top floor of the Harbour Grand hotel, with floor-to-ceiling windows on three sides (hence the name) providing spectacular views, is this intimate, 'fine dining' restaurant, along with a very appealing terrace. The menu focuses primarily on modern European cuisine and typical dishes could include lobster salad, roasted cod fish or US beef striploin; for dessert the 'full moon cake' is a popular choice.

這家優雅舒適的高級食府座落於海逸君綽酒店的頂樓，三邊落地玻璃窗讓客人飽覽180度迷人景觀，另有一個動人的露天用餐區。餐牌以現代歐陸菜為主。特色菜包括龍蝦沙律、燒鱈魚與美國西冷牛扒。甜品更有受歡迎的芒果水晶球。

■ ADDRESS/地址

TEL. 2121 2688
41F, Harbour Grand North Point Hotel,
23 Oil Street, North Point
北角油街23號港島海逸君綽酒店41樓
www.harbourgrand.com/hongkong

■ OPENING HOURS, LAST ORDER
營業時間，最後點菜時間
Lunch/午膳 12:00-14:30 (L.O.)
Dinner/晚膳 18:00-24:00 (L.O.)

■ PRICE/價錢
Lunch/午膳	set/套餐	$ 258
	à la carte/點菜	$ 360-670
Dinner/晚膳	set/套餐	$ 488-788
	à la carte/點菜	$ 360-670

Lil' Siam　NEW

Competition is fierce in these parts but this little Thai restaurant manages to hold its own. Those who knew its big sister, Café Siam, will notice that the menu here shares many of its popular dishes, such as the banana blossom salad, the stir-fried spicy pepper prawns and the roast duck in red curry.　The interior is a pleasant mix of wood, mirrors and orange hues. It seats just 30 so booking ahead is a sensible option.

在激烈的競爭下，這間小小的泰國餐廳仍能站穩陣腳。作為Café Siam的姐妹店，你會留意到大部分受歡迎的菜式，例如蕉蕾沙律、炒胡椒蝦和紅咖喱烤鴨等都能在Lil' Siam的菜單中找到。悦目的裝修以木材、鏡子配搭橙色色調，僅設 30 個座位，訂座是明智之舉。

■ ADDRESS/地址

TEL. 2868 4445
38 Elgin Street, Central
中環伊利近街38號
www.lilsiam.com.hk

■ OPENING HOURS, LAST ORDER
　營業時間，最後點菜時間
Lunch/午膳　12:00-15:00 (L.O.)
Dinner/晚膳　18:00-23:00 (L.O.)

■ PRICE/價錢
Lunch/午膳　set/套餐　　　　　$88
　　　　　à la carte/點菜 $210-400
Dinner/晚膳　à la carte/點菜 $210-400

Linguini Fini NEW

True Italian flavours lie at the heart of this warm and relaxed eatery. It uses organic produce and meats sourced from local farms; the kitchen makes its own pasta, bread and gelato, and cures its own meat. Pasta, especially the linguini fini, is a highlight but they are not averse to also using local ingredients, such as salty egg yolk or dried shrimps. The stylish bar makes a pleasant spot in which to wait for a table.

既舒適又悠閒的環境，洋溢著濃厚意大利氣息。餐廳採用有機食材，並由本地農場採購肉類；意粉、麵包和意大利雪糕都是自家廚房出品，肉類亦是自己醃製。意大利麵當然是焦點所在，尤其是細扁麵；他們並不抗拒使用本地食材，如鹹蛋黃或蝦乾，創作新穎菜式。別具風格的酒吧是等位期間的好去處。

■ ADDRESS/地址

TEL. 2857 1333
1F, The L Place,
139 Queen's Road, Central
中環皇后大道中139號The L Place1樓
www.linguinifini.com

■ ANNUAL AND WEEKLY CLOSING
　休息日期
Closed Sunday
週日休息

■ OPENING HOURS, LAST ORDER
　營業時間，最後點菜時間
11:30-22:30 (L.O.)

■ PRICE/價錢
Lunch/午膳　set/套餐　　　$ 98
　　　　　　à la carte/點菜 $ 185-335
Dinner/晚膳　à la carte/點菜 $ 185-335

Lin Heung Kui
蓮香居

Opened in 2009, this huge eatery on two floors aims to build on the success of the famous Lin Heung Tea House in Wellington Street. It's modest inside, but hugely popular and the dim sum trolley is a must with customers keen to be the first to choose from its extensive offerings. The main menu offers classic Cantonese dishes with specialities such as Lin Heung special duck house style. The pastry shop below is worth a look on the way out.

佔地甚廣的蓮香居於二零零九年開幕，樓高兩層，秉承威靈頓街蓮香樓的輝煌成績。樸素的內部裝潢擋不住人氣，點心車最讓人急不及待從其各式各樣點心中選擇心愛好。菜單上提供傳統廣東菜及特色小菜，如蓮香霸王鴨。離開時路經樓下的中式餅店，亦值得留意。

■ ADDRESS/地址

TEL. 2156 9328
2-3F, 40-50 Des Voeux Road West, Sheung Wan
上環德輔道西40-50號2-3樓

■ OPENING HOURS, LAST ORDER
營業時間，最後點菜時間
06:00-22:30

■ PRICE/價錢
à la carte/點菜　　　　　$ 50-220

Lin Heung Tea House
蓮香樓

A famous name for over 80 years, this restaurant was lightly renovated in 2009. Dim sum is served from 6am to late afternoon, while classic Cantonese dishes are offered at night. Don't underestimate this place: many come early for their dim sum and not only do you need to find a table but the favourites, like steamed egg cake, are gone the second those trolleys roll out. Try a few Lin Heung specials in the evening, like the duck and pork ribs.

八十年來聞名四方的蓮香樓於二零零九年六月稍作裝修。清晨六時至下午供應點心，晚上則供應粵菜。不要低估了這茶樓：很多人清早慕名前來品嘗其點心，你不但要忙著佔桌，更要找尋著名美點，如蒸馬拉糕，點心車甫出現就被掃個片甲不留了。晚上可嚐嚐蓮香精選蓮香霸王鴨及招牌醬燒骨。

■ ADDRESS/地址
TEL. 2544 4556
160-164 Wellington Street, Central
中環威靈頓街160-164號

■ ANNUAL AND WEEKLY CLOSING
　　休息日期
Closed 3 days Lunar New Year
農曆新年休息3天

■ OPENING HOURS, LAST ORDER
　　營業時間，最後點菜時間
06:00-23:00 L.O.22:30

■ PRICE/價錢
à la carte/點菜　　　　　　　$ 120-300

Liu Yuan Pavilion
留園雅敘

🍴🍴

🛋16　📞🍽

If you want to compete with its loyal followers who clearly appreciate the good food here, then it's advisable to arrive having booked ahead. The light, airy décor provides a somewhat sober environment in which to enjoy some seriously tasty Shanghainese cuisine, especially the dim sum. Choose perhaps stir-fried shrimps, Mandarin fish with a sweet and sour sauce, braised meat balls with vegetables in a casserole or braised pig knuckle.

留園雅敘的一眾忠心擁躉顯然非常欣賞這裡的美食，為免向隅建議提早預約。在輕巧樸實的環境中，細意品嚐出色的上海佳餚，除了點心以外，清炒蝦仁，松子桂魚，砂窩獅子頭及紅燒元蹄等經典菜式亦值得一試。

■ ADDRESS/地址

TEL. 2804 2000
3F, The Broadway,
54-62 Lockhart Road, Wan Chai
灣仔駱克道54-62號博匯大廈3樓

■ OPENING HOURS, LAST ORDER
　營業時間，最後點菜時間
Lunch/午膳　12:00-15:00 L.O.14:30
Dinner/晚膳　18:00-23:00 L.O.22:30

■ PRICE/價錢
Lunch/午膳　set/套餐　　　　　$110
　　　　　à la carte/點菜 $150-500
Dinner/晚膳　à la carte/點菜 $200-500

Loaf On
六福菜館

💺36 ☎️

Hidden one block behind the strip of seafood restaurants in Sai Kung is this neat little restaurant, spread over three floors. Their soup of the day depends on what the owner finds and buys from the local fishermen. You can even bring your own seafood and have staff prepare it for you. Besides seafood, Loaf On also offers simple but flavoursome Cantonese dishes like stir-fry prawns with eggs, Loaf On-style chicken, and salt and pepper calamari.

這家小菜館隱藏在西貢的海鮮餐廳一帶的後街，佔地三層。是日例湯視乎店主當天從當地漁民處買到的新鮮食材。你甚至可自行攜帶海鮮，交由店員烹調。除了海鮮，六福菜館還提供簡單而美味的小菜如滑蛋蝦仁、風沙雞及椒鹽鮮魷。

■ ADDRESS/地址

TEL. 2792 9966
49 See Cheung Street, Sai Kung
西貢市場街49號

■ ANNUAL AND WEEKLY CLOSING
　休息日期
Closed 2 days Lunar New Year
農曆新年休息2天

■ OPENING HOURS, LAST ORDER
　營業時間，最後點菜時間
11:00-23:00 L.O. 22:30

■ PRICE/價錢
Lunch/午膳　à la carte/點菜 $150-500
Dinner/晚膳　à la carte/點菜 $200-500

Lobster Bar and Grill
龍蝦吧

The clubby atmosphere here derives from the colonial style furniture and décor: you can even enjoy an aperitif or single malt whisky in a cosy armchair upholstered in Scottish tartan. Specialities are Maine and Spiny lobsters prepared in a choice of styles, as well as a variety of oysters and fish. Also featured are grilled meats and vegetarian options. It's mostly business-orientated at lunchtime but more relaxed, with live music, at night.

殖民地傢具和裝潢襯托出俱樂部般的氣氛：你可以躺在舒適的蘇格蘭格仔扶手椅上享受一杯餐前酒或單一麥芽威士忌。鎮店菜式以不同品種的龍蝦做主題，亦提供多款生蠔，魚類，各式烤肉和素食選擇。午餐時段這裡的食客大都是商務人士，晚上氣氛則較悠閒，更有現場樂隊演奏。

■ ADDRESS/地址

TEL. 2820 8560

6F, Island Shangri-La Hotel, Pacific Place, Supreme Court Road, Admiralty
中區法院道太古廣場
港島香格里拉酒店6樓
www.shangri-la.com

■ OPENING HOURS, LAST ORDER
　　營業時間，最後點菜時間
Lunch/午膳 12:00-14:30 (L.O.)
Dinner/晚膳 18:30-22:30 (L.O.)

■ PRICE/價錢
Lunch/午膳　à la carte/點菜 $500-1,000
Dinner/晚膳　set/套餐　　　 $688
　　　　　　à la carte/點菜 $500-1,000

Lo Chiu (Jordan)
老趙 (佐敦)

The Chinese owner spent several years in Vietnam before arriving in Hong Kong and opening this Vietnamese restaurant back in 1978. He now has two other shops but this is his flagship. Steamed stuffed rice rolls, noodles in beef soup and cold vermicelli with pork, beef or chicken are some of the highlights, but the hotpot curry is also worth trying. The environment is basic but clean and the staff are helpful.

老闆是曾經在越南住過幾年的華僑，回來香港後，在1978年開始經營這餐廳。他現在已擁有兩家分店，但此店依然是他的旗艦店。越式蒸粉包、牛肉湯河，豬肉、牛肉或雞肉凍檬都是不錯的選擇，椰香咖喱也非常值得嘗試。餐廳只有簡單裝修，但侍應服務周到。

■ ADDRESS/地址

TEL. 2384 2143
25-27 Man Yuen Street,
Jordan, Kowloon
九龍佐敦文苑街25-27號

■ ANNUAL AND WEEKLY CLOSING
   休息日期
Closed 4 days Lunar New Year
農曆新年休息4天

■ OPENING HOURS, LAST ORDER
   營業時間，最後點菜時間
12:00-23:00 (L.O.)

■ PRICE/價錢
set/套餐	$ 104-116
à la carte/點菜	$ 65-110

Lo Chiu (Tsim Sha Tsui)
老趙（尖沙咀）

The second branch of this Vietnamese group may have opened in 1999 but its vivid orange colours and chandeliers are more evocative of the 1970s. However, what the room may lack in its levels of comfort, it makes up for in its food and sunny service. The large choice includes traditional Vietnamese soup and noodles but it also purports to be the "king prawn specialist"; these can be served simply grilled on charcoal or with tamarind or chilli paste.

這個越南集團的第二分店在1999年開幕，但她鮮艷的橙色和吊燈更較人想起七零年代。雖然，這間餐廳的環境不算非常舒適，但它的食物質素和陽光般溫暖的服務卻令人倍感自在。豐富的選擇包括傳統越南湯河，它也號稱「大頭蝦專門店」，大頭蝦可簡單地碳烤或加上酸子醬或辣椒蓉。

■ ADDRESS/地址
TEL. 2314 7966
10-12 Hillwood Road,
Tsim Sha Tsui, Kowloon
九龍尖沙咀山林道10-12號

■ ANNUAL AND WEEKLY CLOSING
休息日期
Closed 4 days Lunar New Year
農曆新年休息4天

■ OPENING HOURS, LAST ORDER
營業時間，最後點菜時間
12:00-23:00 L.O. 22:30

■ PRICE/價錢
Lunch/午膳　set/套餐　　　$ 50-85
　　　　　　à la carte/點菜　$ 80-220
Dinner/晚膳　à la carte/點菜　$ 80-220

Loong Toh Yuen
隆濤院

Traditional Shanghainese tea houses were the inspiration behind the charming decorative style of this Chinese restaurant within Hullett House, a colonial-style building dating from 1881. The menu features Cantonese recipes combined with some Hong Kong classics and even a few contemporary touches. Typical dishes would include deep-fried shrimp rolls, roasted Peking duck, and fresh garoupa cooked in two ways.

Hullett House是一棟充滿殖民地風格的建築，歷史可追溯至1881年。而這家位於Hullett House內的中餐館，則從傳統的上海茶館找到其迷人裝潢的靈感。餐牌內的廣東佳餚大多揉合了香港的經典和現代色彩。具代表性的菜式包括沙律皮旦蝦筒、隆濤烤鴨與錦繡東星斑。

■ ADDRESS/地址
TEL. 3988 0107
Hullett House, 2A Canton Road,
Tsim Sha Tsui, Kowloon
九龍尖沙咀廣東道2A Hullett House
www.hulletthouse.com

■ OPENING HOURS, LAST ORDER
   營業時間，最後點菜時間
Lunch/午膳 11:30-14:30 (L.O.)
Dinner/晚膳 18:00-22:30 (L.O.)

■ PRICE/價錢
Lunch/午膳   à la carte/點菜 $400-900
Dinner/晚膳   set/套餐 $588
             à la carte/點菜 $400-900

Luk Yu Tea House
陸羽茶室

Large numbers of both regulars and tourists come to Luk Yu Tea House for the traditionally prepared and flavoursome dim sum, and its three floors fill up quickly. The animated atmosphere and subtle colonial decoration are appealing but no one really stays too long; the serving team in white jackets have seen it all before and go about their work with alacrity. Popular dishes are fried prawns on toast and fried noodles with sliced beef.

陸羽茶室能同時吸引本地常客和外地遊客，可見其過人之處。大量常客和遊客主要是為了以傳統方法製造的美味點心而來，所以佔地三層的茶室經常滿座。生氣盎然的環境和帶點殖民地色彩的裝潢很吸引，但沒有人會長久駐足觀賞——穿著白色外套的侍應們早以見怪不怪，只會敏捷地專注工作。除點心外其他菜式如窩貼蝦及鼓椒牛肉炒麵也值得一試。

■ ADDRESS/地址
TEL. 2523 5464
24-26 Stanley Street, Central
中環士丹利街24-26號

■ ANNUAL AND WEEKLY CLOSING
　休息日期
Closed 4 days Lunar New Year
農曆新年休息4天

■ OPENING HOURS, LAST ORDER
　營業時間，最後點菜時間
07:00-22:00 (L.O.)

■ PRICE/價錢
Lunch/午膳　à la carte/點菜 $ 100-300
Dinner/晚膳　à la carte/點菜 $ 200-300

Lung King Heen
龍景軒

✿ ✿ ✿   ✗✗✗✗

♿ ← ☞ 🅿 ⊟16 📞 🍴 ⬡

It's not just the dim sum that's gaining legendary status here. Every dish is delicately crafted and enticingly presented, and the quality of the ingredients is of the highest order. The delightful serving team describe dishes with great care and obvious pride. Translated as 'view of the dragon', the restaurant offers a panorama of the harbour; its interior is smart and uncluttered, with hand-embroidered silk, columns and glass screens.

龍景軒名副其實，坐擁動人心弦的維港全景；餐廳內部亦時尚整潔，飾以手工刺繡絲綢、圓柱和玻璃屏幕。素負盛名的，絕不只是美味點心那麼簡單，這裡每一度菜都經過精心雕琢，賣相極其吸引，並採用最高級的食材。侍應團隊充滿朝氣，介紹菜式固然仔細，同時亦讓人感受到餐廳令他們引以為傲。

■ ADDRESS/地址

TEL. 3196 8880
4F, Four Seasons Hotel,
8 Finance Street, Central
中環金融街8號四季酒店4樓
www.fourseasons.com/hongkong

■ OPENING HOURS, LAST ORDER
   營業時間，最後點菜時間
Lunch/午膳 12:00-14:30 (L.O.)
Dinner/晚膳 18:00-22:30 (L.O.)

■ PRICE/價錢
Lunch/午膳   set/套餐 $ 450
                à la carte/點菜 $ 350-1,400
Dinner/晚膳   set/套餐 $ 1,280
                à la carte/點菜 $ 400-1,400

European contemporary/時尚歐陸式　　　　　　　　MAP/地圖　25/B-3

Madam Sixty Ate　NEW

Those who like a side order of whimsy with their meal will appreciate this bright, fun and laid-back restaurant, whose interior design and 'concept' are inspired by the life and travels of the eponymous Madam. Surrealist paintings and huge lampshades like upturned cupcakes add to the playfulness. From the open kitchen come artistically presented and creatively named dishes whose influences are kept mostly within Europe.

如果你喜歡在享用食物的同時，伴以一點新奇趣味，這家既清新有趣又閒適的餐廳，一定能夠得到你的歡心。這裡的室內設計和主題意念，都離不開「Madam」的生活風格和遊歷見聞。那些超現實主義的畫作、看似倒置小蛋糕的巨型燈罩，都為室內環境增添了玩味。開放式廚房烹制出的菜式充滿藝術氣息，散發點點歐陸味道，並被冠以創意洋溢的名稱。

■ ADDRESS/地址
TEL. 2527 2558
1F, The Podium, J Senses,
60 Johnston Road, Wan Chai
灣仔莊士敦道60號J Senses 1樓
www.madamsixtyate.com.hk

■ OPENING HOURS, LAST ORDER
　營業時間，最後點菜時間
12:00-23:00 (L.O.)

■ PRICE/價錢

Lunch/午膳	set/套餐	$148-178
	à la carte/點菜	$340-500
Dinner/晚膳	set/套餐	$680
	à la carte/點菜	$430-540

Mak An Kee Noodle (Wing Kut Street)
麥奀記(忠記)麵家 (永吉街)

This narrow shop, at Des Voeux Road and Wing Kut Street, tucked away behind the market, quickly fills up at lunch break time. The regular clientele will happily move up to allow you to share their tables. The legendary beef and wonton noodles is the speciality of the house; using the best quality raw ingredients, these exquisite bowls are bursting with flavour. Furthermore, this quality comes at prices that represent very good value for money.

這家窄小的麵店位於德輔道與永吉街交界，隱藏在街市後方，午飯時間座無虛席。店內常客很樂意稍移座位，與你共用餐桌。其傳統牛腩雲吞麵甚具特色，用料上乘，泡製出每一碗都香濃美味。此外，更是價格相宜，物超所值。

■ ADDRESS/地址

TEL. 2541 6388
37 Wing Kut Street, Central
中環永吉街37號

■ ANNUAL AND WEEKLY CLOSING
　休息日期
Closed 3 days Lunar New Year
農曆新年休息3天

■ OPENING HOURS, LAST ORDER
　營業時間，最後點菜時間
10:30-20:00 (L.O.)

■ PRICE/價錢
à la carte/點菜　　　　$ 18-64

Mak's Noodle
麥奀雲吞麵世家

A small place with a big reputation: Mak Chi Ming's father opened the original Mak's Noodle in 1960, while his grandfather was 'king of the wonton' in the 1930s. The premises may be modest but the operation runs like clockwork. The staff - strict, efficient and overseen by the boss - serve nothing but noodles, with fresh, authentic recipes utilising seasonal vegetables produced to order. Most prized dish is the mouth-watering chutney pork.

地方淺窄的餐廳卻享負盛名：麥志明祖父是30年代的「雲吞麵大王」，父親則於1960年創立了麥奀記老店。店裡地方不大，設備簡單，員工由老闆監督著，既嚴謹又有效率。餐廳供應的只有麵，採用新鮮食材、正宗食譜，以及季節性蔬菜。最特別的菜式是令人垂涎欲滴的炸醬麵。

■ ADDRESS/地址
TEL. 2854 3810
77 Wellington Street, Central
中環威靈頓街77號

■ OPENING HOURS, LAST ORDER
營業時間，最後點菜時間
11:00-20:00 L.O.19:45
■ PRICE/價錢
à la carte/點菜 $ 30-65

Malaysia Port Klang Cuisine
馬拉蓋星馬美食

You'll find this small, friendly, family-run Malaysian restaurant on a busy street; its façade covered with the photos of the local celebrities who have visited. Inside is equally modest but this time the photos shown are of the dishes on offer. The Malaysian community appear much taken with the traditional bah kut teh, the seafood laksa, the special prawn noodle with soup and the stir fry vegetables with shrimp paste sauce.

這家細小、親切、友善的家族式馬來西亞餐廳位處繁忙的街道，門口貼滿了曾光顧的本地名人照片，店內同樣貼滿各式菜餚的照片。馬來西亞人似乎相當喜愛這裡的肉骨茶、海鮮叻沙、特色蝦湯麵與馬拉蓋通菜。

■ ADDRESS/地址
TEL. 2555 6444
143 Sai Yee Street, Mong Kok, Kowloon
九龍旺角洗衣街143號

■ ANNUAL AND WEEKLY CLOSING
　休息日期
Closed Monday
週一休息

■ OPENING HOURS, LAST ORDER
　營業時間，最後點菜時間
12:00-23:00

■ PRICE/價錢
à la carte/點菜　　　　　　$ 100-160

Mandarin Grill + Bar
文華扒房+酒吧

A luminous dining room - Sir Terence Conran's refurbishment has kept the Oriental references; if you want to be seen, this is the place to eat. Alternatively, if you want to see the oyster chefs at work, sit at the bar and watch them – guaranteed freshness! On the other side, behind a window, the kitchen team prepare appealing and contemporary European cuisine. Soufflé lovers adore this place as they have a large selection from which to choose.

明亮的餐廳經過20世紀著名的室內設計師Sir Terence Conran的裝修後，仍然保留文華東方的味道。如果你的用餐不介意張揚，這家餐廳則十分適合。又或者，如果你想看看師傅如何準備生蠔，坐在吧檯觀看吧，生蠔保證新鮮！餐廳的另一邊，你可透過窗戶看到廚房團隊用心準備令人垂涎三尺的當代歐洲菜。梳乎厘的愛好者鍾情於這個地方，因為這裡的選擇琳瑯滿目。

■ ADDRESS/地址
TEL. 2825 4004
1F, Mandarin Oriental Hotel,
5 Connaught Road, Central
中環干諾道中5號文華東方酒店1樓
www.mandarinoriental.com/hongkong

■ ANNUAL AND WEEKLY CLOSING
　休息日期
Closed lunch Saturday and Sunday
週六、日午膳休息

■ OPENING HOURS, LAST ORDER
　營業時間，最後點菜時間
Lunch/午膳 12:00-14:30 (L.O.)
Dinner/晚膳 18:30-22:30 (L.O.)

■ PRICE/價錢
Lunch/午膳　set/套餐　　　$608
　　　　　　à la carte/點菜 $780-1,150
Dinner/晚膳 set/套餐　　　$1,088-1,688
　　　　　　à la carte/點菜 $780-1,150

Man Wah
文華廳

Man Wah exudes a luxuriously intimate yet traditional feel. Tables just off the entrance may have the better views, but everyone can appreciate the décor: brass lanterns hang from the wood ceiling and the room is framed by an ornate screen. The Peking duck is a classic, as is the stir-fried lobster with egg white and scallop mousse. Equally good is pork neck with Kuei Hua flavoured pear, and steamed garoupa with ginger, crabmeat and egg white.

文華廳散發著一種傳統高貴典雅的氣質。雖然近門口的餐桌享有較佳的景觀，但所有食客都可以欣賞這裡的裝潢：木天花板吊著黃銅燈籠，及周邊的華麗屏幕。這裡的北京片皮鴨及海棠龍蝦是名副其實的經典美食，桂花梨黑醋脆豬肉及酥薑珊瑚蒸星斑球亦不遑多讓。

■ ADDRESS/地址

TEL. 2825 4003

25F, Mandarin Oriental Hotel,
5 Connaught Road, Central
中環干諾道中5號文華東方酒店25樓
www.mandarinoriental.com/hongkong

■ OPENING HOURS, LAST ORDER
營業時間，最後點菜時間
Lunch/午膳 12:00-14:30 (L.O.)
Dinner/晚膳 18:30-22:30 (L.O.)

■ PRICE/價錢
Lunch/午膳   set/套餐 $ 468-888
             à la carte/點菜 $ 320-1,100
Dinner/晚膳 set/套餐 $ 588-988
             à la carte/點菜 $ 320-1,100

Mask of Sichuen & Beijing   NEW
面譜京川料理

Beijing opera masks hanging from the ceiling add to the atmosphere of this softly lit, contemporary dining room which has intimate booths as well as large tables. The good-sized menus offer a comprehensive selection of Sichuan and Pekingese dishes, along with some innovative offerings, like stir-fried shredded potato and mango. Diners can decide on their own level of spiciness and there's also a wide selection of vegetarian dishes available.

懸掛在天花的京劇面譜，為柔和的燈光和富現代感的裝潢增添氣氛；這裡既提供私密的卡座，亦有大形餐枱供應。種類繁多的餐牌，既有齊全的川菜選擇，亦有京菜佳餚，更有創新之選，如香芒土豆絲。食客可自選辣度，並有多種素菜提供。

■ ADDRESS/地址

TEL. 2311 9233
Shop 33, GF, KCR East Tsim Sha Tsui Station, Kowloon
九龍尖沙咀尖東站地下33號舖

■ OPENING HOURS, LAST ORDER
營業時間，最後點菜時間
Lunch/午膳 12:00-15:30 (L.O.)
Dinner/晚膳 17:45-23:30 (L.O.)

■ PRICE/價錢
Lunch/午膳 set/套餐 $52-58
          à la carte/點菜 $200-510
Dinner/晚膳 à la carte/點菜 $200-510

May's Sawaddee Thailand NEW
旺泰特食

On the ground floor of a residential building in the heart of Sai Kung sits this long, narrow, simply decorated but comfortable Thai restaurant. From the hospitable, all-female service team comes an extensive menu of authentic Thai dishes, whose highlights include yellow chicken curry in bread, fried crab with curry, Tom Yum Goong, and fried rice with minced meat and herbs, all made using fresh, good quality ingredients.

位於西貢市中心的住宅大廈地下，這是一家店內空間既長又窄，裝修簡約但舒適的泰國餐廳。員工是全女班，服務殷勤，提供多款正宗泰國菜式，推介有黃咖喱雞配包、咖哩炒蟹、冬蔭功、肉碎香葉炒飯等，全部均以優質新鮮材料炮製。

■ ADDRESS/地址
TEL. 2791 0522
24 Man Nin Street, Sai Kung
西貢萬年街24號

■ OPENING HOURS, LAST ORDER
　營業時間，最後點菜時間
Lunch/午膳 12:00-15:00 (L.O.)
Dinner/晚膳 18:00-22:30 (L.O.)

■ PRICE/價錢
Lunch/午膳　set/套餐　　$ 38
　　　　　　à la carte/點菜 $ 50-230
Dinner/晚膳
à la carte/點菜　　　　$ 50-230

Megan's Kitchen   NEW
美味廚

Can't decide between Cantonese or a hotpot? Or perhaps you'd like both? Megan's Kitchen can help as it offers a grand selection of Cantonese dishes, like steamed pork belly with mui choy or braised oxtail Chinese style, but is also known for its hotpots, which come with high quality ingredients like seafood or Japanese beef. The dining room has a warm, contemporary feel and there are several well-equipped private rooms.

廣東菜還是火鍋？還是想兩者兼得？美味廚讓你不再苦惱。它除了有各式廣東小菜如梳乎里梅菜扣肉和中式燴牛尾，火鍋亦同樣聞名，更有海鮮、和牛等高級配料。大廳設計感覺溫馨時尚，並備有多個設備齊全的私人客房。

■ ADDRESS/地址
TEL. 2866 8305
5F, Lucky Centre,
165-171 Wan Chai Road, Wan Chai
灣仔灣仔道165-171樂基中心5樓
www.meganskitchen.com

■ OPENING HOURS, LAST ORDER
　營業時間，最後點菜時間
Lunch/午膳 12:00-14:30 (L.O.)
Dinner/晚膳 18:00-23:00 (L.O.)

■ PRICE/價錢
Lunch/午膳　set/套餐　　　　$ 100
　　　　　à la carte/點菜 $ 120-550
Dinner/晚膳　à la carte/點菜 $ 120-550

Mesa 15 NEW

🛋20

Opened by a noted Andalusian chef, along with some local partners, Mesa 15 offers a tempting range of creative Spanish dishes designed for sharing – aim for 3 per person plus a dessert. The signature dishes are mini pork rib burgers with red pepper jam and the 12 hour crispy suckling pig with pickled cabbage. The small dining room is crisply decorated in whites and greys and comes with high marble-topped tables.

由著名安達盧西亞大廚與本地班底合作，Mesa 15專門設計多款可讓數人分享的創新西班牙菜式，3人分吃再加一客甜品剛剛好。招牌菜式包括迷你豬肋漢堡配紅椒醬，以及12小時脆皮烤豬配酸菜。小小的餐廳以白和灰作主要色調，並襯以雲石面高桌。

■ ADDRESS/地址
TEL. 2530 1890
15 Hollywood Road, Central
中環荷利活道15號

■ OPENING HOURS, LAST ORDER
營業時間，最後點菜時間
Lunch/午膳 12:00-14:30 (L.O.)
Dinner/晚膳 18:30-22:30 (L.O.)

■ PRICE/價錢
Lunch/午膳 set/套餐 $158
à la carte/點菜 $200-480
Dinner/晚膳 à la carte/點菜 $200-480

Ming Court
明閣

A fascinating collection of replica Ming Dynasty bronzes, as well as some fine Chinese landscape paintings, lend elegance to the stylish interior with its curved walls. Highlights of the sophisticated and expertly prepared Cantonese cooking include stir-fried sliced giant garoupa stuffed with shrimp paste, and pan-fried chicken filled with minced chicken and black truffles. Be sure to reserve your table in the main dining room.

餐廳陳列著一系列青銅器仿製品，以及一些筆法細緻的中國山水畫，令本已獨具風格的裝潢更顯高雅。菜單包括精心炮製的精美廣東菜式。招牌菜有：脆芝士龍蝦伴醋香鮑魚天使麵。切記預訂在主廳的座位。

■ ADDRESS/地址
TEL. 3552 3300
6F, Langham Place Hotel,
555 Shanghai Street, Mong Kok, Kowloon
九龍旺角上海街555號朗豪酒店6樓
www.hongkong.langhamplacehotels.com

■ OPENING HOURS, LAST ORDER
　營業時間，最後點菜時間
Lunch/午膳 11:00-14:30 (L.O.)
Dinner/晚膳 18:00-22:30 (L.O.)
■ PRICE/價錢
Lunch/午膳　set/套餐　　　$278-528
　　　　　　à la carte/點菜 $200-500
Dinner/晚膳 set/套餐　　　$398-958
　　　　　　à la carte/點菜 $350-1,100

Mirror NEW

🛏10 📞🍴

After working in Alain Ducasse's empire for over a decade, the French owner-chef spent two years teaching in a local culinary school before opening this restaurant. His cuisine is inspired by childhood memories, in dishes such as frog's legs with garlic cream, and his set menus try to use as many local ingredients as possible. The room has a homely but comfortable feel and sits somewhat at odds with the bars that share the building.

法裔店東兼主廚追隨Alain Ducasse麾下逾10年，並曾在本地廚藝學院任教兩年，才正式開設這間餐廳。他的菜式都是從兒時回憶中獲取靈感，例如田雞腿配蒜蓉忌廉醬；而他的套餐都是盡量利用本地食材。室內設計帶出舒適的家居感覺，與大廈內的其他酒吧相映成趣。

■ ADDRESS/地址

TEL. 2573 7288

6F, Tiffan Tower,
197-199 Wan Chai Road, Wan Chai
灣仔灣仔道197-199號天輝中心6樓
www.themirror.hk

■ ANNUAL AND WEEKLY CLOSING
　休息日期
Closed 6 days Lunar New Year and
Sunday
農曆新年6天及週日休息

■ OPENING HOURS, LAST ORDER
　營業時間，最後點菜時間
Dinner/晚膳 18:30-22:30 (L.O.)

■ PRICE/價錢
set/套餐　　$538-1,198

Mist

The stainless steel and glass façade hint at the equally chic interior, which comes with walls lined with stone and mirrors, and colour courtesy of the red leather dining chairs. The classic ramen noodle is here given a modern makeover, with many of the dishes displaying an element of fusion. Dinner offers the most interesting menu but then lunch represents excellent value. Can't find your chopsticks? Simply pull out the drawer.

由不銹鋼和玻璃組成的外觀可知內裏的裝潢必定同樣時尚新潮——牆身以石材和鏡子砌成線條，配上紅色皮革椅子，色彩強烈。這裡為傳統日本拉麵換上現代新裝，很多菜式都具備fusion（融合異國特色）的元素。晚餐選擇較吸引，但午餐則絕對物超所值。找不到筷子？拉開抽屜吧！

■ ADDRESS/地址

TEL. 2881 5006
4 Sun Wui Road, Causeway Bay
銅鑼灣新會道4號
www.mist.com.hk

■ OPENING HOURS, LAST ORDER
　營業時間，最後點菜時間
Lunch/午膳　12:00-15:00 (L.O.)
Dinner/晚膳　18:00-23:00 (L.O.)

■ PRICE/價錢

Lunch/午膳	set/套餐	$80-150
	à la carte/點菜	$220-300
Dinner/晚膳	set/套餐	$428
	à la carte/點菜	$220-300

Nanhai No.1
南海一號

It's highly appropriate that this maritime-themed restaurant – which opened in 2010 and takes as its inspiration a culinary voyage around China and the South Seas – commands such terrific harbour views, thanks to its floor-to-ceiling windows. But the cuisine is not just limited to seafood; the contemporary dishes also have a strong Cantonese element. The Eyebar is an equally good-looking spot that makes the most of the top-floor vistas.

這家以海為主題的餐廳於2010年開張，靈感來自中國及南海一帶的美食航程。落地玻璃讓海港美景一覽無遺。她的美食當然不限於海鮮，創新菜式帶有強烈廣東菜元素。頂樓的Eyebar酒吧景觀同樣出色，讓你飽覽落地玻璃下的廣闊景色。

■ ADDRESS/地址

TEL. 2487 3688
30F, iSquare, 63 Nathan Road,
Tsim Sha Tsui, Kowloon
九龍尖沙咀彌敦道63號iSquare30樓
www.elite-concepts.com

■ OPENING HOURS, LAST ORDER
營業時間，最後點菜時間
Lunch/午膳 11:30-15:00 L.O.14:30
Dinner/晚膳 18:00-23:30 L.O.22:30

■ PRICE/價錢

Lunch/午膳	set/套餐	$480-980
	à la carte/點菜	$300-900
Dinner/晚膳	set/套餐	$480-980
	à la carte/點菜	$300-900

208

Nha Trang (Central)
芽莊 (中環)

If you're not here bang on midday then you'll probably find yourself queuing as this fun, fast and frantic Vietnamese restaurant really pulls in the crowds. It has a bright, fresh feel, a mix of individual and communal tables and a young service team who are well organised and efficient. The healthy menu ranges from Vietnamese street snacks and salad rolls through to 'broken rice platters' and lemongrass grilled fish, all at affordable prices.

午市時，你若不早前來，便需要在這家有趣、快速、如臨大敵的餐廳前排隊了。店內感覺明亮而清新，設有小餐桌和可能與人共用的大餐桌，年輕的侍應們工作有條理而有效率。健康菜單從越南街頭小吃與粉卷，到越南碎米飯和香茅燒魚都有，價錢也相當合理。

■ ADDRESS/地址

TEL. 2581 9992
88-90 Wellington Street, Central
中環威靈頓街88-90號
www.nhatrang.com.hk

■ OPENING HOURS, LAST ORDER
營業時間，最後點菜時間
12:00-22:30 (L.O.)

■ PRICE/價錢
à la carte/點菜　　　　　$ 140-250

Nha Trang (Tsim Sha Tsui) NEW
芽莊 (尖沙咀)

On the ground floor of the Ocean Terminal sits this branch of these popular Vietnamese eateries. The dishes blend Southeast Asian flavours and herbs with touches of French influence, as well as street food. Ingredients such as 'broken rice' and fish sauce are imported directly from Vietnam. It's a pleasant, comfortable environment in which to enjoy the good value food and the harbour views; lunchtimes are very busy.

備受歡迎的越南餐廳集團旗下分店，座落於海運大廈地下。菜式揉合了東南亞風味、香草和法國菜的影響，以至越南街頭小食的特色。所採用的原材料如碎米和魚露，均是由越南直接入口。這裡是享受實惠美食和維港景致的好去處；午飯時間特別繁忙。推介菜有越南碎米飯和越式涼伴元蹄。

■ ADDRESS/地址
TEL. 2199 7779
Shop G51, GF, Ocean Terminal,
Harbour City, Canton Road,
Tsim Sha Tsui, Kowloon
九龍尖沙咀廣東道海港城
海運大廈地下G51號舖
www.nhatrang.com.hk

■ OPENING HOURS, LAST ORDER
營業時間，最後點菜時間
12:00-22:30 (L.O.)
■ PRICE/價錢
à la carte/點菜　　　　　$ 140-250

Nicholini's
意寧谷

This stylish circular room has large windows that offer a peek between the adjoining tower blocks, allowing views over the bay. At the back is a large Venetian scene and some intriguing glass sculptures which add a little opulence to proceedings. The cooking mixes traditional Northern Italian recipes and contemporary influences. Recommended dishes include three-way scallops and wild mushroom lasagne. There's a popular buffet at lunch.

時尚的圓形餐室擁有寬大的窗戶，於鄰近的摩天大樓間，一窺維港美景。餐廳後方的巨型威尼斯佈景和迷人的玻璃塑像，散發著豪華莊重的氣息。烹調方式融合北義大利傳統煮法及現代元素；切勿錯過其出色義大利麵！推薦菜式包括三式帶子及焗野菌千層麵。午市的自助餐亦十分受歡迎。

■ ADDRESS/地址

TEL. 2521 3838

8F, Conrad Hotel, Pacific Place,
88 Queensway, Admiralty
香港金鐘道88號太古廣場港麗酒店8樓
www.conradhotels.com

■ ANNUAL AND WEEKLY CLOSING
　　休息日期
Closed Saturday lunch
週六午膳休息

■ OPENING HOURS, LAST ORDER
　　營業時間，最後點菜時間
Lunch/午膳 12:00-15:00 (L.O.)
Dinner/晚膳 18:30-23:00 (L.O.)

■ PRICE/價錢
Lunch/午膳　set/套餐　　　　$368
　　　　　　à la carte/點菜 $ 560-1,100
Dinner/晚膳　set/套餐　　　$728-828
　　　　　　à la carte/點菜 $ 560-1,100

Nobu

This branch of the über-fashionable, international Nobu brand boasts an impressive ceiling fashioned from sea urchin spines and there are images of cherry blossom behind the bar. At lunch, bento boxes are the popular choice. At dinner, Mr Matsuhisa's beguiling blend of Japanese and South American tastes continues to work its fashionable magic by featuring sushi and sashimi, good quality seafood and fine salsas.

這家享譽國際的Nobu餐廳分店有著以海膽刺裝飾的天花，讓人印象深刻，背景更配有櫻花美景裝飾。午餐時間最受歡迎的是便當。而晚餐方面，主廚松久信幸融合日本和南美風味，炮製的嶄新口味更是迷人。菜式包括壽司、刺身、優質的海鮮及辛香番茄醬。

■ ADDRESS/地址

TEL. 2313 2340
2F, Intercontinental Hotel,
18 Salisbury Road, Tsim Sha Tsui,
Kowloon
九龍尖沙咀梳士巴利道18號
洲際酒店2樓

■ OPENING HOURS, LAST ORDER
　營業時間，最後點菜時間
Lunch/午膳 12:00-14:30 (L.O.)
Dinner/晚膳 18:00-23:00 (L.O.)

■ PRICE/價錢
Lunch/午膳　set/套餐　　　$298-596
　　　　　　à la carte/點菜 $300-900
Dinner/晚膳　set/套餐　　　$888-1,188
　　　　　　à la carte/點菜 $350-1,200

Noodle Concepts　NEW
麵創坊

The concept here is relatively straightforward: they offer around 16 different types of noodles in a bright, uniformly fitted, Western-style restaurant. Established by a local photographer in 2009, the place now also provides a range of Cantonese dishes and some Chinese snacks. The noodles come with plenty of choice in both soup and sauce – the chef is particularly proud of his beef brisket and yellow curry with its secret recipe.

原來的概念倒是相當直接，只是在明亮、一致的西式裝潢中，供應約16款不同麵食。於2009年由一名本地攝影師創辦，現在同時供應一系列廣東小菜和中式小吃。麵的湯底和醬汁均有多款選擇，大廚更以牛腩及秘製黃咖喱自豪。

■ ADDRESS/地址

TEL. 3486 8525
Shop 2, Tai Kut House,
7 Greig Road, Quarry Bay
鰂魚涌基利路7號太吉樓2號舖

■ ANNUAL AND WEEKLY CLOSING
　　休息日期
Closed 3 days Lunar New Year
農曆新年休息3天

■ OPENING HOURS, LAST ORDER
　　營業時間，最後點菜時間
12:00-21:30 (L.O.)

■ PRICE/價錢
Lunch/午膳　set/套餐　　　　$40-70
　　　　　　à la carte/點菜 $75-280
Dinner/晚膳　à la carte/點菜 $75-280

Noodle Shop NEW
麵棧

Table sharing is required if you want to enjoy a quick, simple but satisfying meal at this lively, soberly furnished dining room. Mr Lai prepares authentic northern cuisine which he learnt from the locals when he lived in Mainland China. His noodles and dumplings (600 of which are sold daily) are freshly made each day and his soy milk is also famous. Lamb dumplings and noodles with minced pork both come highly recommended.

在這家充滿生氣的簡約餐廳，要享受一頓快捷、簡單又滿足的美食，就要跟素未謀面的人同枱而座。老闆黎先生做得一手正宗北方菜，是他在內地居住時跟當地人學習的。他的麵條和水餃(日售600隻)均是每天新鮮製造，另外豆漿亦十分有名。特別推薦羊肉水餃和炸醬麵。

■ ADDRESS/地址
TEL. 2412 0513
12 Lo Tak Court, Tsuen Wan,
New Territories
新界荃灣路德圍12號

■ ANNUAL AND WEEKLY CLOSING
　休息日期
Closed 10 days Lunar New Year
農曆新年休息10天

■ OPENING HOURS, LAST ORDER
　營業時間，最後點菜時間
11:00-23:00 (L.O.)

■ PRICE/價錢
à la carte/點菜　　　　　$ 18-40

Olala (St. Francis Street)
一碗麵 (聖佛蘭士街)

Olala has this part of chic Wan Chai covered, with its charcuterie shop and traiteur. But it is the noodle shop on the corner that's the best of the bunch. Its creator, Mr Chow, imports many of the ingredients from Europe; bones from the Iberico hams form the basis of the big bowls of noodles which are becoming legendary. Best sellers are the deluxe braised beef noodles, Olala's signature shrimp noodle and, for dessert, mango sponge cake.

"一碗麵" 坐落在灣仔充滿時尚風格的一角，鄰近有肉店與小餐館。但最為出色的就是這家在角落的麵店。伊比利亞火腿的骨頭，正正就是這裡馳名大碗麵條湯底的主要材料，除此以外，亦有紅燒牛肉等不同變化。別忘了嚐嚐這裡的小吃，例如蒜泥白肉。

■ ADDRESS/地址

TEL. 2294 0426
33 St. Francis Street, Wan Chai
灣仔聖佛蘭士街33號

■ ANNUAL AND WEEKLY CLOSING
   休息日期
Closed 4 days Lunar New Year
農曆新年休息4天

■ OPENING HOURS, LAST ORDER
   營業時間，最後點菜時間
11:30-22:30 (L.O.)

■ PRICE/價錢
à la carte/點菜 $ 100-200

Olé   NEW

As the name somewhat suggests, both the decorative style and the menu of this Spanish restaurant have an unapologetically traditional look. The tiles, white walls and knick-knacks give it a certain charm and extra colour is provided by a plethora of paintings. The kitchen prepares the classics such as garlic shrimps, seafood paella and squid with ink sauce with aplomb; go for the churros with hot chocolate sauce for dessert.

單看店名就知道，無論裝修還是菜式都會是地地道道的西班牙風味。瓷磚、白牆配以小擺設就是魅力所在，無處不在的掛畫更添幾分色彩。廚房鬆容地炮製蒜蓉蝦、海鮮炒飯和墨汁墨魚等經典菜式。甜品建議一試churros配熱朱古力醬。

■ ADDRESS/地址

TEL. 2523 8624
1F, Shun Ho Tower,
24-30 Ice House Street, Central
中環雪廠街24-30號順豪大廈1樓
www.ad-caterers.com

■ ANNUAL AND WEEKLY CLOSING
休息日期
Closed 4 days Lunar New Year and Sunday
農曆新年4天及週日休息

■ OPENING HOURS, LAST ORDER
營業時間，最後點菜時間
Lunch/午膳 12:00-14:30 (L.O.)
Dinner/晚膳 18:30-23:00 (L.O.)

■ PRICE/價錢
Lunch/午膳   set/套餐 $148
              à la carte/點菜 $280-550
Dinner/晚膳   à la carte/點菜 $280-550

One Dim Sum
一點心

The owner may be young but he's been involved in the dim sum business for quite a few years and has clearly learnt something because there is often a queue here, despite the shop being able to accommodate up to 40 people. The décor is simple and the two chefs, who have around 30 years of experience, prepare mostly traditional dishes such as steamed prawn dumpling, barbecued pork buns and steamed rice noodles with deep-fried flour roll.

店東雖然相當年輕，但他從事點心專門店已多年，亦顯然對自己的生意有一定的了解，因為儘管店內能容納約40人，卻仍然大排長龍。店內裝潢簡潔，而兩名有30多年經驗的主廚，則努力為客人準備經典點心如薄皮鮮蝦餃、蜜汁叉燒包與炸兩腸粉等。

■ ADDRESS/地址
TEL. 2789 2280
15 Playing Field Road,
Mong Kok, Kowloon
九龍旺角運動場道15號

■ ANNUAL AND WEEKLY CLOSING
　休息日期
Closed 5 days Lunar New Year
農曆新年休息5天

■ OPENING HOURS, LAST ORDER
　營業時間，最後點菜時間
11:00-01:00 (L.O.)

■ PRICE/價錢
à la carte/點菜　　　　　　　$ 30-50

One Harbour Road
港灣壹號

One Harbour Road may be set in a hotel, but its graceful ambience will make you think you're on the terrace of an elegant 1930s Taipan mansion. The airy feel comes courtesy of split-level dining offering views of the harbour, and the sound of running water softens the bold statement of the huge pillars. Cantonese menus offer a wide variety of well-prepared meat and fish dishes. To see how they're done, consider booking the Chef's Table.

雖然港灣壹號位於酒店內，但這裡的氣氛，令你恍如置身於30年代的優雅大班府第。分層用餐讓你同時飽覽海景，享受明亮又開揚的環境。大型蓮花池，以及潺潺的流水聲，軟化了龐大柱子給人的硬朗感覺。這裡的粵菜包括精心準備、種類繁多的肉類和魚類菜式。如想一睹烹調過程，可考慮預訂「廚師餐桌」。

■ ADDRESS/地址

TEL. 2584 7722
8F, Grand Hyatt Hotel,
1 Harbour Road, Wan Chai
灣仔港灣道一號君悅酒店8樓
www.hongkong.grand.hyatt.com

■ OPENING HOURS, LAST ORDER
　營業時間，最後點菜時間
Lunch/午膳　12:00-14:30 (L.O.)
Dinner/晚膳　18:30-22:30 (L.O.)

■ PRICE/價錢
Lunch/午膳　set/套餐　　　　$440-550
　　　　　　à la carte/點菜 $400-750
Dinner/晚膳　set/套餐　　　　$880
　　　　　　à la carte/點菜 $450-750

On Lee
安利

There can't be many locals who don't know this place. It began in 1966 and has moved around, but never far from its current position. Virtually opposite the temple, it has evolved a little from 'milk tea and toast with butter', although these are still on the menu. Now it's fish balls and beef flanks with handmade noodles and their own chilli sauce. The food arrives quickly so you've hardly time to spot your favourite celebrity signature on the wall.

若你住在這一區，肯定聽過這家茶餐廳。自1966年開業以來，安利在附近搬遷多次，但都離現在的地點不遠。這家在寺廟對面的小店，供應的食物從「奶茶配奶油多」已改良了不少，不過這些經典套餐仍然存在於餐單上。現在餐廳的招牌菜已是魚蛋、牛腩配上手打麵，以及他們自製的辣椒醬。上菜快得讓你無暇在牆上找出你最愛明星的簽名。

■ ADDRESS/地址
TEL. 2513 8398
22 Main Street East, Shau Kei Wan
筲箕灣東大街22號

■ OPENING HOURS, LAST ORDER
  營業時間，最後點菜時間
07:00-19:00 (L.O.)

■ PRICE/價錢
à la carte/點菜 $ 20-70

On Lot 10

It's not quite as small as it looks as there's more space upstairs, but this is still a very intimate French restaurant. What it lacks in size, it makes up for in quality. The keen chef tours the markets daily to compile his good value menu of traditional Gallic home cooking; specialities include whole fish with crushed potatoes and roasted chicken with black truffle and sweet peas. Choice is limited at lunch so dinner is the best time to visit.

這家法國餐廳看似地方細小，但其實樓上別有洞天--另有更多座位設於其中，氣氛親切。其優質出品更讓它絲毫不顯遜色。充滿熱情的主廚每天穿梭市場，準備其獨具傳統法國家常菜風格的實惠菜單；店內特色法國菜包括原條魚焗薯蓉、黑松露菌蜜糖豆烤雞。中午時段選擇有限，建議於晚餐時段光顧。

■ ADDRESS/地址

TEL. 2155 9210
34 Gough Street, Central
中環歌賦街34號

■ ANNUAL AND WEEKLY CLOSING
　休息日期
Closed Saturday lunch,
Sunday and Public Holidays
週六午膳、週日及公眾假期休息

■ OPENING HOURS, LAST ORDER
　營業時間，最後點菜時間
Lunch/午膳　12:15-14:45 (L.O.)
Dinner/晚膳　19:00-22:30 (L.O.)

■ PRICE/價錢
Lunch/午膳　set/套餐　　　$ 128
　　　　　　à la carte/點菜 $ 370-550
Dinner/晚膳　à la carte/點菜 $ 370-550

8½ Otto e Mezzo - Bombana

✿ ✿ ✿   ✗✗✗

🍽30   📞🍴   🍇

Fellini's film about the search for inspiration is behind the name of chef-owner Umberto Bombana's bright and bold restaurant. It is an exquisitely framed and thoughtfully lit space, with a chic, urbane feel. The Italian cooking is equally sophisticated; the homemade pasta dishes and Tajima beef specialities are not to be missed. The 'ageing cellar' for the hams and cheeses is an attractive feature. 70% of the large wine list is Italian.

費里尼那齣有關尋找靈感的電影，正是主廚兼老闆Umberto Bombana為這家裝修色彩鮮豔又大膽的餐廳命名的來源。餐廳開業於2010年初，不論裝潢還是照明都經過深思熟慮，帶有都市時尚感。餐廳的意大利菜式同樣精美；自製意大利麵與田島牛特製菜式都是必然之選。火腿與芝士的發酵窖亦甚為吸引。餐廳備有大量美酒讓顧客挑選，當中七成佳釀更來自意大利。

■ ADDRESS/地址

TEL. 2537 8859

Shop 202, 2F, Alexandra House,
18 Chater Road, Central
中環遮打道18號歷山大廈2樓202號舖
www.ottoemezzobombana.com

■ ANNUAL AND WEEKLY CLOSING
   休息日期
Closed Sunday
週日休息

■ OPENING HOURS, LAST ORDER
   營業時間，最後點菜時間
Lunch/午膳 12:00-15:00
Dinner/晚膳 18:00-23:00

■ PRICE/價錢

Lunch/午膳	set/套餐	$420-890
	à la carte/點菜	$520-800
Dinner/晚膳	set/套餐	$890
	à la carte/點菜	$520-800

Peking Garden (Central)
北京樓（中環）

Divided into two large and warmly lit rooms; one more traditionally decorated, the other better suited for bigger family groups. Be sure to time your visit for the noodle-making demonstration, performed by a chef each evening in the restaurant at 8.30pm. The signature dish is, of course, the Peking duck which is prepared with great care. Other dishes to look out for are deep-fried prawns in chilli sauce, and diced steak with walnuts.

餐廳劃分為兩個溫暖明亮的大廳；一邊裝潢風格較為傳統，另一邊則較為適合大家族聚餐。緊記要算準時間，欣賞每晚8時30分的師傅即席拉麵表演。這裡的招牌菜當然是經過精心炮製的北京填鴨。其他值得一試的小菜有宮爆明蝦及琥珀牛柳粒。

■ ADDRESS/地址
TEL. 2526 6456
BF, Alexandra House,
18 Chater Road, Central
中環遮打道18號歷山大廈地庫
www.maxims.com.hk

■ OPENING HOURS, LAST ORDER
　營業時間，最後點菜時間
Lunch/午膳 11:30-15:00 L.O.14:45
Dinner/晚膳 18:00-23:30 L.O.22:45

■ PRICE/價錢
à la carte/點菜　　　　　$ 260-600

Peking Garden (Kowloon)
北京樓 (九龍)

✕✕ ✕✕

⊟ 24

A huge, boisterous Peking restaurant with eight rooms and 500 seats, where the staff are either supervising with calm deliberation, or pushing trolleys and serving. The special dishes are the barbecued Peking duck with pancake, and the poached fish with bamboo shoots and salted cabbage - but look out also for the sliced fish with rice wine sauce and fried hand-made noodles with shredded pork.

這家熱鬧大型的北京樓分為8個部分，可容納500個座位。員工分工合作，有的沉著地監督；有的推著餐車；有的在奉菜。招牌菜有北京填鴨，雪筍湯爆魚絲等。值得一試的還有北京糟溜魚片和炒手拉麵。

■ ADDRESS/地址
TEL. 2735 8211
3F, Star House, 3 Salisbury Road, Tsim Sha Tsui, Kowloon
九龍尖沙咀梳士巴利道3號星光行3樓
www.maxims.com.hk

■ OPENING HOURS, LAST ORDER
營業時間，最後點菜時間
Lunch/午膳 11:30-15:00 L.O.14:45
Dinner/晚膳 17:30-23:30 L.O.23:00

■ PRICE/價錢
Lunch/午膳　set/套餐　　　　$ 105
　　　　　　à la carte/點菜 $ 335-535
Dinner/晚膳　à la carte/點菜 $ 335-535

Peking Garden (Tai Koo Shing)
北京樓（太古城）

Head for the City Plaza's indoor ice rink to find this smart restaurant. The interior hits the gold standard, its glitter an ornately ubiquitous statement - just what's required to draw in all those shoppers. The accomplished cuisine is mostly Peking, and the hallmark dish is Peking duck, but spice is nice here too: tuck into fried prawns with chilli sauce. Sichuan and Shanghai elements are also on the menu, though dim sum is low key.

向太古城溜冰場的方向走，便會找到這家時尚的餐廳。餐廳的內部實在金璧輝煌：發出閃閃生輝、無所不在的光芒，如此華麗的氣派正正吸引了購物者到此用餐。餐廳的菜式大部分是北京菜，招牌菜是北京填鴨，而這裡的川菜亦頗美味：不妨試試京爆明蝦球。有些菜式含四川和上海元素，但點心則較少。

■ ADDRESS/地址

TEL. 2884 4131
2F, Cityplaza II, Tai Koo Shing
太古城太古城中心第2期2樓
www.maxims.com.hk

■ OPENING HOURS, LAST ORDER
營業時間，最後點菜時間
Lunch/午膳 11:30-15:30 L.O.14:45
Dinner/晚膳 18:00-23:30 L.O.23:00

■ PRICE/價錢
Lunch/午膳	set/套餐	$188
	à la carte/點菜	$160-530
Dinner/晚膳	set/套餐	$438-488
	à la carte/點菜	$180-530

Petrus
珀翠

Petrus is firmly in the classical European style with moulded ceilings, chandeliers, elaborately draped curtains and fine table settings; it also offer great views from its perch on the 56th floor. The professional service blends in perfectly and at dinner you're accompanied by a harpist. All this is matched by very proficient French cooking that relies on a roll-call of top quality ingredients. The wine list has over 20,000 bottles.

Petrus的經典歐陸格調，充分表現在雕有線條的天花、吊燈、高雅的窗簾及排列優雅的餐桌之上。餐廳座落於酒店56樓，可飽覽海港美景，其服務專業之餘，在晚飯時段更有豎琴演奏伴隨用膳。這一切配上一流的法式烹調，與絕對新鮮的食材可謂無與倫比。此外，其美酒清單更逾20,000瓶。

■ ADDRESS/地址

TEL. 2820 8590
56F, Island Shangri-La Hotel, Pacific Place, Supreme Court Road, Admiralty
中區法院道太古廣場
港島香格里拉酒店56樓
www.shangri-la.com

■ OPENING HOURS, LAST ORDER
營業時間，最後點菜時間
Lunch/午膳 12:00-14:30 (L.O.)
Dinner/晚膳 18:30-22:30 (L.O.)

■ PRICE/價錢
Lunch/午膳	set/套餐	$448
	à la carte/點菜	$870-1,500
Dinner/晚膳	set/套餐	$1,380
	à la carte/點菜	$870-1,500

Pierre

The top floor of the Mandarin Oriental provides suitably chic surroundings for celebrated French chef Pierre Gagnaire's culinary pyrotechnics. The intricate and innovative dishes and their component parts arrive in a number of vessels, all carefully explained by the charming staff. The views are terrific and the room itself is stylish, moodily lit and very comfortable. The focus here is on enjoyment, with an atmosphere free from pomposity.

文華東方酒店頂樓的環境，與法國名廚Pierre Gagnaire讓人驚歎的美味菜式非常合襯。精緻而創新的菜式與配菜以不同容器盛載而上，全部由殷勤的侍應細心介紹。餐廳景觀迷人，而餐廳本身的裝潢也甚具現代感，配合富情調的照明，非常舒適。在這裡，你大可盡情融入美食，專心享受美食。

■ ADDRESS/地址

TEL. 2825 4001

25F, Mandarin Oriental Hotel,
5 Connaught Road, Central
中環干諾道中5號文華東方酒店25樓
www.mandarinoriental.com/hongkong

■ ANNUAL AND WEEKLY CLOSING
　　休息日期
Closed Saturday lunch, Sunday
and Public Holidays
週六午膳、週日及公眾假期休息

■ OPENING HOURS, LAST ORDER
　　營業時間，最後點菜時間
Lunch/午膳 12:00-14:30 (L.O.)
Dinner/晚膳 19:00-22:30 (L.O.)

■ PRICE/價錢

Lunch/午膳	set/套餐	$448-1,488
	à la carte/點菜	$1,360-1,650
Dinner/晚膳	set/套餐	$1,448
	à la carte/點菜	$1,360-1,650

Prawn Noodle Shop NEW
蝦麵店

It was while living in New Zealand that the owners, Mr and Mrs Sham, met a Malaysian man of Chinese descent who passed on his secret for cooking prawn noodles. They duly returned to Hong Kong and opened a shop in the '90s, before moving to this address. They listened well, as their shop is now famous for the Penang-style prawn noodles, which come with many toppings and a choice of four delicious base soups - try the spicy seafood curry.

店主沈氏伉儷早年在紐西蘭居住時，遇到一名馬來西亞華僑，向他們傳授了烹調蝦麵的秘訣。於90年代回港後，就開設了蝦麵店，隨後再搬至現址。他們可謂盡得真傳，讓其馬來西亞式蝦麵遠近馳名；這裡每碗麵都有豐富配料，並備有四個湯底可供選擇 — 推介辣海鮮咖哩。

■ ADDRESS/地址
TEL. 2520 0268
2 Landale Street, Wan Chai
灣仔蘭杜街2號

■ ANNUAL AND WEEKLY CLOSING
　 休息日期
Closed 3 days Lunar New Year,
Sunday and Public Holidays
農曆新年3天、週日及公眾假期休息

■ OPENING HOURS, LAST ORDER
　 營業時間，最後點菜時間
11:30-20:00 (L.O.)

■ PRICE/價錢
à la carte/點菜　　　　　　$ 30-55

Red Seasons (Lam Tei)
季季紅 (藍地)

Red Seasons restaurant is renowned for its roast suckling pig – it comes stuffed with rice and dried shrimps, must be ordered in advance and is perfect for a large party. It's just one of a number of specialities, along with pork patties with lotus root and pork ribs with plum sauce. Such is their reputation that reservations need to be made well in advance. The restaurant even has its own small temple at the back.

季季紅最著名的菜式是蝦禾米乳香豬－－乳豬內釀了飯和蝦米，須提前預訂，十分適合大型派對。其他鎮店名菜包括有香煎蓮藕餅與冰淋醬烤骨。由於酒樓名氣甚廣，請提早訂座。酒樓後方更設有小嗣堂。

■ ADDRESS/地址
TEL. 2462 7038
1 Lam Tei Main Street, Tuen Mun, New Territories
新界屯門藍地大街 1號
www.redseasons.com.hk

■ OPENING HOURS, LAST ORDER
　營業時間，最後點菜時間
05:00-23:00 (L.O.)

■ PRICE/價錢
Lunch/午膳　set/套餐　　　　$ 127-155
　　　　　　à la carte/點菜 $ 50-250
Dinner/晚膳　à la carte/點菜 $ 120-250

Regal Palace
富豪金殿

A makeover in 2011 left this grand dining room on the third floor of the Regal Hotel feeling a lot fresher and brighter. With its vast windows and twinkling glass crystals, it provides suitably elegant surroundings to match the classic Cantonese cooking. Chef Ip's long-standing tenure of the top job has kept the regulars happy. It's well worth heading straight for the 'award' or 'signature' dishes on the menu.

經過2011年的全新裝修後,這家位於富豪酒店3樓的豪華酒家更見清新亮麗。巨大的玻璃窗與閃爍的水晶玻璃裝飾,優雅的環境配合著這裡的經典粵菜。長久以來,這裡的主廚一職都由名廚葉師傅擔任,一直都令常客十分滿意。值得一試菜單上的「得獎」與「招牌」菜式。

■ ADDRESS/地址
TEL. 2837 1773
3F, Regal Hotel, 88 Yee Wo Street,
Causeway Bay
銅鑼灣怡和街88號富豪酒店3樓
www.regalhotel.com

■ OPENING HOURS, LAST ORDER
營業時間,最後點菜時間
Lunch/午膳 12:00-15:00 (L.O.)
Dinner/晚膳 18:00-23:00 (L.O.)

■ PRICE/價錢

Lunch/午膳	set/套餐	$398-598
	à la carte/點菜	$240-1,100
Dinner/晚膳	set/套餐	$398-598
	à la carte/點菜	$260-1,100

Sabah
莎巴

It may have an unremarkable façade, but at least it's easy to find thanks to the huge horizontal neon sign. It's equally modest inside which alerts you to the fact that diners don't come for the interior design but for the authentic Malay specialties. Satay, king prawns with butter and deep-fried egg yolk, beef Rendang and Hainanese chicken rice are some of the highlights. And it's always worth saving room here for the banana fritters.

這家餐廳的外觀也許毫不起眼,但是靠著巨大的霓虹燈招牌,我們可輕易找到它。內部的裝潢與外觀一樣平凡,但吸引眾多食客的並不是餐廳的室內設計,而是正宗的馬拉菜。精選菜式包括沙嗲、金絲奶油大蝦、巴東牛肉與海南雞飯。主廚秘方炮製的炸香蕉也十分惹味。

■ ADDRESS/地址

TEL. 2143 6626
98-102 Jaffe Road, Wan Chai
灣仔謝菲道98-102號

■ ANNUAL AND WEEKLY CLOSING
　　休息日期
Closed 4 days Lunar New Year
農曆新年休息4天

■ OPENING HOURS, LAST ORDER
　　營業時間,最後點菜時間
11:00-23:30 (L.O.)

■ PRICE/價錢

Lunch/午膳	set/套餐	$60
	à la carte/點菜	$130-330
Dinner/晚膳	à la carte/點菜	$130-330

Sang Kee Congee & Noodles (Sheung Wan)
生記清湯牛腩麵家 (上環)

The same menu is available here as in the original premises which still operate just a few steps away in Burd Street and opened over forty years ago. However, as this ten-year old sibling is somewhat larger, it's a little easier to get a table here without waiting too long. Piping hot bowls of congee and tender beef brisket noodles draw the crowds, while the ladies who run it do so with alacrity and efficiency.

在這裡，菜單與相隔數步，早於四十年前已開幕的畢街總店相同。不過，由於這位年僅十歲的「弟弟」面積較大，在這裡不用久等就能取得座位。店裡不斷送上的一碗碗熱騰騰的粥和牛腩麵吸引大量食客，勤快的女店員動作敏捷、效率高。

■ ADDRESS/地址
TEL. 2541 8199
20 Hillier Street, Sheung Wan
上環禧利街20號

■ ANNUAL AND WEEKLY CLOSING
　休息日期
Closed 1 week Lunar New Year,
Sunday and Public Holidays
農曆新年7天、週日及公眾假期休息

■ OPENING HOURS, LAST ORDER
　營業時間，最後點菜時間
07:00-21:00

■ PRICE/價錢
à la carte/點菜 $ 20-50

Ser Wong Fun
蛇王芬

This restaurant was established 70 years ago and is now under the stewardship of the fourth generation, so it is little wonder that there has been a book celebrating the family history and their cherished recipes. Regulars flock here for the snake soup and snake banquets in winter. No less than 15 varieties of double-boiled soups and a vast array of seasonal pot dishes are also offered; add to that barbecue dishes and assorted seafood.

七十年前開店的蛇王芬如今由第四代傳人主理，更有出版書籍介紹家族歷史及其著名菜式。熟客經常來此品嚐蛇羹，冬天甚至品嚐蛇宴。超過十五種老火燉湯任君選擇，亦提供一系列煲仔飯；此外更提供燒烤雜錦海鮮。

■ ADDRESS/地址
TEL. 2543 1032
30 Cochrane Street, Central
中環閣麟街30號

■ ANNUAL AND WEEKLY CLOSING
　休息日期
Closed 4 days Lunar New Year
農曆新年休息4天

■ OPENING HOURS, LAST ORDER
　營業時間，最後點菜時間
11:00-22:30 (L.O.)

■ PRICE/價錢
Lunch/午膳　à la carte/點菜 $ 70-100
Dinner/晚膳　à la carte/點菜 $ 150-180

Shanghai Garden
紫玉蘭

❌❌

🚌120 ◐🍴

It is known for its range of classic dishes mostly from Shanghai, but dishes from Sichuan and Beijing also feature. The décor in the two large dining rooms may not be that noteworthy but it is the cuisine that's the attraction here and it is hugely popular with local office staff at lunchtime. Specialities include deep-fried Mandarin fish with sweet and sour sauce, sautéed freshwater shrimp, and stewed pork with preserved vegetables.

紫玉蘭聞名於它的經典上海和蘇杭佳餚，同時亦有少量京川菜式；相較兩個大型餐室的裝飾，這裡的菜餚似乎更吸引，因此飯店於午飯時間極受當地白領歡迎。馳名美食包括蘇浙大班松鼠桂魚、上海清炒河蝦仁及太湖陳家梅干菜燒肉。

■ ADDRESS/地址
TEL. 2524 8181
1F, Hutchison House,
10 Harcourt Road, Central
中環夏慤道10號和記大廈1樓
www.maxims.com.hk

■ OPENING HOURS, LAST ORDER
營業時間，最後點菜時間
Lunch/午膳 11:30-14:30 (L.O.)
Dinner/晚膳 17:30-23:00 (L.O.)

■ PRICE/價錢
à la carte/點菜　　　　$ 180-520

Shanghai Wing Wah   NEW
上海榮華川菜館

Owner-chef Mr Yeung may be Cantonese himself but such was his love of Shanghainese cuisine that when he opened this neighbourhood restaurant in a market street back in '75 he wanted it to serve home-style Shanghainese specialities, along with some Sichuan dishes. The dining room still retains that '70s look and some of the tiling is original. Dishes to look out for are sautéed eel with chives, and twice-cooked pork with pepper and chilli.

店東兼大廚楊先生是廣東人，卻偏鍾情上海菜。早於1975年於鄰近街市之處創辦這家街坊小館，目的就是讓大家都能嚐到上海家常菜，並有數款川菜。餐廳仍維持70年代風貌和保留部份原裝的瓷磚。推介韮王鱔糊和回鍋肉。

■ ADDRESS/地址

TEL. 2341 0583
15 Shung Yan Street,
Kwun Tong, Kowloon
九龍觀塘崇仁街15號
www.shwingwah.com

■ ANNUAL AND WEEKLY CLOSING
    休息日期
Closed 3 days Lunar New Year
農曆新年休息3天

■ OPENING HOURS, LAST ORDER
    營業時間，最後點菜時間
11:30-22:30 (L.O.)

■ PRICE/價錢
à la carte/點菜 $ 80-150

Shanghai Xiao Nan Guo (Kowloon Bay)
上海小南國 (九龍灣)

What started off as a small family business in Shanghai has now grown into an international chain, with branches all over China and Hong Kong and even in Tokyo. This Kowloon outpost provides a stylish and contemporary environment in which to enjoy the flavoursome dishes. Along with drunken chicken in Shaoxing wine, look out for grandma's braised pork belly and pan-fried crispy pork soup bun. Dim sum is available at both lunch and dinner.

從上海一家小規模經營的家族生意開始，餐廳如今已成為國際知名的連鎖店，在中國、香港甚至東京都有分店。位於九龍的新店裝潢時尚，令你更投入享受佳餚。除了紹興花雕醉雞，更應嚐嚐外婆紅燒肉及灌湯生煎包。午餐及晚餐時段均供應點心。

■ ADDRESS/地址

TEL. 2545 0880

Unit 2, Level 6, Megabox,
38 Wang Chiu Road, Kowloon Bay,
Kowloon
九龍九龍灣宏照道38號
Megabox6樓2號舖

■ OPENING HOURS, LAST ORDER
營業時間，最後點菜時間
Lunch/午膳 11:30-15:00 L.O. 14:30
Dinner/晚膳 18:00-23:00 L.O. 22:30

■ PRICE/價錢
à la carte/點菜　　　　　$ 200-850

Shang Palace
香宮

✿✿   ᴪᴪᴪ

                         ♿ ☞♟ ⊟24 ☏⊪

Four golden statues by the entrance welcome you to this sumptuous room that vividly evokes the grandeur of the Sung Dynasty. Red lacquered walls, antique paintings and classic lanterns only add to the authentic atmosphere. Highlights of the Cantonese menu include lobster, garoupa and scallop dumpling in supreme soup; pan-fried lamb chop with goose liver paste; braised Wu Xi spare rib casserole, and sautéed rice with crab meat and egg white.

大門的四個金色塑像歡迎你來到這家豪華的餐廳，宋朝的顯赫氣派活靈活現。紅色漆牆、古董國畫，以及傳統燈籠交織出古色古香的氣氛。這裡的粵菜亦同樣精巧，更提供不錯的素食菜式。烹調技巧出色，特色美色包括高湯龍皇果、鵝肝醬煎紐西蘭羊架、無錫焗排骨煲及宮廷兩儀飯。

■ ADDRESS/地址
TEL. 2733 8754
Lower level, Kowloon Shangri-La Hotel, 64 Mody Road, East Tsim Sha Tsui, Kowloon
九龍尖東麼地道64號
九龍香格里拉酒店地庫1樓
www.shangri-la.com

■ OPENING HOURS, LAST ORDER
營業時間，最後點菜時間
Lunch/午膳 12:00-15:00 (L.O.)
Dinner/晚膳 18:00-23:00 (L.O.)

■ PRICE/價錢
Lunch/午膳　set/套餐　　　$288-788
　　　　　　à la carte/點菜 $300-1,000
Dinner/晚膳 set/套餐　　　$788
　　　　　　à la carte/點菜 $300-1,000

Shek Kee Kitchen NEW
石記廚房

 8

During the day, the shop sells Cha Chan Tang dishes, but we recommend it for the traditional, home-style Cantonese cooking it serves in the evening. The owner-chef goes to the market each day in search of the freshest ingredients and some of his regulars even call him directly to order specific dishes for that night. Specialities are braised pork belly with preserved vegetables, and roasted chicken with fermented bean curd.

在日間，這家餐廳賣的是普通的茶餐廳食物，但我們要推介的是他們在晚間提供的家庭式廣東小菜。大廚兼東主每天都親自往街市選購最新鮮的食材，部分熟客更會直接打電話找他預訂當晚的菜式。推介有梅菜扣肉和南乳吊燒雞。

■ ADDRESS/地址
TEL. 2571 3348
GF, 15-17 Ngan Mok Street, Tin Hau
天后銀幕街17號地下

■ OPENING HOURS, LAST ORDER
營業時間，最後點菜時間
Lunch/午膳 07:00-15:00 (L.O.)
Dinner/晚膳 18:00-23:00 (L.O.)

■ PRICE/價錢
Lunch/午膳　set/套餐　　$ 36-43
Dinner/晚膳　à la carte/點菜 $ 60-380

She Wong Yee
蛇王二

Their signature snake soup has long been renowned and in winter around 1,200 bowls are served each day, up until midnight. Regulars are quick to occupy one of the few tables for this memorable experience and it is no surprise that the recipe has remained unchanged for years. These days, those regulars come also for the famed barbecued meats and speciality sausages with rice; the roast goose and double-boiled soups are good too.

此著名蛇羹集團一向聞名四方，冬天平均每天賣出多達1200碗，營業至深夜零時。熟客急不及待佔駐其中一張桌，享受一貫的美味，不出所料，製法多年來從未改變。如今，熟客對其著名燒味及燒臘配飯亦趨之若鶩，燒鵝還有燉湯更具水準。要先在外面等等才有座位？你的等待將是有意義的。

■ ADDRESS/地址

TEL. 2831 0163
24 Percival Street, Causeway Bay
銅鑼灣波斯富街24號

■ ANNUAL AND WEEKLY CLOSING
　休息日期
Closed 3 days Lunar New Year
農曆新年休息3天

■ OPENING HOURS, LAST ORDER
　營業時間，最後點菜時間
11:30-00:00 (L.O.)

■ PRICE/價錢
à la carte/點菜　　　　　　$ 50-150

Sister Wah　NEW
華姐清湯腩

With just six round tables, Sister Wah's diminutive dimensions are in direct contrast to the size of its reputation – this is one of the most famous beef brisket noodle shops. Hence, this family-run shop is always full and it is easy to see why: there are around 20 items on the menu which include Dan Dan noodles and Drunken chicken, but chief among them is the beef brisket in a clear soup (and be smart when you order and ask for 牛坑腩).

只有六張圓檯的華姐清湯腩，規模與其名氣形成鮮明對比 — 這裡是最馳名的牛腩麵家之一。正因如此，這間家庭式經營的小店經常滿座，這也難怪：餐牌上約有二十種食品，包括擔擔麵和醉雞，但招牌菜當然是清湯腩(點菜時記得指明要牛坑腩是你的精明之選)。

■ ADDRESS/地址
TEL.2807 0181
Shop A1, 13 Electric Road, Tin Hau
天后電氣道13號A1號舖

■ ANNUAL AND WEEKLY CLOSING
　　休息日期
Closed 6 days Lunar New Year
農曆新年休息6天

■ OPENING HOURS, LAST ORDER
　　營業時間，最後點菜時間
11:00-23:00 (L.O.)

■ PRICE/價錢
à la carte/點菜　　　　$ 22-50

Siu Shun Village Cuisine
肇順名匯河鮮專門店

Specialities such as stir-fried freshwater lobster with ginger and shallots; steamed pork spare ribs; fresh prawns in XO sauce, and the fish lips casserole draw plenty of locals to this restaurant specialising in Shun Tak cuisine. Located in a shopping mall, it's always crowded and noise levels can reach the lively end of the scale. Imitation bamboo and birdcage lampshades add to the somewhat eccentric decorative style.

這裡的著名菜式包括薑葱龍蝦球、檀香骨、XO醬炒花枝鮮蝦球、瓦撐煎焗魚咀吸引很多香港人來此品嘗順德菜。餐廳位於商場內，經常座無虛席，從吵鬧聲可見其熱鬧氣氛。仿竹及雀籠燈罩令這裡的裝潢風格更顯特色。

■ ADDRESS/地址
TEL. 2798 9738
7F, MegaBox, 38 Wang Chiu Road,
Kowloon Bay, Kowloon
九龍灣宏照道38號MegaBox7樓

■ OPENING HOURS, LAST ORDER
營業時間，最後點菜時間
Lunch/午膳 09:00-16:30 (L.O.)
Dinner/晚膳 18:00-23:30 (L.O.)

■ PRICE/價錢
Lunch/午膳　à la carte/點菜 $ 100-550
Dinner/晚膳　à la carte/點菜 $ 140-550

Snow Garden (Causeway Bay)
雪園 (銅鑼灣)

✖️🍴

🍱 16　📞🍴

Established in 1992 at this sleek business address and known for its traditional Shanghainese cuisine, this is a restaurant that operates like clockwork and whose staff are warm and attentive. The long-standing chef's specialities are steamed herring and deep-fried chicken skin with four spices; braised sea cucumber with shrimp roe; and yellow fish with sweet and sour sauce. Dishes arrive carefully prepared and bursting with flavour.

餐廳於1992年創辦於此商業區熱點，以精心烹調的上海菜馳名，人流絡繹不絕，員工態度親切熱誠。四寶片皮雞、蝦子花膠及糖醋黃魚都是歷久不衰的廚師精選。每道菜式都經過精心制作，色香味俱全。

■ ADDRESS/地址
TEL. 2881 6837
2F, China Taiping Tower,
8 Sunning Road, Causeway Bay
銅鑼灣新寧道8號中國太平大廈2樓
www.snow-garden.com

■ ANNUAL AND WEEKLY CLOSING
　　休息日期
Closed 3 days Lunar New Year
農曆新年休息3天

■ OPENING HOURS, LAST ORDER
　　營業時間，最後點菜時間
Lunch/午膳 11:30-14:45 (L.O.)
Dinner/晚膳 18:00-22:45 (L.O.)

■ PRICE/價錢
Lunch/午膳　set/套餐　　　　$100
　　　　　　à la carte/點菜 $250-700
Dinner/晚膳 set/套餐　　　　$500
　　　　　　à la carte/點菜 $250-700

Spoon by Alain Ducasse

Fantastic views, stylish seating, a ceiling lined with spoons and an impressive glass cellar holding around 600 wines – characteristics of this fashionable outpost of the Alain Ducasse empire. The carefully prepared, French cuisine suits this environment well. Signature dishes include steamed duck foie gras with fruit condiment and brioche, and baked suzuki with asparagus, black truffle and Argenteuil sauce.

美妙景觀、時尚雅座、排列著匙羹的天花板，加上擺放了接近600瓶佳釀令人嘆為觀止的玻璃酒櫃，打造成名廚艾倫杜卡斯（Alain Ducasse）美食王國的香港分部，實為潮流時尚之選。精心炮製的當代法國菜與優美環境相得益彰。招牌菜包括蒸法國鴨肝伴乾果醬配牛油包及焗鱸魚伴青露筍跟黑松露菌。

■ ADDRESS/地址

TEL. 2313 2256

GF, Intercontinental Hotel,
18 Salisbury Road, Tsim Sha Tsui,
Kowloon
九龍尖沙咀梳士巴利道18號
洲際酒店地下
www.hongkong-ic.intercontinental.com

■ OPENING HOURS, LAST ORDER
　　營業時間，最後點菜時間
Sunday lunch/週日午膳 12:00-14:30
Dinner/晚膳 18:00-23:30 (L.O.)

■ PRICE/價錢
Sunday lunch/週日午膳 set/套餐 $558
　　　　　　à la carte/點菜 $800-1,420
Dinner/晚膳 set/套餐 $1,180
　　　　　　à la carte/點菜 $800-1,420

Spring Moon
嘉麟樓

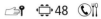

An elegant and luxurious Cantonese restaurant, which appears to be very much at home in The Peninsula. Admire the tropical hardwood or the bamboo flower arrangements while sipping tea at the tea bar, or dine in the restaurant or on the more intimate mezzanine floor where refined service oversees authentic dishes with flavour. There are 25 different teas available and you can even call upon the services of a 'tea sommelier'.

嘉麟樓位於半島酒店內，是一家優雅豪華的粵菜餐廳，令人感覺舒適。食客可以邊在"茶檔"茗茶，邊欣賞餐廳內的熱帶硬木或竹花排列。你可以選擇在餐廳內或在較隱蔽的私家房內用餐，完善的服務配合味道濃郁的原味菜餚。這裏有25種茶可供選擇，你甚至可要求「茗茶師」為你調配名茶。

■ ADDRESS/地址
TEL. 2315 3160
1F, The Peninsula Hotel, Salisbury Road,
Tsim Sha Tsui, Kowloon
九龍尖沙咀梳士巴利道半島酒店1樓
www.peninsula.com

■ OPENING HOURS, LAST ORDER
營業時間，最後點菜時間
Lunch/午膳 11:30-14:30 (L.O.)
Dinner/晚膳 18:00-22:30 (L.O.)

■ PRICE/價錢
Lunch/午膳	set/套餐	$ 368-448
	à la carte/點菜	$ 300-800
Dinner/晚膳	set/套餐	$ 928-1,988
	à la carte/點菜	$ 500-1,500

Steik World Meats

✕✕ ✕✕

🍽 26

There may be lobster, oysters, prawns and scallops on the menu but the vast majority come here for the beef. The assorted cuts come mostly from the USA, Australia, Scotland and Ireland; try the 'Four Nations of Beef' tasting menu. The dry-ageing is done in-house and in-view above the part-open kitchen. The restaurant is contemporary, but undoubtedly masculine in style; ask for one of the booths. Its discreet location adds to the clubby feel.

餐牌上不乏龍蝦、蠔、虎蝦和帶子，但大部份客人都是慕牛肉之名而來。這裡的牛扒主要來自美國、澳洲、蘇格蘭及愛爾蘭，可試試齊集上述四國牛肉的套餐。半開放式廚房設有dry-ageing（風乾）櫃，既可自行風乾牛肉，又可吸引客人注目。餐廳設計時尚，風格充滿陽剛味，廂座很受歡迎。獨特的位置也令餐廳更添俱樂部感覺。

■ ADDRESS/地址

TEL. 2530 0011
Level 3, K11, 18 Hanoi Road,
Tsim Sha Tsui, Kowloon
九龍尖沙咀河內道18號K11 3樓
www.epicurean.com.hk

■ OPENING HOURS, LAST ORDER
　　營業時間，最後點菜時間
Lunch/午膳 12:00-15:00 (L.O.)
Dinner/晚膳 18:00-23:30 L.O.22:30

■ PRICE/價錢
Lunch/午膳　set/套餐　　$138-276
　　　　　　à la carte/點菜 $250-1,000
Dinner/晚膳 set/套餐　　$538-728
　　　　　　à la carte/點菜 $250-1,000

St. George

The beams, vaulted ceiling, chandeliers and fireplaces add character and intimacy to this comfortable and discreet first floor dining room, while the atmosphere evokes colonial Hong Kong. The private dining rooms are equally appealing and also come furnished with antiques. By contrast, the cuisine is far more contemporary, with the kitchen adding plenty of original touches and Asian influences to the largely French specialities.

橫樑、拱形天花、吊燈與壁爐為這間位於一樓，既舒適又隱密的餐廳增加不少親切感，餐廳的氣氛讓人聯想起昔日的殖民地風格。餐廳的私人宴會廳，以古董做裝飾，格調同樣典雅華麗。與裝潢剛好相反，餐廳的菜式非常大膽創新，於傳統菜式加入亞洲風味，炮制款式新穎的法式佳餚。

■ ADDRESS/地址

TEL. 3988 0220
Hullett House, 2A Canton Road,
Tsim Sha Tsui, Kowloon
九龍尖沙咀廣東道2A Hullett House
www.hulletthouse.com

■ ANNUAL AND WEEKLY CLOSING
　休息日期
Closed Sunday
週日休息

■ OPENING HOURS, LAST ORDER
　營業時間，最後點菜時間
Lunch/午膳　12:00-14:30 (L.O.)
Dinner/晚膳　19:00-22:30 (L.O.)

■ PRICE/價錢
Lunch/午膳　set/套餐　　　$288-528
　　　　　　à la carte/點菜 $750-1,100
Dinner/晚膳　set/套餐　　　$588-1,288
　　　　　　à la carte/點菜 $750-1,100

Summer Palace
夏宮

They've created a charming environment here in this 5th floor room, with its crystal chandeliers, traditional Chinese screens and well-placed tables. The Cantonese menu features all the true classics and the kitchen uses carefully chosen ingredients prepared without fussiness or over-elaboration. To drink, there's a varied selection of wines by the glass, Chinese liquors and exquisite teas.

他們在這位於五樓的空間營造了迷人的環境，配上水晶吊燈、傳統中國屏風及精心佈置的餐桌。粵菜菜譜提供所有經典名菜，廚房精心挑選食材，烹調時井井有條，毫不過火。餐飲方面具杯裝餐酒、中國酒和高級茗茶。

■ ADDRESS/地址

TEL. 2820 8553

5F, Island Shangri-La Hotel, Pacific Place, Supreme Court Road, Admiralty
中區法院道太古廣場
港島香格里拉酒店5樓
www.shangri-la.com

■ OPENING HOURS, LAST ORDER
營業時間，最後點菜時間
Lunch/午膳 11:30-14:30 (L.O.)
Dinner/晚膳 18:30-22:30 (L.O.)

■ PRICE/價錢
Lunch/午膳　set/套餐　　　　$590
　　　　　à la carte/點菜 $280-1,100
Dinner/晚膳　à la carte/點菜 $280-1,100

Sun Kau Kee Noodle Shop
新九記粥麵

Most residents of Wan Chai will know this shop as it's been here for around twenty years and, although it's now under the stewardship of the former managers and chef, little has really changed in all that time. This is one of the few places to offer congee hotpot so try it and you can be assured of a table; if you want noodles then you'll just have to join the queue. It's also worth sampling the beef flank with tendons.

大部分灣仔居民都認識這已有約二十年歷史的店鋪。這裡雖然掌管的經理和廚師都不同了，但除此之外改變不大。這是少數提供火鍋以粥做湯底的地方，試試看，絕不會讓你失望。如果你想吃麵，就要花時間排隊了。這裡的牛筋腩也非常有名。

■ ADDRESS/地址
TEL. 2865 2827
9 Tai Wong Street East, Wan Chai
灣仔大王東街9號

■ ANNUAL AND WEEKLY CLOSING
　　休息日期
Closed 10 days Lunar New Year and Sunday
農曆新年10天及週日休息

■ OPENING HOURS, LAST ORDER
　　營業時間，最後點菜時間
11:00-01:00

■ PRICE/價錢
à la carte/點菜 　　　　$ 20-65

Sun Sin NEW
新仙清湯腩咖喱專門店

Never mind directions – just follow your nose and those enticing beef aromas will lead you to this small noodle shop in Yau Ma Tei's busiest street. Sun Sin is famous for its well-priced beef brisket in a clear soup and for the curry with its secret recipe. The owner buys high quality beef each morning from a local supplier and it's then cooked for hours. As she sells over three hundred portions each day, don't be surprised when it's all gone.

就算不辨方向，只要跟著你的鼻子，誘人的牛腩香氣就會把你帶到這家位於油麻地最繁忙地段的小麵店。新仙以價廉物美的清湯腩和秘製咖喱聞名。店主每天早上向本地肉商購入高質素的牛腩，並耗時數小時烹煮，每天賣出超過 300 碗，還隨時售罄。

■ ADDRESS/地址
TEL. 2332 6872
37 Portland Street,
Yau Ma Tei, Kowloon
九龍油麻地砵蘭街37號

■ OPENING HOURS, LAST ORDER
營業時間，最後點菜時間
11:30-01:00
■ PRICE/價錢
à la carte/點菜 $ 25-90

Sun Tung Lok
新同樂

✿✿　　　　　　　　　　　　　　　　　　XX X X

🛋️48　◑🍴

After 40 years in Happy Valley, Sun Tung Lok is now comfortably installed on the fourth floor of the Miramar shopping centre. A contemporary colour palette of grey, brown and beige is used to good effect in this stylish restaurant; ask for one of the three booths for extra privacy. 80% of the menu is Cantonese; examples include rib of beef with house gravy, stuffed crab shell, and roast suckling pig.

在跑馬地經營了40年後，新同樂現在於美麗華商場的4樓重新開張。充滿時代感的灰色、咖啡色與米色在這家摩登酒家裡被巧妙運用。設有3個廂坐，以供需要多點私隱的客人選擇。八成菜式是粵菜，包括燒汁乾逼牛肋骨、鮮蘑菇焗釀蟹蓋及燒乳豬件。

■ ADDRESS/地址
TEL. 2152 1417
4F, Miramar Shopping Centre,
132 Nathan Road, Tsim Sha Tsui,
Kowloon
九龍尖沙咀彌敦道132號
美麗華商場4樓
www.suntunglok.com.hk

■ OPENING HOURS, LAST ORDER
　　營業時間，最後點菜時間
Lunch/午膳 11:30-15:00 (L.O.)
Dinner/晚膳 18:00-23:00 (L.O.)

■ PRICE/價錢
Lunch/午膳　set/套餐　　　　$180-450
　　　　　　à la carte/點菜 $280-5,000
Dinner/晚膳　set/套餐　　　　$568-768
　　　　　　à la carte/點菜 $280-5,000

Sun Yuen Hing Kee
新園興記

This traditionally styled, simple but well maintained barbecue shop has been run by the same family since the mid 1970s. Over the years they've built up quite an appreciative following so the small place fills quickly. The appetising looking suckling pigs hanging next to the kitchen are not the only draw here: roasted pork, duck and pigeon all have their followers, as does the soft-boiled chicken. It's located next to Sheung Wan market.

這家格調傳統，簡單而又保養得宜的燒味店自70年代中一直由同一家族經營。多年來，他們已累積了不少忠實顧客，所以小小的地方很快便座無虛席。這裡受歡迎的不僅是掛在廚房旁邊，賣相令人垂涎欲滴的乳豬、燒肉、烤鴨、乳鴿，和白切雞都各有忠實擁躉。燒味店位於上環街市旁邊。

■ ADDRESS/地址

TEL. 2541 2207
327-329 Queen's Road Central, Sheung Wan
上環皇后大道中327-329號

■ ANNUAL AND WEEKLY CLOSING
　休息日期
Closed 5 days Lunar New Year
農曆新年休息5天

■ OPENING HOURS, LAST ORDER
　營業時間，最後點菜時間
08:00-19:45 (L.O.)

■ PRICE/價錢
à la carte/點菜　　　　　$ 25-150

Superior Rice Roll Pro Shop
第一腸粉專賣店 NEW

You can't argue with the name. Opened in 2011, this lively and compact shop, with just six tables and a high turnover of customers each day, specialises in delicious and good value rice rolls, all cooked 'à la minute'. The simple menu on the wall offers around 14 items, eight of which are rice roll dishes. We recommend in particular the pork and ginger rice roll, shredded roasted duck rice roll, and the turnip pudding.

名符其實，就是這個意思。這家生氣勃勃的小店在2011年開業，只有六張餐桌，每天食客流量極高，專賣美味又實惠的腸粉，全部即叫即做。牆上簡單的餐牌提供14種食物，其中8種都是腸粉。我們特別推薦薑汁豬潤拉腸、名爐鴨絲拉腸和第一籠蘿糕。

■ ADDRESS/地址
TEL. 2380 7700
373 Portland Street,
Prince Edward, Kowloon
九龍太子砵蘭街373號

■ OPENING HOURS, LAST ORDER
營業時間，最後點菜時間
10:30-23:00 (L.O.)

■ PRICE/價錢
à la carte/點菜 $ 10-28

Sushi Fuku-suke NEW
鮨 福助

Thanks to the understated elegance and simplicity of its decoration, along with the immaculate table settings, this traditional Japanese restaurant would not look out of place in Ginza, Tokyo's smartest district, which is where the sushi chef previously worked. Lunch is based around a reasonably priced set menu; at dinner two omakase menus are offered and are composed of sushi or sashimi along with a variety of hot side dishes.

鮨 福助的裝修雅緻而簡約、座位陳設整潔，令這間傳統日本餐廳即使在東京最繁盛的銀座區，亦不會顯得格格不入，而那裡正是其壽司師傅曾經工作過的地方。餐廳午間以價錢實惠的定食為主，晚間則提供兩個廚師推介套餐，當中包括壽司或刺身，伴以多種熱盤美食。

■ ADDRESS/地址
TEL. 2955 0005
11/F, Macau Yat Yuen Centre,
525 Hennessy Road, Causeway Bay
銅鑼灣軒尼詩道525號
澳門逸園中心11樓

■ OPENING HOURS, LAST ORDER
營業時間，最後點菜時間
Lunch/午膳 12:00-15:00 L.O.14:45
Dinner/晚膳 18:00-23:00 L.O.22:45

■ PRICE/價錢
Lunch/午膳　set/套餐　　　$160-280
Dinner/晚膳　set/套餐　　　$800-1,200
　　　　　à la carte/點菜 $260-1,000

Sushi Sase   NEW
鮨 佐瀨

The Japanese owner-chef worked in Sapporo for 18 years before coming to Hong Kong and, once through the sliding door, customers will instantly feel they've made the journey in reverse. Pale wood, a grey stone floor and the elegant sushi counter all respectfully create the traditional look. Only set menus are offered; the omakase (chef's choice) may be pricey but is worth it. Along with the sushi are a number of appealing hot dishes.

日籍店東兼大廚來港前已在札幌工作18年。甫拉開店門即如進入時空之旅，室內以淡雅的木材為主調，襯以石板地和雅緻的壽司吧，處處體現傳統氣派。店內只供應套餐，由廚師選定的omakase價格也許昂貴，但絕對物有所值。除了壽司亦伴有多款熱盤。

■ ADDRESS/地址
TEL. 2815 0455
49 Hollywood Road, Central
中環荷里活道49

■ ANNUAL AND WEEKLY CLOSING
　　休息日期
Closed 2-5 January and
3 days Lunar New Year
1月2-5日及農曆新年休息3天

■ OPENING HOURS, LAST ORDER
　　營業時間，最後點菜時間
Lunch/午膳 12:00-14:30 (L.O.)
Dinner/晚膳 18:00-22:30 (L.O.)

■ PRICE/價錢
Lunch/午膳　set/套餐　　$ 300-1,380
Dinner/晚膳　set/套餐　　$ 1,050-1,450

Sushi Ta-ke　NEW
竹 寿司

10

A striking and artfully lit interior comes as no surprise when one considers the expertise of the three owners: one is an interior designer, one a lighting designer and the third a restaurateur. In partnership with Mamoru Sugiyama, owner-chef of Sushiko Honten in Tokyo, the restaurant focuses on sushi and sashimi but also serves hot dishes like Matsuba crab; grilled dishes, such as swordfish or Wagyu beef, are also popular.

竹壽司的室內燈光設計既突出又別具藝術氣息，如果知道三個東主的背景，你自會明白其因由：一個是室內設計師、一個是燈光設計師，第三個是飲食業專家。與東京銀座壽司幸本店(Sushiko Honten)東主及主廚杉山 衛(Mamoru Sugiyama)先生合作，餐廳主要供應壽司及刺身，同時亦提供熱盤如松葉蟹，其燒物如劍魚或和牛同樣受歡迎。

■ ADDRESS/地址

TEL. 2577 0611
12F, Cubus, 1 Hoi Ping Road, Causeway Bay
銅鑼灣開平道1號Cubus12樓
www.sushitake.com.hk

■ ANNUAL AND WEEKLY CLOSING
休息日期

Closed Lunar New Year
年初一休息

■ OPENING HOURS, LAST ORDER
營業時間，最後點菜時間

Lunch/午膳 12:00-15:00 L.O.14:30
Dinner/晚膳 18:00-24:00 L.O.23:00

■ PRICE/價錢

Lunch/午膳	set/套餐	$ 180-380
	à la carte/點菜	$ 400-1,550
Dinner/晚膳	set/套餐	$ 1,200-1,500
	à la carte/點菜	$ 400-1,550

Tai Wing Wah
大榮華

 20

Anyone travelling all the way to Yuen Long (in the north of New Territories) can seek reward for doing so by visiting this restaurant. It's above its own cake shop, which specialises in moon cakes and Chinese sausages, and serves dim sum and 'Walled Village' cuisine, alongside classic Cantonese dishes. Try the roast duck with bean paste and coriander; claypot rice with lard and premium soy sauce; and, above all, the steamed sponge cake.

很多人長途跋涉來到元朗（新界北部），只有一個原因：為了大榮華而來。餐廳位於其餅店樓上，餅店專門售賣月餅和臘腸。除了全日提供的點心外，還提供圍村菜及經典粵菜。香荽豆醬燒米鴨及砵仔豬油頭抽撈飯絕對不容錯過，當然少不了奶黃馬拉糕。

■ ADDRESS/地址

TEL. 2476 9888
2F, 2-6 On Ning Road,
Yuen Long, New Territories
新界元朗安寧路2-6號2樓

■ OPENING HOURS, LAST ORDER
營業時間，最後點菜時間
06:30-23:30 (L.O.)

■ PRICE/價錢
à la carte/點菜 $ 70-450

Takeya NEW
竹家

The Japanese owner-chef was originally posted to Hong Kong as an engineer but having settled here and married a local girl he switched careers and together they opened this little yakitori shop in Hung Hom. Seating just 15, it's an intimate spot, made warmer with all that bamboo. There's extensive choice available and particularly recommended is the pork liver from Kagoshima, the Japanese cream cheese and the dried fish roe.

日籍店主兼大廚原本是工程師，獲公司派駐香港工作多年，其後定居香港並展開新的生活方式，與太太在紅磡開辦日式串燒小店。雖然店內只有15個座位，但是店主利用竹子為主題，以有限的空間打造出親密又溫暖的小餐室。店內串燒種類繁多，特別推介鹿兒島豬肝、日本芝士及魚子乾。

■ ADDRESS/地址
TEL. 2365 8878
Shop 1, On Wah Building,
31C1 Tak Man Street, Whampoa Estate,
Hung Hom, Kowloon
九龍紅磡黃埔新村德民街31C1
安華樓1號舖

■ ANNUAL AND WEEKLY CLOSING
　　休息日期
Closed 14 days Lunar New Year
農曆新年休息14天

■ OPENING HOURS, LAST ORDER
　　營業時間，最後點菜時間
Dinner/晚膳 18:00-22:30 (L.O.)

■ PRICE/價錢
à la carte/點菜　　　　　　$ 150-400

Tak Lung
得龍

Tak Lung moved to its current San Po Kong location in 1963, and this successful operation is now being run by the second-generation owner. It comes divided into two dining rooms; try to get a table in the brighter main room. Business remains brisk thanks to the sensible prices and the popularity of signature dishes such as baked oyster in port wine, sweet and sour pork and 'grandpa chicken' which involves a 100 year old recipe from Guangzhou.

得龍大飯店於1963年搬遷至新蒲崗現址，這家成功的飯店現在由第二代繼承人經營。飯店由兩個舖位組成，盡可能選擇在較明亮的一邊。由於價錢相宜，招牌菜又廣受歡迎，這裡客似雲來。招牌菜包括砵酒焗桶蠔、山楂咕嚕肉，以及按有100年歷史的廣州食譜炮製的古法太爺雞。

■ ADDRESS/地址

TEL. 2320 7020
25-29 Hong Keung Street,
San Po Kong, Kowloon
九龍新蒲崗康強街25號
www.taklung.com.hk

■ ANNUAL AND WEEKLY CLOSING
　休息日期
Closed 3 days Lunar New Year
農曆新年休息3天

■ OPENING HOURS, LAST ORDER
　營業時間，最後點菜時間
06:00-23:30 L.O.23:00

■ PRICE/價錢
Lunch/午膳　set/套餐　　　$ 30-42
　　　　　　à la carte/點菜　$ 80-250
Dinner/晚膳　à la carte/點菜　$ 80-250

Tam's Yunnan Noodles (Sham Shui Po)
譚仔雲南米線 (深水埗)

It's easy to see why there are now more than ten branches of this family-owned noodle business. For a start, the concept works well: you choose your own spice level and the ingredient you would like added to your clear soup – the choice ranges from beef slices and tofu to cabbage or meatballs. Then you simply find a space and share a table with others. If it's too busy you can always just cross the street to find another of their shops.

不難發現這家家庭式經營的麵店迅速擴張至十多家分店的原因。一開始，概念就對了：你可以選擇適合自己的辣度和喜歡加到清湯裡的材料。選擇繁多，從牛肉片到豆腐到椰菜或肉丸都有。然後，你只需找個空位，與其他食客「搭枱」。餐廳經常都很忙碌，但在對面街就可輕易找到其另一家分店。

■ ADDRESS/地址

TEL. 2708 7055
107 Fuk Wing Street,
Sham Shui Po, Kowloon
深水埗福榮街107號

■ ANNUAL AND WEEKLY CLOSING
　休息日期
Closed 5 days Lunar New Year
農曆新年休息5天

■ OPENING HOURS, LAST ORDER
　營業時間，最後點菜時間
10:30-24:00 (L.O.)

■ PRICE/價錢
à la carte/點菜 $ 25-50

T'ang Court
唐閣

Rich silks and contemporary art line the walls of the lavishly furnished main dining room, on the first floor above the hotel's grand lobby. There's also a dramatic staircase leading up to a second floor of tables and exclusive private dining rooms named after famous Tang Dynasty poets. The cooking displays considerable skill, with particular emphasis on seafood. The service is also well structured and polished.

豐厚的絲緞配合富當代氣息的牆身，裝潢豪華的主菜廳位於酒店大堂樓上。一道極盡奢華的樓梯連上二樓各餐桌，更設有以唐代著名詩人命名的貴賓廳。菜餚極具功夫，海鮮更是當中首推菜式。服務經過精心編排。

■ ADDRESS/地址
TEL. 2375 1133
1F, The Langham Hotel, 8 Peking Road, Tsim Sha Tsui, Kowloon
九龍尖沙咀北京道8號朗廷酒店1樓
www.hongkong.langhamhotels.com

■ OPENING HOURS, LAST ORDER
營業時間，最後點菜時間
Lunch/午膳 12:00-15:00 L.O. 14:30
Dinner/晚膳 18:00-23:00 L.O. 22:30

■ PRICE/價錢
Lunch/午膳   à la carte/點菜 $ 160-2,000
Dinner/晚膳   set/套餐 $ 460-920
              à la carte/點菜 $ 300-2,000

Tasty (Happy Valley)
正斗粥麵專家 (跑馬地)

This is worth searching out because it's more than your average noodle experience. It has a sophisticated air, with polished wood enhancing a feeling of exclusivity. Customers call over the colourfully uniformed waitresses for the legendary wonton noodles; the range of congee toppings is comprehensive and chef's special dim sum includes roast pork bun with saucy filling and rice noodle with beef in a black bean and pepper sauce.

這裡值得你花時間走一趟，因為此店有非一般的水準。這裡氣氛濃厚，服務員制服色彩繽紛，拋光的木飾更添一種獨特感覺。許多客人被口碑載道的雲吞麵深深吸引，粥的種類也很全面，特別推介廚師精制點心流汁叉燒飽及豉椒牛河。

■ ADDRESS/地址

TEL. 2838 3922
21 King Kwong Street, Happy Valley
跑馬地景光街21號

■ OPENING HOURS, LAST ORDER
營業時間，最後點菜時間
11:30-24:00 (L.O.)

■ PRICE/價錢
à la carte/點菜 $ 60-160

Tasty (Hung Hom)
正斗粥麵專家 (紅磡)

It's quite modest and simple inside, with dark wood walls and Chinese decorations but it's all enlivened by friendly and efficient waitresses. You can't reserve here and it's often so busy you're forced to queue. It's worth it, though, for the quality of the noodles, soup, congee and dim sum. Try dishes like salted lean pork and preserved egg congee or stir-fried rice noodle with beef. You won't be disappointed and you won't pay much either.

餐廳裝潢樸實簡單，深木色的牆身和中國傳統擺設。友善而高效率的女侍應更增加餐廳活力。這裡食客眾多，但沒有訂座服務，因此經常需要排隊輪候。不過，這裡的麵、 湯、粥和點心都是優質美食，實在值得排隊等候。推介菜式包括皮蛋瘦肉粥或乾炒牛河。此外，這裡的菜式價錢相宜，絕對不會令你失望！

■ ADDRESS/地址

TEL. 3152 2328
Shop 111, 1F, Whampoa Plaza,
Site 8, Hung Hom, Kowloon
九龍紅磡黃埔花園第8期1樓111號舖

■ OPENING HOURS, LAST ORDER
　營業時間，最後點菜時間
11:30-23:30 (L.O.)

■ PRICE/價錢
à la carte/點菜　　　　　$ 75-150

Tasty (IFC)
正斗粥麵專家（國際金融中心）

Over 1,000 customers a day, many of whom work in IFC, crowd into this Tasty, so be prepared to queue and share a table before tucking into the hallmark shrimp wonton or the much-loved beef and rice noodle stir fry. Also recommended from the vast choice is congee with prawns. The interior is pretty vivid: its walls are covered with 30,000 chopsticks, handmade chairs with intricate floral patterns and eye-catching metal pots.

這裡每日有逾千名顧客，當中很多是在IFC工作，要一嚐這間正斗粥麵專家，就要做好可能需要排隊和搭枱的準備。熱門菜包括招牌鮮蝦雲吞麵，或極受歡迎的干炒牛河。此外，在芸芸選擇中，我們亦推介生猛大蝦粥。餐廳裡的牆壁佈滿一萬五千雙筷子，手工椅子上有複雜精細的花卉圖案，還有引人注目的金屬壺。

■ ADDRESS/地址

TEL. 2295 0101

Shop 3016, Podium Level 3, IFC Mall,
1 Harbour View Street, Central
中環港景街1號國際金融中心商場
3樓3016號舖

■ OPENING HOURS, LAST ORDER
　營業時間，最後點菜時間
11:30-22:45 (L.O.)

■ PRICE/價錢
à la carte/點菜　　　　　$ 75-150

Tasty (Kowloon Bay)
正斗粥麵專家（九龍灣）

Old black and white photos of local streets are here to remind diners that this growing chain began life as a street food business back in the 1950s. This branch, located within the Telford Plaza shopping mall, is delightfully decorated with Chinese inspired furniture and the kitchen is on view behind the window. The menu offers a large selection of traditional congee, noodles in soup, fried noodles and dim sum served all day.

香港街道的黑白照，提醒著顧客這家正不斷發展的連鎖麵店，其實早在50年代已由街頭小店開始經營。這家位於德福廣場的分店，採用中式傢俬，顧客可透過店內的大玻璃窗清楚看到廚房的情況。餐牌羅列了許多全日供應的傳統粥品、湯麵、炒麵與點心。

■ ADDRESS/地址
TEL. 2795 2828
Shop F1, Level 1, Telford Plaza 1, Kowloon Bay
九號灣德福廣場第1期1樓F1號舖

■ OPENING HOURS, LAST ORDER
營業時間，最後點菜時間
11:30-23:00 L.O.22:45

■ PRICE/價錢
à la carte/點菜　　　　　　$ 70-170

Thai Basil

Shoppers in Pacific Place mall can seek sustenance here from a wide ranging menu of straightforward dishes which include the likes of deep-fried soft shell crab tempura and char-grilled tiger prawns in yellow curry. Don't miss the sticky banana pudding with honey ice cream to boost those energy levels. The simple décor and friendly young team of servers help create a relaxed atmosphere in this large, and at times noisy, dining room.

於太古廣場購物的人士可在此一慰飢腸，餐單提供林林總總的選擇，從較簡單的菜式一如軟殼蟹米紙卷，或是大虎蝦黃咖喱，任君選擇。別錯過讓你精神百倍的雪糕香蕉布甸。簡約的裝潢，加上友善年輕的侍應團隊，營造出悠閒的氣氛。這裡全日開放，但偌大的餐廳在繁忙時間可能會較為嘈吵。

■ ADDRESS/地址

TEL. 2537 4682

Shop 001, LG, Pacific Place,
88 Queensway, Admiralty

香港金鐘道88號太古廣場地庫1樓1號舖

■ OPENING HOURS, LAST ORDER
　　營業時間，最後點菜時間
11:30-22:30 (L.O.)

■ PRICE/價錢
à la carte/點菜　　　　　　$ 220-450

Thai Chiu
泰潮

Hainannese chicken; tom yum kung with seafood; fried egg with herbs and the various different styles of curry are just some of the highlights from an extensive menu prepared by native Thai chefs at this simple little restaurant. It's made up of two modest dining rooms, both decorated in bright green and yellow, with plastic tables and small stools. But the food is good and the prices are competitive.

海南雞、海鮮冬蔭功、香草炒蛋及一系列咖喱只是選擇繁多的菜單的其中一部分，一律由這家簡樸小餐廳的泰藉廚師主理。餐廳由兩個飯廳組成，都以亮綠及黃色裝潢，加上膠桌和小板凳。食物美味，價錢相宜。

■ ADDRESS/地址
TEL. 2314 3333
101-103 Fuk Wing Street,
Sham Shui Po, Kowloon
九龍深水涉福榮街101-103號

■ ANNUAL AND WEEKLY CLOSING
　休息日期
Closed 3 days Lunar New Year
農曆新年休息3天

■ OPENING HOURS, LAST ORDER
　營業時間，最後點菜時間
12:00-23:30 L.O.23:00

■ PRICE/價錢

Lunch/午膳	set/套餐	$40
	à la carte/點菜	$60-150
Dinner/晚膳	set/套餐	$40
	à la carte/點菜	$60-150

The Bostonian NEW
美岸海鮮廳

Exuding confidence and sophistication, The Bostonian is a handsome fellow offering all the things you'd expect from an American restaurant: plenty of hearty salads, lots of Maine lobster, assorted seafood and, of course, a huge choice of prime beef from the grill. It's unlikely anyone will leave still hungry. This is also the place to come to experience two other great American inventions: brunch, accompanied by live jazz.

散發著自信和涵養，令人印象甚佳的美岸海鮮廳，其提供的菜式完全符合你對美式餐廳的期望：豐盛的沙律、大量波士頓龍蝦、雜錦海鮮，不可或缺的，當然是選擇繁多的特級烤牛肉。在這裡，人人都不會餓著肚子離開。這裡也是體驗美國另外兩樣偉大發明的好去處：早午合餐，配以現場演奏爵士樂。

■ ADDRESS/地址
TEL. 2375 1133
BF, The Langham Hotel,
8 Peking Road, Tsim Sha Tsui,
Kowloon
九龍尖沙咀北京道8號朗廷酒店地庫
www.hongkong.langhamhotels.com

■ OPENING HOURS, LAST ORDER
營業時間，最後點菜時間
Lunch/午膳 12:00-14:30 (L.O.)
Dinner/晚膳 18:00-23:00 (L.O.)

■ PRICE/價錢
Lunch/午膳　à la carte/點菜 $520-1,000
Dinner/晚膳　à la carte/點菜 $520-1,000

The Chairman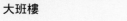
大班樓

The Chairman looks to small suppliers and local fishermen for its ingredients and much of its produce is also organic. Showing respect for the provenance of ingredients, and using them in such flavoursome dishes as steamed crab with aged Shaoxing or braised bean curd with morel and Chinese mushrooms, has clearly attracted a loyal following. The restaurant is divided into four different sections and service is reassuringly experienced.

大班樓的食材來自小型供應商和本地漁民，大部分都是有機材料。如此重視採購，更將精挑細選的材料用於美味菜式，如雞油花雕蒸大花蟹、野生羊肚菌炆腐皮，吸引不少忠實擁躉。餐廳分成四個不同用餐區，服務令人賓至如歸。

■ ADDRESS/地址

TEL. 2555 2202
18 Kau U Fong, Central
中環九如坊18號
www.thechairmangroup.com

■ ANNUAL AND WEEKLY CLOSING
　休息日期
Closed 3 days Lunar New Year
農曆新年休息3天

■ OPENING HOURS, LAST ORDER
　營業時間，最後點菜時間
Lunch/午膳 12:00-14:30
Dinner/晚膳 18:00-22:30

■ PRICE/價錢
Lunch/午膳　set/套餐　　　$ 158-178
　　　　　　à la carte/點菜 $ 300-450
Dinner/晚膳　à la carte/點菜 $ 300-450

The Chinese Restaurant
凱悅軒

As the name more than suggests, this restaurant, located on the 3rd floor of the Hyatt Regency, offers Chinese cuisine. Dishes such as double boiled crab meat soup; fried prawns with premium soy sauce; roast barbecued pork and crispy chicken Loong Kong are among the specialities. At lunch, the all-you-can-eat dim sum is a bestseller. The décor adds Chinese influences to a contemporary palette. There's also a large terrace.

餐廳一如其名，坐落凱悅酒店三樓，供應中菜。四寶燉萬壽果、頭遍生抽焗花竹蝦、蜜汁叉燒及脆皮龍崗雞均屬名菜之列。中午時分的任食點心最受歡迎。餐廳裝潢在現代色彩中加上一抹中國特色。餐廳亦有大型露台。

■ ADDRESS/地址

TEL. 2311 1234
3F, Hyatt Regency, 18 Hanoi Road, Tsim Sha Tsui, Kowloon
九龍尖沙咀河內道18號凱悅酒店3樓
www.hongkong.tsimshatsui.hyatt.com

■ OPENING HOURS, LAST ORDER
　營業時間，最後點菜時間
Lunch/午膳 11:30-14:30 (L.O.)
Dinner/晚膳 18:30-22:30 (L.O.)

■ PRICE/價錢
Lunch/午膳　set/套餐　　　　　$218-318
　　　　　　à la carte/點菜 $260-1,420
Dinner/晚膳　à la carte/點菜 $260-1,420

The Drawing Room

The Drawing Room is a warm and stylish restaurant on the first floor of the chic JIA boutique hotel. The striking and original pieces from local artists are quite a feature and the bar sets the mood – this is a place to be seen. Choose from the two daily changing Italian set menus created with the best available ingredients. This is accompanied by an impressive wine list of more than 700 labels covering most regions of Italy.

位於時尚酒店JIA的一樓，溫暖而具流行風格。本地藝術家創作了讓人一見難忘的原創金屬藝術品，甚具特色，酒吧更別具情調，這裡的一切都是賞心悦目的視覺饗宴。可從兩款每日更替的菜單中選擇，全由當日最佳新鮮食材炮製。此外，伴隨著美食是超過700款的佳釀，網羅自意大利各大產區。

■ ADDRESS/地址

TEL. 2915 6628
1F, 1-5 Irving Street, Causeway Bay
銅鑼灣伊榮街1-5號1樓
www.thedrawingroom.com.hk

■ ANNUAL AND WEEKLY CLOSING
　休息日期
Closed 3 days Lunar New Year
and Sunday
農曆新年3天及週日休息

■ OPENING HOURS, LAST ORDER
　營業時間，最後點菜時間
Dinner/晚膳 18:00-23:00 (L.O.)

■ PRICE/價錢
Dinner/晚膳   set/套餐 $680-860
             à la carte/點菜 $570-800

The New Sangeet   NEW

🍴

💺 10 📞🍽

The 'old' Sangeet was established in 1999 but moved to
its current post here in a busy shopping mall in 2007.
The dining room has an agreeably contemporary edge and
there's live music every evening from 8pm. The kitchen
focuses on more northerly parts of India and so they make
much use of the tandoor oven. They also offer a small
selection of Indo-Sino dishes. For those battling time's
winged chariot, there's a lunchtime buffet.

「舊」Sangeet 早於1999年開業，2007年才搬到現在的商場。店內
設計具時尚色彩，每晚8時起更有現場音樂演奏。廚房主打印度北部
菜式，巧用傳統泥爐烹調。另外亦提供數款中印混合菜式。無懼與時
間競賽的你，還可選擇午市的自助餐。

■ ADDRESS/地址

TEL. 2367 5619
Shop UG06-08, Toyo Mall,
Inter-Continental Plaza,
94 Granville Road, Tsim Sha Tsui,
Kowloon
九龍尖沙咀加連威老道94號
明輝中心尖東廣場上層06-08號舖

■ OPENING HOURS, LAST ORDER
  營業時間，最後點菜時間
11:00-23:30 (L.O.)

■ PRICE/價錢

Lunch/午膳	set/套餐	$ 88
	à la carte/點菜	$ 160-500
Dinner/晚膳	set/套餐	$ 110
	à la carte/點菜	$ 160-500

The Press Room

A local newspaper once occupied these premises but it's now home to a typically French brasserie that offers a pleasant, relaxed atmosphere. The panelling and high ceiling is enlivened by some interesting contemporary Chinese art. There's still plenty to read, from a large menu of classics that covers everything from soups and salads to grills and seafood. Also newsworthy is the exclusively French wine list offering plenty of choice by the glass.

這物業範圍曾是某本地報社的所在位置，但如今已變身為法式小菜館，氣氛舒適宜人。木鑲板及高天花襯以有趣的現代中國藝術裝飾。餐牌提供眾多選擇，從餐湯、沙律、烤肉、海鮮，應有盡有。此外，不可不提的是其精選法國佳釀，種類繁多，任君選擇。

■ ADDRESS/地址

TEL. 2525 3444
108 Hollywood Road, Central
中環荷里活道108號
www.thepressroom.com.hk

■ OPENING HOURS, LAST ORDER
   營業時間，最後點菜時間
12:00-23:00 (L.O.)
Weekends/週末 10:00-23:00

■ PRICE/價錢
Lunch/午膳   set/套餐 $ 132
                 à la carte/點菜 $ 350-520
Dinner/晚膳   à la carte/點菜 $ 350-520

The Square
翠玉軒

One always feels a sense of anticipation as one climbs the small staircase up to The Square and expectations will now be heightened thanks to a comprehensive makeover that has given it a handsome new look. Meanwhile, the menu offers a very diligently prepared selection of Cantonese dishes, including such specialities as braised conpoy with bean curd, signature crispy fried chicken and vegetable purée broth, and golden crispy prawns with tangerine sauce.

緩步通往翠玉軒的梯級之際，內心不期然泛起盼望，既是對其精緻美味佳餚的懷念嚮往，更多的是對其全新裝潢後的熱切期待。餐廳的粵菜菜式烹調甚見巧思，美食包括瑤柱豆腐菜茸羹，招牌脆皮雞及柑橘脆蝦球。

■ ADDRESS/地址
TEL. 2525 1163
Shop 401, 4F, Exchange Square Podium, Central
中環交易廣場平台4樓401號舖
www.maxims.com.hk

■ OPENING HOURS, LAST ORDER
營業時間，最後點菜時間
Lunch/午膳 11:00-15:00 (L.O.)
Dinner/晚膳 18:00-22:45 (L.O.)

■ PRICE/價錢
Lunch/午膳	set/套餐	$218-868
	à la carte/點菜	$170-600
Dinner/晚膳	set/套餐	$298-868
	à la carte/點菜	$170-600

The Steak House

One of the most sophisticated grill rooms in town, with its own dramatic wine bar and a spectacular wine list, 70% of which is from the USA, including an impressive number of top Californian wines. The ingredients used here are unimpeachable: beef sourced from Australia, the U.S. and Japan is supplemented by great seafood. You even get to choose your knife from 10 different models. Service is both professional and friendly.

城中功力最到家的扒房之一--The Steak House，擁有一流的酒吧，讓人目不暇給的齊全酒牌，當中70%產自美國，更包括了許多頂級加州葡萄酒。這裡採用的全是一流食材：來自澳洲、美國與日本的牛肉，配合鮮美的海鮮。你甚至可以從10種餐刀中挑選最適合自己的款式！服務既專業又友善。

■ ADDRESS/地址

TEL. 2313 2405

LF, Intercontinental Hotel,
18 Salisbury Road, Tsim Sha Tsui,
Kowloon
九龍尖沙咀梳士巴利道18號
洲際酒店地庫1樓

■ OPENING HOURS, LAST ORDER
營業時間，最後點菜時間
Sunday lunch/週日午膳 12:00-14:30
Dinner/晚膳 18:00-23:00 (L.O.)

■ PRICE/價錢
Sunday lunch/週日午膳
set/套餐 $598-1,018
Dinner/晚膳 à la carte/點菜 $750-2,100

Tim Ho Wan (Mong Kok)
添好運 (旺角)

It would not be an exaggeration to say that this little dim sum shop has brought life into this quiet street in Mong Kok. In 2009, two chefs joined forces and opened here; it has been a success ever since, hence the queue outside. There's no doubt about their ingredients; special mention can be given to the steamed dumpling 'chiu chow style', the steamed egg cake and, most definitely, the baked bun with barbecued pork. The wait will be worth it.

説這家小小的點心店為旺角較為靜寂的街角增添了生氣，這個說法並不為過。2009年，兩位師傅聯手創辦此店。值得留意的有潮洲蒸粉果、香滑馬拉糕，酥皮焗叉燒包更是絕對不能錯過。你會發現，這裡的點心絕對不負期望。

■ ADDRESS/地址
TEL. 2332 2896
8 Kwong Wa Street, Mong Kok, Kowloon
九龍旺角廣華街8號

■ ANNUAL AND WEEKLY CLOSING
休息日期
Closed 3 days Lunar New Year
農曆新年休息3天

■ OPENING HOURS, LAST ORDER
營業時間，最後點菜時間
10:00-21:15 (L.O.)

■ PRICE/價錢
à la carte/點菜　　　　　$ 30-50

Tim Ho Wan (Sham Shui Po)
添好運 (深水埗)

2010 saw the opening of this second branch of Tim Ho Wan, this time in a more residential area. Although able to accommodate more customers than the original, it didn't take long before queues started appearing here too. The 25 different dim sum choices are reasonably priced and carefully prepared. Highlights include steamed shrimp dumpling, baked bun with bbq pork and steamed beef balls. There are four small private rooms on the first floor.

這家坐落於住宅區的首家添好運分店於2010年中開張。儘管這家分店比總店能容納更多客人，相信不用多久便會出現人龍。25款價錢實惠的點心由廚師精心炮製。出名的點心包括蝦餃、酥皮焗叉燒包和陳皮牛肉球。一樓還設有4個小型貴賓房。

■ ADDRESS/地址
TEL. 2788 1226
9-11 Fuk Wing Street,
Sham Shui Po, Kowloon
九龍深水埗福榮街9-11號

■ ANNUAL AND WEEKLY CLOSING
　休息日期
Closed 3 days Lunar New Year
農曆新年休息3天

■ OPENING HOURS, LAST ORDER
　營業時間，最後點菜時間
08:00-22:00

■ PRICE/價錢
à la carte/點菜　　　　　$ 30-50

Tim's Kitchen
桃花源小廚

Success lead to Tim's Kitchen moving to these premises in 2010 – it's in the same area as before but, with two floors and a capacity of 100, much larger; chef-owner Tim's son designed the room. Plenty of choice is offered, such as popular specialities like Crystal prawn, pomelo skin and pork stomach, which showcase the kitchen's respect for the ingredients. Lunch dim sum is a 'must-try'. A branch opened in Shanghai in 2011.

桃花源小廚的成功令其開辦新店──新店位於同區，佔地2層，可容納100人，比舊店大得多。店主兼廚師黎先生的兒子設計了色彩豐富、現代化的房間，他的女兒則提供專業服務。現時，此店提供更多菜式以供選擇，當然少不了鎮店菜式如玻璃蝦球、柚皮及豬肚，每種都能證明廚房對優質材料的高度重視。其午市點心也不容錯過。酒家更進軍內地市場，於2011年在上海開辦分店。

■ ADDRESS/地址

TEL. 2543 5919
84-90 Bonham Strand, Sheung Wan
上環文咸東街84-90號
www.timskitchen.com.hk

■ ANNUAL AND WEEKLY CLOSING
    休息日期
Closed Sunday
週日休息

■ OPENING HOURS, LAST ORDER
    營業時間，最後點菜時間
Lunch/午膳 11:30-14:30 (L.O.)
Dinner/晚膳 18:00-22:30 (L.O.)

■ PRICE/價錢
Lunch/午膳 à la carte/點菜 $ 150-300
Dinner/晚膳 à la carte/點菜 $ 250-850

Tin Lung Heen NEW
天龍軒

Occupying a large section of the 102nd floor of the Ritz Carlton is this striking Cantonese restaurant, appropriately named 'Dragon in the sky'. Filling such a dramatic space could be daunting but the pleasant staff do make it feel more intimate. The menu focuses on traditional, familiar dishes; the chefs, unlike in Tosca next door, are mere shadows glimpsed occasionally through the lattice screens. There are several charming private rooms.

高處於香港麗思卡爾頓酒店 102 樓，這間極具氣派的粵菜廳以氣勢十足的「天龍」命名。空間感之大幾乎讓人無所適從，但殷勤的服務人員即時讓你倍感親切。菜單着重傳統菜式。與相鄰的Tosca相反，您只能在屏風後隱約看見大廚的身影。另設有多個精緻的私人包廂。

■ ADDRESS/地址

TEL. 2263 2270
102F, The Ritz Carlton Hotel,
1 Austin Road West, Kowloon
九龍尖沙咀柯士甸道西1號
麗思卡爾頓酒店102樓
www.ritzcarlton.com/hongkong

■ OPENING HOURS, LAST ORDER
　營業時間，最後點菜時間
Lunch/午膳 12:00-14:30 (L.O.)
Dinner/晚膳 18:00-22:30 (L.O.)

■ PRICE/價錢
à la carte/點菜　　　　　$245-2,100

Tokoro

♿ ☞ 🅿 ⛺10 🚇 ◔⑂

Based around the robatayaki concept of the Japanese barbecue, with many raw ingredients on display here for you to select. Once that's done, you take your seat either at a counter or in one of three bird cages which swivel if you want to face the kitchen. Interaction between guests and chefs makes for an animated atmosphere and there's plenty of sake on hand to lubricate things further. There is also a small but lively and contemporary sushi bar.

這家以爐端燒為主題的餐廳特色是展示多種原材料供食客挑選。選料後可隨意選擇座位,既可以坐在櫃檯用餐,亦可選擇三個可旋轉至面向廚房的鳥籠的其中一個。客人和廚師之間的互動令這裡充滿生氣。餐廳提供多種清酒,並設有一個時尚的小型壽司吧。

■ ADDRESS/地址

TEL. 3552 3330

3F, Langham Place Hotel,
555 Shanghai Street, Mong Kok,
Kowloon

九龍旺角上海街555號朗豪酒店3樓

www.tokoro.com.hk

■ OPENING HOURS, LAST ORDER
    營業時間,最後點菜時間
Lunch/午膳 12:00-14:30 (L.O.)
Dinner/晚膳 18:30-22:30 (L.O.)

■ PRICE/價錢

Lunch/午膳	set/套餐	$178-288
	à la carte/點菜	$300-500
Dinner/晚膳	set/套餐	$558-958
	à la carte/點菜	$300-500

Tosca   NEW

It is not just the incomparable views from its lofty location within the Ritz Carlton hotel that set Tosca apart – its strikingly glamorous interior, dominated by the large open kitchen, is as dramatic as any production of Puccini's opera. There's a pleasing southern Italian accent to the extensive menu and the kitchen makes good use of top quality, seasonal ingredients; the appealingly presented desserts, such as baba and cannoli, are a particular strength.

座落於麗思卡爾頓酒店高層位置的Tosca，有著俯瞰全景的氣勢，但她的獨特之處猶過於此，富麗堂皇的裝修和大型開放式廚房，加起來比普契尼的歌劇還要扣人心弦。豐富的菜單帶著讓人喜悅的南意情調。廚房能善用頂級時令食材，精美得令人垂涎的甜品，如巴巴蛋糕（baba）和甜酥卷（cannoli）更是一絕。

■ ADDRESS/地址

TEL. 2263 2270
102F, The Ritz Carlton Hotel,
1 Austin Road West, Kowloon
九龍尖沙咀柯士甸道西1號
麗思卡爾頓酒店102樓
www.ritzcarlton.com/hongkong

■ OPENING HOURS, LAST ORDER
　營業時間，最後點菜時間
Lunch/午膳 12:00-14:30 (L.O.)
Dinner/晚膳 18:00-22:30 (L.O.)

■ PRICE/價錢
à la carte/點菜 $710-960

Trattoria Doppio Zero   NEW

The pasta course is usually the highlight at this modern trattoria, which is appropriate as it is named after the ultra-fine flour used to make it. But specialities don't just include traditional pairings like tagliatelle Bolognese – the kitchen is not afraid of adding the occasional Asian hint, with dishes like spaghetti neri with cuttlefish, tomatoes and Thai chillies. A good value set lunch pulls in the local office crowd.

意粉是這家摩登意大利小館的焦點所在，並以制造意粉所用的頂級麵粉為餐廳命名，可謂名符其實。但餐廳的特色菜並不局限於傳統配搭如肉醬寬麵，他們亦勇於添加一些亞洲元素，如新鮮墨魚汁製成的意粉，加上墨魚、蕃茄和泰國辣椒香葱烹調。其超值的午市套餐更是本地白領的首選。

■ ADDRESS/地址

TEL. 2851 0682
GF, The Pemberton,
22 Bonham Strand, Sheung Wan
上環文咸東街22號柏廷坊地下
www.doppiozero.com.hk

■ OPENING HOURS, LAST ORDER
營業時間，最後點菜時間
11:00-23:00 (L.O.)

■ PRICE/價錢
Lunch/午膳   set/套餐 $100-125
             à la carte/點菜 $245-575
Dinner/晚膳 à la carte/點菜 $470-660

Trusty Congee King
靠得住

The owner, Mr Lam, opened his first shop after his friends were so impressed by his ability to throw together a quick congee meal that they suggested he should start selling it. His was purported to be the first congee shop in Hong Kong to use a fish soup base for congee. These days, his specialities are salted meat rice dumpling and poached fresh fish skin. With a name that includes the words 'trusty' and 'king', how can you go wrong?

店鋪主人林先生的友人無不讚嘆他的巧手粥品，紛紛提議他開店經營，於是他開了第一間店。靠得住據説是全港首家採用魚湯煮粥底的粥店。而這家店的另一推薦就是鹹肉粽及皇牌魚皮。出品一如其名——「靠得住」。怎會令你失望？

■ ADDRESS/地址
TEL. 2882 3268
7 Heard Street, Wan Chai
灣仔克街7號

■ ANNUAL AND WEEKLY CLOSING
　休息日期
Closed 2 days Lunar New Year
農曆新年休息2天

■ OPENING HOURS, LAST ORDER
　營業時間，最後點菜時間
11:00-23:00

■ PRICE/價錢
à la carte/點菜　　　　　$ 30-70

Tsim Chai Kee (Queen's Road)
沾仔記 (皇后大道中)

The simple but neat and clean basement room is hidden away somewhat, with steps leading down from its narrow entrance. However, that doesn't stop hordes of business types trooping in for the good value, straightforward cooking. So chat with your new 'friends' at your table and tuck into dishes such as king prawn wonton noodle, fresh minced fish ball or fresh sliced beef noodle; choose between yellow or flat white noodles or vermicelli.

以往位於干諾道的沾仔記於2008年遷至此處。簡約雅潔的地下室有樓梯連至其窄小入口。人們前來只為一嚐其物有所值、簡單直接的美食。於繁忙時段，您大概要「搭抬」與一眾新朋友同枱品嚐其招牌雲吞麵及鮮鯪魚球，食店並提供麵、河、米粉以供選擇。

■ ADDRESS/地址

TEL. 2581 3369
153 Queen's Road Central, Central
中環皇后大道中153號

■ OPENING HOURS, LAST ORDER
   營業時間，最後點菜時間
09:00-21:00 (L.O.)

■ PRICE/價錢
à la carte/點菜 $ 17-25

Tsim Chai Kee (Wellington Street)
沾仔記 (威靈頓街)

This highly regarded, simple noodle shop may have been here since 1998 but it's still looking good. The staff are as bright as their aprons; the popular side booths are quickly snapped up and the regulars know to eat outside peak times when the pace is less frenetic. The attraction is the handmade fish balls, the generously filled wontons and the fresh beef served with the noodles. It's easy to spot – just look for the lunchtime queues.

享負盛名的沾仔記於1998年開業，裝修簡單，但依然整潔舒適。侍應制服明亮潔淨。卡位非常受歡迎，經常滿座；熟客會在非繁忙時間光顧，氣氛則較為輕鬆。著名菜式包括自製的鮮鯪魚球、餡料豐富的招牌雲吞，以及鮮牛肉麵。餐廳容易尋找，午市時段外面大排長龍的那家就是了！

■ ADDRESS/地址
TEL. 2850 6471
98 Wellington Street, Central
中環威靈頓街98號

■ ANNUAL AND WEEKLY CLOSING
休息日期
Closed 4 days Lunar New Year
農曆新年休息4天

■ OPENING HOURS, LAST ORDER
營業時間，最後點菜時間
09:00-22:00 (L.O.)

■ PRICE/價錢
à la carte/點菜　　　$ 17-25

Tulsi NEW
羅勒

Those in Quarry Bay who are partial to Indian food have but one place to choose from. Fortunately that place is Tulsi, a warm and cosy restaurant, opened in 2009, that also represents good value for money. The experienced chef looks to northern India for most of his influences and the specialities include Nawabi chicken and Jheenga Shola. The popularity of the set lunch explains the full house most weekdays.

鰂魚涌區的老饕想一嚐印度菜，大抵只有一個選擇，它就是於 2009 年開業的Tulsi，環境舒適親切而且價廉物美。經驗豐富的大廚尤其精於印度北部菜餚，特色菜包括Nawabi雞肉和Jheenga Shola。午餐廣受歡迎，平日午市大多數都座無虛席。

■ ADDRESS/地址

TEL. 2561 2968
Shop 1, GF, Hoi Kwong Court,
13-15 Hoi Kwong Street, Quarry Bay
鰂魚涌海光街13-15號海光苑地下1號舖
www.tulsi.com.hk

■ ANNUAL AND WEEKLY CLOSING
   休息日期
Closed Sunday lunch
週日午膳休息

■ OPENING HOURS, LAST ORDER
   營業時間，最後點菜時間
Lunch/午膳 11:00-14:45 (L.O.)
Dinner/晚膳 18:00-22:45 (L.O.)

■ PRICE/價錢
Lunch/午膳   set/套餐 $58-68
               à la carte/點菜 $85-220
Dinner/晚膳   set/套餐 $100
               à la carte/點菜 $85-220

Uno Más

Kick back with friends and absorb the atmosphere, while the open kitchen prepares classic tapas like boquerones (anchovies) or croqueta de jamon (ham croquettes) alongside grilled dishes like octopus Gallega. Fine imported charcuterie is good, as are the olives, and there are also more substantial dishes like paella available, with a well chosen list of Spanish wines. Sitting here, one could almost be on Las Ramblas, not Lockhart Road.

和三五知己一同安坐於這裡，享受Uno Más的氣氛吧。開放式廚房裡烹調著西班牙醋醃鯷魚或西班牙火腿炸件（croqueta de jamon），以及燒烤菜式，如烤西班牙八爪魚（Gallega）。精美的進口雜肉（charcuterie）和橄欖同樣出色。其他精彩菜式還有西班牙大鍋飯、以及精挑細選的西班牙餐酒。坐在這裡，感覺就像身處蘭布拉大道，而非駱克道。

■ ADDRESS/地址

TEL. 2527 9111
1F, 54-62 Lockhart Road, Wan Chai
灣仔駱克道54-62號1樓
www.uno-mas.com

■ OPENING HOURS, LAST ORDER
　營業時間，最後點菜時間
Lunch/午膳　12:00-15:00 (L.O.)
Dinner/晚膳　18:00-23:00 (L.O.)

■ PRICE/價錢
Lunch/午膳　set/套餐　　　$138
　　　　　　à la carte/點菜 $300-650
Dinner/晚膳　à la carte/點菜 $300-650

Wagyu Kaiseki Den

🕭 🏷 🍴24 ⛓ 🕭🍴 🐝

Don't let the name confuse you - Wagyu beef is not the only ingredient. In fact, its just one of numerous imported items that appears on the daily changing, Kaiseki menu, where some modern touches sit alongside more traditional elements. Seasonality and freshness are fundamental to the passionate Japanese chef here; watch Hiroyuki Saotome and his team perform by reserving at the counter. Charming service and fine decoration add to the experience.

別讓店名混淆了印象—和牛並非唯一食材。其實,每天更新的懷石餐單,依從傳統而帶點現代修飾,更包羅無數每天新鮮進口的食材,而和牛只是其中之一。對充滿熱情的主廚五月女広之來說,食材的時令性及新鮮程度是基本要素。預訂櫃檯位置,看看他和團隊如何施展渾身解數吧。迷人精緻的裝潢,令用餐體驗更臻完美。

■ ADDRESS/地址
TEL. 2851 2820
263 Hollywood Road, Sheung Wan
上環荷李活道263號

■ ANNUAL AND WEEKLY CLOSING
    休息日期
Closed 3 days Lunar New Year
and Sunday
農曆新年3天及週日休息

■ OPENING HOURS, LAST ORDER
    營業時間,最後點菜時間
Dinner/晚膳 18:30-23:00 (L.O.)

■ PRICE/價錢
Dinner/晚膳 set/套餐 $ 1,780

Wang Fu
王府

It's all about charming Madame Wang (that's not her real name but that's what everybody calls her): she helps make the dumplings, cooks them and oversees the eating of them. Hers was one of the first shops on Wellington Street and her Pekingese dumplings are renowned. Pork and chive or even tomato and egg are part of an extensive range and this is the only place you'll find winter melon dumplings. Check the kitchen window for the day's special.

一切都靠著王女士（不是她的真名，不過大家都這樣叫）：她幫忙包餃子、煮餃子，看著大家吃餃子。王府是威靈頓街最早期的店鋪之一，北京水餃更是遠近馳名。韭菜豬肉或蕃茄蛋都屬眾多選擇之一，而且，這是你唯一可以找到冬瓜水餃的店鋪。看看廚房的窗子，就可見到每日精選。

■ ADDRESS/地址
TEL. 2121 8006
65 Wellington Street, Central
中環威靈頓街65號

■ ANNUAL AND WEEKLY CLOSING
　休息日期
Closed 4 days Lunar New Year
農曆新年休息4天

■ OPENING HOURS, LAST ORDER
　營業時間，最後點菜時間
11:00-22:30 (L.O.)

■ PRICE/價錢
à la carte/點菜　　　　$ 30-120

Whisk

☞ 📷26 📞🍴 🍇

The appropriately named Whisk brings together contemporary French cooking techniques with modern twists and Asian influences to create dishes with an appealing blend of flavours, such as steamed escargot with spinach, galangal and radish or wagyu beef sirloin 'Rossini' with truffle potatoes. The location for this informal but elegant environment is equally apposite as it is found on the 5th floor of the urbane and vibrant Mira Hotel.

恰如其名的Whisk，以當代法國菜烹調技巧，揉合現代元素和亞洲菜特色，造出多款創新菜式，為味覺帶來新享受，例如法式菠菜蒸蝸牛伴高良薑及蘿蔔或和牛鵝肝伴菠菜卷及黑松露薯。這家位於The Mira 酒店五樓的餐廳，營造了一個優雅中帶點無拘無束的用餐環境，與酒店富活力和時代感的形象互相呼應。

■ ADDRESS/地址
TEL. 2315 5999
5F, The Mira Hotel, 118 Nathan Road, Tsim Sha Tsui, Kowloon
九龍尖沙咀彌敦道118號The Mira 5樓
www.themirahotel.com

■ OPENING HOURS, LAST ORDER
營業時間，最後點菜時間
Lunch/午膳 12:00-14:30 (L.O.)
Dinner/晚膳 18:00-22:30 (L.O.)

■ PRICE/價錢
Lunch/午膳   set/套餐 $218
   à la carte/點菜 $550-1,750
Dinner/晚膳 set/套餐 $880
   à la carte/點菜 $550-1,750

Wing Hap Lung
永合隆

Take care with the slippery floor and slide gently towards one of the 8 small tables of this tiny shop, which was established more than 40 years ago. Moreish suckling pig and succulent roasted pig are the best sellers but they also serve bbq pork, Peking duck, goose legs and wings; most come simply presented on steamed white rice. It boasts a pleasant neighbourhood atmosphere and there is often a queue outside for takeaway orders.

小心地滑！進入這家有40多年歷史只有八張小桌的細小燒臘店時要步步為營。乳豬和多汁的燒肉最受歡迎，亦有叉燒、燒鴨、鵝掌翼等選擇，大部分都配白飯。這裡有著親切的街坊氣氛，也經常可見排隊外賣的人龍。

■ ADDRESS/地址
TEL. 2380 8511
392 Portland Street, Mong Kok, Kowloon
九龍旺角砵蘭街392號

■ ANNUAL AND WEEKLY CLOSING
　　休息日期
Closed Lunar New Year
年初一休息

■ OPENING HOURS, LAST ORDER
　　營業時間，最後點菜時間
11:00-22:00

■ PRICE/價錢
à la carte/點菜　　　　　　$ 40-140

Wing Lai Yuen   NEW
詠藜園

    🚻 **P** 🍽16 📞🍴

The film business glitterati used to flock to the original shop in San Po Kong for the authentic Sichuan Dan Dan noodles. A decade ago the Yeung family moved it to its current address in Whampoa Garden, where the Dan Dan noodles are still the main attraction today, although these days you can decide whether or not you want them spicy. Along with other Sichuan dishes are a few Shanghainese specialities too.

早在新蒲崗原舖已吸引影星名人為嚐正宗四川擔擔麵蜂擁而至。10年前，楊氏家族決定遷址到現在的黃埔花園。直至今日擔擔麵仍然是主打，分別是你可以決定要不要辣。另外還供應多款川菜和數款上海美食。

■ ADDRESS/地址
TEL. 2320 6430
Shop 102-105, 1F, Whampoa Plaza,
Site 8, Hung Hom, Kowloon
九龍紅磡黃埔花園第8期1樓102-105號舖

■ OPENING HOURS, LAST ORDER
　　營業時間，最後點菜時間
Lunch/午膳 11:00-15:30 (L.O.)
Dinner/晚膳 18:00-22:30 (L.O.)

■ PRICE/價錢
à la carte/點菜　　　　　$ 60-300

Wing Wah
永華雲吞麵家

This simple operation has been maintaining high standards for well over 50 years now, the secret being that they do everything from scratch upstairs, making their noodles by hand using bamboo. So proud are they of their skills that there's a photographic display of their craft on the walls. Finest offerings include shrimp wonton and barbecued pork noodle, a coconut milk dessert with honeydew melon and sago and drinks like sweet herbal tea.

這家簡單的餐廳營運至今逾50年，依然保持一貫的高水準，成功秘訣在於一手包辦所有工作，在樓上用竹昇手打麵條便可見一斑。他們以自家技術深感自豪，牆上貼著製作過程的照片。招牌美食包括鮮蝦雲吞麵及炸醬麵，甜品方面首推蜜瓜椰汁西米露或多款桑寄茶。

- ■ ADDRESS/地址
TEL. 2527 7476
89 Hennessy Road, Wan Chai
灣仔軒尼詩道89號

- ■ ANNUAL AND WEEKLY CLOSING
  休息日期
Closed 3 days Lunar New Year
農曆新年休息3天

- ■ OPENING HOURS, LAST ORDER
  營業時間，最後點菜時間
12:00-04:00 (L.O.)
Sunday/週日 12:00-01:00 (L.O.)

- ■ PRICE/價錢
à la carte/點菜 $ 40-70

Wooloomooloo Steakhouse (Wan Chai)

Carnivores can choose between Black Angus beef from Australia or USDA Prime beef from the USA at this fun branch of the growing chain. Cuts range from rib-eye and sirloin to porterhouse and New York strip and you also choose the sauce to accompany your meat. Finish with some equally hearty desserts like apple crumble and you'll be sure to leave feeling sated. Make time to have a drink on the rooftop terrace, which offers 270° views.

喜愛肉類的你，大可前往這家連鎖店，在澳洲黑安格斯牛肉和美國的USDA頂級牛肉之間選取心頭好。種類從rib-eye，sirloin，porterhouse到New York strip steak應有盡有，還有不同醬汁可供選擇。蘋果脆批等甜品可為你豐盛的一餐畫上完美的句號，定令你捧腹而回。你更可抽空到天台平台享受一杯，同時欣賞270° 美景。

■ ADDRESS/地址

TEL. 2893 6960
31F, The Hennessy, 256 Hennessy Road, Wan Chai
灣仔軒尼詩道256號The Hennessy 31樓
www.wooloo-mooloo.com

■ OPENING HOURS, LAST ORDER
營業時間，最後點菜時間
Lunch/午膳　12:00-14:30 (L.O.)
Dinner/晚膳　18:00-23:00 (L.O.)

■ PRICE/價錢
Lunch/午膳　set/套餐　　　$178
　　　　　　à la carte/點菜　$330-700
Dinner/晚膳　à la carte/點菜　$420-900

Xin Dau Ji (Jordan)
新斗記 (佐敦)

Formerly located in Woosung Street, this restaurant, in the heart of Jordan, is known for its seafood and roasted suckling pig, items for which its customers will travel some distance. But the main appeal is clearly the seafood which is bought from the fish market every day and placed in the tank on the ground floor just by the entrance. Look out for the pictures of Old Kowloon in the large first floor dining room.

餐館本來位於吳松街，現時坐落佐敦的中心位置。最著名的是海鮮和燒乳豬，不少顧客為此遠道前來。不過，最吸引的顯然是海鮮，每天從魚市場新鮮購買，然後放進地下入口旁的大魚缸裡。餐館的一樓掛著多幅九龍舊貌的照片，讓人懷舊一番。

■ ADDRESS/地址
TEL. 2388 6020
18 Cheong Lok Street, Jordan, Kowloon
九龍佐敦長樂街18號

■ ANNUAL AND WEEKLY CLOSING
　休息日期
Closed Lunar New Year
年初一休息

■ OPENING HOURS, LAST ORDER
　營業時間, 最後點菜時間
Dinner/晚膳 18:00-03:00 L.O. 02:30

■ PRICE/價錢
à la carte/點菜　　　　　$ 200-1,000

Xin Dau Ji (Sha Tin) NEW
新斗記 (沙田)

⌐⊅♟ ⊂⊃ 36 ◔⫣

Photos of old Hong Kong add a hint of nostalgia to this lively and noisy Cantonese restaurant in Sha Tin, which is a sister branch to the Jordan original. Famous for its roasted suckling pig, it also offers a good selection of wok-fried and claypot dishes; other highlights among the authentic Cantonese specialities include preserved steamed chicken, 'ju-ju style' vegetables in hotpot, and stewed bitter melon with frog.

沙田新斗記內一幅幅老香港的相片為這間熱鬧的粵菜館添上懷舊氣息，這是佐敦總店的分店，以金牌即燒乳豬遠近馳名，並提供大量鑊炒小菜及煲仔菜式以供選擇。其他馳名的傳統粵菜菜式包括秘制貴妃雞、啫啫唐生菜煲及涼瓜炆田雞。

■ ADDRESS/地址
TEL. 3102 2282
86 Chik Fuk Street, Tai wai,
Sha Tin, New Territories
新界沙田大圍積福街86號

■ ANNUAL AND WEEKLY CLOSING
　　休息日期
Closed Lunar New Year
年初一休息

■ OPENING HOURS, LAST ORDER
　　營業時間，最後點菜時間
Lunch/午膳 11:00-15:45 (L.O.)
Dinner/晚膳 18:00-22:45 (L.O.)

■ PRICE/價錢
à la carte/點菜 $ 150-1,000

Xi Yan Sweets
囍宴 甜 · 藝

Created by interior designer/celebrity chef Jacky Yu, this vibrant place makes quite a statement in its vivid red, while the well thumbed menu indicates just how popular it has become. Most tables have the Zhenjiang spare ribs, along with the Sichuan spicy chicken and Dan Dan noodles. Desserts are renowned, such as poached pear in osmanthus wine served with tofu ice cream and the glutinous custard dumpling with sweet potato ginger soup.

令人食指大動的餐牌顯示這家餐廳的受歡迎程度。由著名室內設計師兼名廚余健志打造的美食空間以鮮紅作宣言。幾乎每一桌都會點上一道秘製鎮江骨，金牌口水雞及招牌擔擔拉麵。這裡的甜品亦非常出名，包括桂花陳酒燴梨伴豆腐雪糕與蕃薯湯漏黃湯圓。

■ ADDRESS/地址

TEL. 2833 6299
8 Wing Fung Street, Wan Chai
灣仔永豐街 8 號
www.xiyan.com.hk

■ ANNUAL AND WEEKLY CLOSING
　休息日期
Closed Lunar New Year
年初一休息

■ OPENING HOURS, LAST ORDER
　營業時間，最後點菜時間
11:30-22:30 (L.O.)

■ PRICE/價錢
Lunch/午膳　set/套餐　　　　$ 90-110
　　　　　　à la carte/點菜 $ 160-280
Dinner/晚膳　à la carte/點菜 $ 160-280

Yan Toh Heen
欣圖軒

The authentic Cantonese specialties include golden scallops with minced shrimp and pear; double boiled Black chicken with mushrooms and abalone, and wok-fried lobster with crab roe and milk. Also included in the extensive choice is the 'ihealth menu' - a collaboration between the Intercontinental hotel and the Hong Kong Adventist hospital. It's all served in an elegant room with lovely views and attractive table settings.

這家水準一流的中菜廳精心炮製的粵式佳餚包括龍帶玉梨香、鮮松茸鮑魚燉竹絲雞、龍皇炒鮮奶。此外，由洲際酒店與港安醫院合作的健康餐單「ihealth餐單」更有大量不同選擇。客人用膳的大廳裝潢優雅，景致宜人，餐桌擺設吸引。

■ ADDRESS/地址

TEL. 2313 2243
GF, Intercontinental Hotel,
18 Salisbury Road, Tsim Sha Tsui,
Kowloon
九龍尖沙咀梳士巴利道18號
洲際酒店地下

■ OPENING HOURS, LAST ORDER
　營業時間，最後點菜時間
Lunch/午膳　12:00-14:30 (L.O.)
Dinner/晚膳　18:00-23:00 (L.O.)

■ PRICE/價錢
Lunch/午膳　set/套餐　　　$ 518
　　　　　　à la carte/點菜 $ 250-1,900
Dinner/晚膳　set/套餐　　　$ 988-1,968
　　　　　　à la carte/點菜 $ 350-1,900

Yat Tung Heen (Jordan)
逸東軒 (佐敦)

✗✗✗

💺24

Despite its basement setting, this spacious restaurant is warm and atmospheric, thanks to the soft colours and subtle lighting. A highly personable manager heads up a friendly and efficient team. The menu is strictly Cantonese and the best of the signature dishes include pan-fried chicken with dried mandarin peel; roasted crispy goose; fried rice with assorted meat and conpoy wrapped in lotus leaves, and fried prawns balls and diced onion with preserved beancurd paste.

雖然位於酒店地庫，但柔和的色調和精心設計的燈光，令佔地甚廣的逸東軒洋溢著溫暖舒服的氣氛。親切有禮的經理，帶領一班態度友善，工作效率高的員工。餐廳提供純粹粵菜，著名菜式包括陳皮煎軟雞、脆皮燒鵝、荷葉飯、干燒明蝦球等。

■ ADDRESS/地址
TEL.2710 1093
B2F, Eaton Hotel, 380 Nathan Road,
Jordan, Kowloon
九龍佐敦彌敦道380號
逸東酒店地庫2樓
www.hongkong.eatonhotels.com

■ OPENING HOURS, LAST ORDER
營業時間，最後點菜時間
Lunch/午膳 11:00-15:30 (L.O.)
Dinner/晚膳 18:00-22:30 (L.O.)

■ PRICE/價錢
Lunch/午膳	set/套餐	$ 108-238
	à la carte/點菜	$ 350-750
Dinner/晚膳	set/套餐	$ 368-980
	à la carte/點菜	$ 350-750

Yat Tung Heen (Wan Chai)
逸東軒 (灣仔)

🍽 240   📞🍴

The business community who occupy the Great Eagle Centre can count themselves lucky to be sharing their building with this restaurant. The menu is firmly Cantonese and along with the classics such as abalone, it offers some real gems such as smoked duck breast with citron honey, healthy double-boiled soup and casserole rice in an 'old style' (don't miss the simmered rice with eel, abalone, spring onions and bean curd paste). Dim sum is good too.

租用了鷹君中心的商務客應暗自慶幸能與此餐廳共用同一大廈。餐牌上的菜式貫徹粵菜風格，除了必備的鮑魚外，有些菜式實不容錯過，例如原盅燉湯、蜂蜜柚子煙鴨胸及瓦罉煲飯（特別是麵醬蔥白鮑魚黃鱔煲飯）。 午市供應的各式美味點心亦不防一試。

■ ADDRESS/地址

TEL. 2878 1212
2F, Great Eagle Centre,
23 Harbour Road, Wan Chai
灣仔港灣道23號鷹君中心2樓

■ OPENING HOURS, LAST ORDER
營業時間，最後點菜時間
11:00-23:00 (L.O.)

■ PRICE/價錢
Lunch/午膳   set/套餐 $ 150-980
               à la carte/點菜 $ 200-700
Dinner/晚膳   à la carte/點菜 $ 200-700

Yellow Door Kitchen
黃色門廚房

Take the lift to this inconspicuous restaurant where the closely set tables will have you practically sharing your neighbour's food! You'll feel instantly at home with the friendly service, and even more relaxed when you try the tasty Sichuan cooking, prepared by the all-female team. Don't be afraid to tackle the evening tasting menu of eight starters, six main courses, dim sum and dessert, all in small, delicious portions.

乘搭升降機來到這家不甚起眼的餐廳，裡面的餐枱緊緊排列在一起，使你幾乎可以分享鄰座的食物！親切的服務令你賓至如歸；美味的四川菜由全女班團隊炮製。放膽試試包含八道前菜、六道主菜、點心和甜品的套餐，全部都是份量小而美味的菜式。

■ ADDRESS/地址
TEL. 2858 6555
6F, 37 Cochrane Street, Central
中環閣麟街37號6樓
www.yellowdoorkitchen.com.hk

■ ANNUAL AND WEEKLY CLOSING
　休息日期
Closed 3 days Lunar New Year, Sunday
and Public Holidays
農曆新年3天、週日及公眾假期休息

■ OPENING HOURS, LAST ORDER
　營業時間，最後點菜時間
Lunch/午膳 12:00-14:30 (L.O.)
Dinner/晚膳 18:30-22:30 (L.O.)

■ PRICE/價錢
Lunch/午膳　à la carte/點菜 $ 120-250
Dinner/晚膳　set/套餐　　　 $ 298

Yè Shanghai (Admiralty)
夜上海（金鐘）

Surrounded by watch and jewellery shops, and with a bijou chocolate shop at the entrance, this large dining room, with floor to ceiling windows, is elegantly decorated. Attentive staff will guide you through the intricacies of the menu which specialises not only in the cuisine of Shanghai but also its neighbouring provinces of Jiangsu and Zhejiang. Try the deep-fried sweet and sour yellow fish with pine nuts or the baked stuffed crab shell.

餐廳附近盡是鐘錶和珠寶店，入口處則設有一家小巧的巧克力店。餐廳佔地寬廣，設有落地玻璃，裝修優雅，侍應樂於為你介紹餐單上的繁複菜式；特色美食不但包括上海菜，更有江蘇及浙江菜。建議一試松子黃魚及蟹粉釀蟹蓋。

■ ADDRESS/地址
TEL. 2918 9833
Shop 332, 3F, Pacific Place,
88 Queensway, Admiralty
香港金鐘道88號太古廣場3樓332號舖
www.elite-concepts.com

■ OPENING HOURS, LAST ORDER
　營業時間，最後點菜時間
Lunch/午膳　11:30-14:30 (L.O.)
Dinner/晚膳　18:00-22:30 (L.O.)
■ PRICE/價錢
Lunch/午膳　set/套餐　　　　$ 340-398
　　　　　　à la carte/點菜 $ 160-530
Dinner/晚膳　à la carte/點菜 $ 160-530

Yè Shanghai (Kowloon)
夜上海（九龍）

✿ ✿   ✗✗✗✗

        ♿   👝   🖳·80   📞🍽

Expertly balanced, subtle cooking is provided here, drawing not only on Shanghai but also the neighbouring provinces of Jiangsu and Zhejiang. Specialities include braised Tianjin cabbage with ham, stir-fried river shrimps with longjin tea and steamed pork belly wrapped in lotus leaves. Contemporary décor recalls 1930s Shanghai in its use of dark woods, subdued lighting and semi-private alcoves. A busy, sophisticated operation.

這裡的烹調水準專業，技術精湛，不但提供上海菜，更涵蓋江蘇及浙江菜。特色美食包括金華火腿津白，龍井蝦仁及稻草扎肉。餐廳以當代風格設計，燈光昏暗，採用深色木材，設有半掩餐室，散發著三十年代上海的味道。餐廳生氣勃勃，營運順暢，服務非常周到。

■ ADDRESS/地址
TEL. 2376 3322
6F, Marco Polo Hotel, Harbour City,
Canton Road, Tsim Sha Tsui, Kowloon
九龍尖沙咀廣東道海運大廈
馬哥孛羅酒店6樓
www.elite-concepts.com

■ OPENING HOURS, LAST ORDER
    營業時間，最後點菜時間
Lunch/午膳 11:30-15:00 L.O.14:30
Dinner/晚膳 18:00-23:00 L.O.22:30
■ PRICE/價錢
à la carte/點菜 $ 250-500

Yuè NEW
粵

It may seem like nothing more than a mezzanine area of the City Garden hotel but it's well worth coming up here for the Cantonese food. The experienced chef's respect for the traditions of Cantonese cuisine is clearly demonstrated in dishes like double-boiled jus of almonds with fish maw, fried rice with prawns and barbecue pork, and seared garoupa with layered egg white. There are a number of different sized private rooms.

看起來只是城市花園酒店的間層，並沒什麼特別，定讓不少人忽略了這間中菜廳，但絕對值得前來一嚐這裏的廣東菜。資深大廚對傳統粵菜的尊重完全反映在各樣菜式上，例如杏汁花膠燉蹄筋、師傅炒飯和雪嶺紅梅映松露等。餐廳更設有不同大小的廂房以供各類宴會之用。

■ ADDRESS/地址
TEL. 2806 4918
1F, City Garden Hotel,
9 City Garden Road, North Point
北角城市花園道9號城市花園酒店1樓
www.citygarden.com.hk

■ OPENING HOURS, LAST ORDER
營業時間，最後點菜時間
Lunch/午膳 11:00-15:00 (L.O.)
Dinner/晚膳 18:00-23:00 (L.O.)

■ PRICE/價錢
à la carte/點菜 $ 160-670

Yue Kee
裕記

Over 40,000 geese are needed each year to satisfy demand at this large, second-generation family business, which opened back in 1958. The restaurant has 50 tables, which are divided between eight simply decorated rooms; the geese are sourced from eight different farms in Mainland China. If contentment is indicated by the amount of noise generated, then clearly these roasted geese are much appreciated by the customers.

這裡每年需購入超過40,000隻鵝以確保供應。這家第二代家族經營的大型餐館自1958年開業，共有50桌，分佈於8個佈置簡潔的房間內；這裡的鵝來自中國內地8個不同的農場。若聲浪與滿足程度成正比，這裡的燒鵝肯定非常受客人欣賞。

■ ADDRESS/地址
TEL. 2491 0105
9 Sham Hong Road, Sham Tseng,
New Territories
新界深井深康路9號
www.yuekee.com.hk

■ ANNUAL AND WEEKLY CLOSING
  休息日期
Closed 3 days Lunar New Year
農曆新年休息3天

■ OPENING HOURS, LAST ORDER
  營業時間，最後點菜時間
11:00-23:15 (L.O.)

■ PRICE/價錢
à la carte/點菜 $ 150-550

Yung Kee
鏞記

🍽️ 100   📞🍴

Yung Kee has been a veritable institution for decades. It can seat over 650 people and is spread over four floors, with each one offering a different environment. So you can enjoy the bustle of the simple ground floor, more formality upstairs or the discreet luxury of the top floor VIP room. It takes an army of waiters to serve the traditional Cantonese dishes, with roast goose being the house speciality, along with 'cloudy tea' smoked pork.

鏞記屹立數十載，早已聲名遠播。這裡可容納超過650人，佔地共四層，每層環境都各有特色。你可以選擇裝潢簡潔、人流絡繹不絕的地下大堂、較爾雅的上層餐室、甚至頂樓的豪華貴賓房。餐廳提供傳統廣東菜，由龐大的侍應隊伍為你服務。招牌菜式是鏞記燒鵝與松子雲霧肉。

■ ADDRESS/地址

TEL. 2522 1624
32-40 Wellington Street, Central
中環威靈頓街32-40號
www.yungkee.com.hk

■ ANNUAL AND WEEKLY CLOSING
   休息日期
Closed 3 days Lunar New Year
農曆新年休息3天

■ OPENING HOURS, LAST ORDER
   營業時間，最後點菜時間
11:00-23:30 L.O.23:00

■ PRICE/價錢
à la carte/點菜 $ 220-600

Yung Kee Siu Choi Wong
容記小菜王

Despite being hidden behind a local market, this restaurant's fame is widely spread - look around and you'll see the shop decked out with photos of the owner and all the famous celebrities who have visited. Must-tries would be their crispy roasted pork and special Yung Kee dish (chives with dried prawns and squid) or the baked fish intestine with egg. It's always busy, so be prepared to share your table with others.

雖然隱藏在本地街市後，你會發現這家餐廳遠近馳名，不容小覷——看看四周，你會看見店內滿佈店主和來訪著名藝人的合照。不能錯過其脆皮燒肉及小炒王（韭黃蝦乾炒鮮魷），或是雞蛋焗魚腸。餐廳經常滿座，要有和陌生人同檯的心理準備。

■ ADDRESS/地址
TEL. 2387 1051
108 Fuk Wa Street,
Sham Shui Po, Kowloon
九龍深水埗福華街108號

■ ANNUAL AND WEEKLY CLOSING
　　休息日期
Closed 4 days Lunar New Year
農曆新年休息4天

■ OPENING HOURS, LAST ORDER
　　營業時間，最後點菜時間
Dinner/晚膳 17:30-02:00 L.O.01:45

■ PRICE/價錢
à la carte/點菜　　　　$ 120-200

Zuma

☶   🍽   🗳14   🚗   ℋ

Currently caught in the zeitgeist of fashion and celebrity, Zuma is spread across 2 floors with a cool sake bar and lounge hovering above the main dining room and linked by a dramatic spiral staircase. Dishes are prepared in three distinct areas: the open kitchen, the sushi bar and the robata grill, allowing a mix of calm precision and dramatic flourish. Over 1,000 wines and 40 types of sake and shochu are available. A DJ plays at weekends.

餐廳風格緊貼名人和時尚潮流，共分為兩層：主餐室樓上設有型格的燒酒吧及酒廊，以螺旋形樓梯連接，設計獨特。廚房包括三個部分：開放式廚房、壽司吧，以及爐端燒，廚藝精巧，味道一流。餐廳提供超過一千種葡萄酒及四十種不同的日本酒及燒酒，週末更有DJ在場打碟。

■ ADDRESS/地址
TEL. 3657 6388
5-6F, The Landmark, 15 Queen's Road, Central
中環皇后大道中15號置地廣場5-6樓
www.zumarestaurant.com

■ OPENING HOURS, LAST ORDER
營業時間，最後點菜時間
Lunch/午膳 12:00-15:00 (L.O.)
Dinner/晚膳 18:00-23:00 (L.O.)

■ PRICE/價錢
Lunch/午膳	set/套餐	$ 290-480
	à la carte/點菜	$ 400-1,000
Dinner/晚膳	set/套餐	$ 970-1,480
	à la carte/點菜	$ 400-1,000

HOTELS
酒店

HOTELS BY ORDER OF COMFORT
酒店 — 以舒適程度分類

City Garden   NEW
城市花園

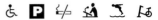

A relatively quiet location combined with convenient transport links make the City Garden hotel a worthy address on Hong Kong Island. Located in a residential area, the hotel is just a short stroll from Fortress Hill MTR and its accommodation is both fair in size and in price. The Garden Café offers an extensive international buffet at lunch and dinner, while Yuè, on the first floor, is the place for authentic Cantonese cooking.

RESTAURANTS/ 餐廳

Recommended/推薦			Also/其他
Yuè/ 粵	✿	✕✕	Garden Café/ 綠茵閣

座落在相對寧靜的地段，再加上便利的交通網絡，城市花園酒店盡享其港島區的優越地利。位於住宅區內，與炮台山港鐵站咫尺之遙，客房空間充裕又收費合理；綠茵閣餐廳提供豐富的午、晚市自助環球美食，而一樓的"粵"中菜廳則提供傳統廣東佳餚。

■ ADDRESS/地址

TEL. 2887 2888
FAX. 2571 7452
9 City Garden Road, North Point
北角城市花園道9號
www.citygarden.com.hk

■ ROOMS AND SUITES/客房及套房
Rooms/客房 ＝598
Suites/套房 ＝15

■ PRICE/價錢

👤	$ 900-2,850
👥	$ 900-2,850
Suites/套房	$ 3,000-4,000
☕	$ 148

Conrad
港麗

& < ☞ **P** ⇥ 🏋 🏊 🚴

With its enviable location above the Pacific Place shopping and entertainment complex, this hotel adeptly mixes the traditional with the modern. The vast oval lobby superbly showcases Chinese vases and bronze sculptures. Bedrooms are located between the 40th and 61st floors, ensuring sweeping views; the suites are particularly spacious and have elegantly marbled bathrooms. An outdoor swimming pool offers an equally dramatic panorama of the city.

RESTAURANTS/ 餐廳

Recommended/推薦		Also/其他
Golden Leaf/ 金葉庭	✗✗✗	Brasserie on the Eight/ 懷歐敘
Nicholini's/ 意寧谷	✗✗✗✗	Garden Café/ 咖啡園
		Lobby Lounge/ 樂敘廊

酒店位處集購物娛樂於一身的太古廣場之上，巧妙地混合了傳統和現代元素。龐大的橢圓形大堂展示著中式花瓶及銅像，優雅而壯麗。寢室全在40至61樓之間，坐擁遼闊美景，而套房則特別寬敞，設有雲石浴室。室外游泳池同樣讓你飽覽香港全景。

■ ADDRESS/地址

TEL. 2521 3838
FAX. 2521 3888
Pacific Place, 88 Queensway, Admiralty
香港金鐘道88號太古廣場
www.conradhotels.com

■ ROOMS AND SUITES/客房及套房
Rooms/客房 ＝467
Suites/套房 ＝46

■ PRICE/價錢

👤	$ 5,000-6,000
👥	$ 5,000-6,000
Suites/套房	$ 6,800-41,000
☕	$ 308

Crowne Plaza
皇冠假日

Upper level bedrooms at this modern, corporate-minded hotel have the best views and that includes the Happy Valley racetrack on the south side. All the bedrooms are decently proportioned and come with glass-walled bathrooms and impressive amenities including a large choice of pillow. On the top floor you will find Club@28, a chic bar for the fashionable crowd, as well as a small but very pleasant swimming pool and fitness room.

RESTAURANTS/ 餐廳

Recommended/推薦	Also/其他
	Kudos

這家為商務顧客精心設計的摩登酒店，高層客房均坐擁香港島最出色的景觀，南邊的高層客房更可飽覽跑馬地馬場全景。所有房間都寬敞舒適，襯以玻璃牆壁的浴室。他們的設施應有盡有，包括多種枕頭以供選擇、酒店頂層有為一眾時尚人士而設的Club@28酒吧，還有小型而舒適的泳池和健身室。

■ ADDRESS/地址
TEL. 3980 3980
FAX. 3980 3900
8 Leighton Road, Causeway Bay
銅鑼灣禮頓道8號
www.cphongkong.com

■ ROOMS AND SUITES/客房及套房
Rooms/客房 ＝253
Suites/套房 ＝10

■ PRICE/價錢

👤	$ 1,550-2,200
👥	$ 1,550-2,200
Suites/套房	$ 4,200-4,850
☕	$ 188

De Edge NEW
隆堡滿景

♿ ≤ ℯ

This tall, thin hotel with just four bedrooms on each floor opened in 2011 and is ideally suited to those on short business trips. Bedrooms are compact but neat and functional; the only decision to make is whether you want more space or better views, as the ones facing the harbour are slightly smaller than those with city views - unless you go for an Executive room. Glo is their diminutive restaurant with a decidedly modern edge.

RESTAURANTS/ 餐廳

Recommended/推薦	Also/其他
	Glo

這家外形高狹的酒店於2011年開幕，每層只提供四間客房，是商務公幹短暫停留的理想選擇。這裡的客房十分精巧，整潔之餘亦提供多項實用設施；你或許要在較多的空間和較好的景觀之間作出取捨，因為海景客房的空間略小於市區景觀客房，而入住行政客房則無此煩惱。Glo 是它的小型餐廳，充滿時尚氣息。

■ ADDRESS/地址
TEL. 3559 9988
FAX. 3559 9999
94-95 Connaught Road West,
Sheung Wan
上環干諾道西94-95號
www.hoteldeedge.com.hk

■ ROOMS AND SUITES/客房及套房
Rooms/客房 ＝90

■ PRICE/價錢

👤	$ 950-4,500
👥	$ 950-4,500
☕	$ 118

East
東隅

Describes itself as a 'lifestyle business hotel' and the water feature by the entrance tells you it's a little different. It has it all: an uncluttered lobby, a chic bar and relaxed dining room serving international cuisine; plus a stunning rooftop terrace bar named 'Sugar', as this was once a sugar factory. Bedrooms are minimalist but elegant and use plenty of glass and wood to create a warm, tasteful feel; corner rooms have great views.

RESTAURANTS/ 餐廳

Recommended/推薦	Also/其他
	Feast

標榜為一家品味商務酒店，東隅入口處的水飾已顯出一點兒與別不同。整潔的大堂，時尚的酒吧，提供國際美食氣氛輕鬆的餐廳，加上一個可觀看迷人維港景色的天台酒吧 "Sugar" 一名字靈感源自酒店前身的糖廠，絕對切合你所需。客房佈置採用簡約而優雅的風格，利用大量玻璃與木材來塑造溫暖而具品味的感覺。位處轉角的客房景觀尤佳。

■ ADDRESS/地址

TEL. 3968 3968
FAX. 3968 3933
29 Taikoo Shing Road, Island East
港島東太古城道29號
www.east-hongkong.com

■ ROOMS AND SUITES/客房及套房
Rooms/客房 ＝339
Suites/套房 ＝6

■ PRICE/價錢

👤	$ 1,388-3,200
👥	$ 1,388-3,200
Suites/套房	$ 3,500-6,000
☕	$ 168

Eaton Smart
逸東智

This friendly establishment is clearly a firm favourite with marrying couples as it hosts over 700 wedding receptions each year! It is located near both the Jade Market and the Tin Hau temple; its large glass atrium lobby on the 4th floor opens out onto a pleasant terrace. Bedrooms are compact but neatly kept and demonstrate a degree of environmental awareness. The small swimming pool is located on the hotel's roof.

RESTAURANTS/ 餐廳

Recommended/推薦	Also/其他
Yat Tung Heen (Jordan)/ 逸東軒 (佐敦) ✗✗✗	Metro Buffet & Grill
	Yagura

每年有超過700個婚宴在這裡舉行，可見這家設備完善的酒店，確實大受新婚人士歡迎。酒店鄰近玉器市場和天后廟；寬敞的玻璃大堂設於四樓，外接景致怡人的花園。客房面積雖不算大，但整潔舒適，亦能感受到酒店對環境保護的關注。此外，酒店天台設有小型游泳池。

■ ADDRESS/地址
TEL. 2782 1818
FAX. 2385 8132
380 Nathan Road, Kowloon
九龍彌敦道380號
www.hongkong.eatonhotels.com

■ ROOMS AND SUITES/客房及套房
Rooms/客房 ＝445
Suites/套房 ＝20

■ PRICE/價錢

👤	$ 2,350-3,200
👥	$ 2,350-3,200
Suites/套房	$ 6,000
☕	$ 138

Four Seasons
四季

Standing majestically over the harbour, Four Seasons offers some of the most spacious accommodation in Hong Kong. Bedrooms come either with contemporary detailing or a more Asian feel; bathrooms are large and luxurious. The Blue Bar is the stylish setting for cocktails and live music; the spa is impressive and leads out to the two swimming pools, each kept at a different temperature. Comfort levels are matched by the high standards of service.

RESTAURANTS/ 餐廳

Recommended/推薦			Also/其他
Caprice	✿✿✿	✗✗✗✗	The Lounge
Lung King Heen/ 龍景軒	✿✿✿	✗✗✗	

四季酒店坐擁壯麗維港景色，提供一些香港最寬敞的時尚客房。部份客房以現代風格佈置，有些則融合東方情懷，更設有大型豪華浴室。Blue Bar專為享受雞尾酒和現場音樂而設。水療設施令人印象難忘，更設有兩個溫度不同的泳池。舒適的環境與高質素服務互相輝映。

■ ADDRESS/地址

TEL. 3196 8888
FAX. 3196 8899
8 Finance Street, Central
中環金融街8號
www.fourseasons.com/hongkong

■ ROOMS AND SUITES/客房及套房
Rooms/客房 =399
Suites/套房 =54

■ PRICE/價錢

👤	$ 4,500-6,500
👥	$ 4,500-6,700
Suites/套房	$ 9,300-63,000
☕	$ 250

Grand Hyatt
君悅

There's a classic 1930s feel to the lobby of this grand hotel, which has been a fixture here in Wan Chai for over 20 years and is perfectly located for the Convention and Exhibition Centre. Bedrooms, by contrast, are more contemporary in look, being minimalist in their decoration, with deluxe rooms offering particularly good views. There are 14 'Plateau' rooms in a Japanese style, with direct access to the pleasant spa.

RESTAURANTS/ 餐廳

Recommended/推薦		Also/其他	
Grand Hyatt Steakhouse	✕✕✕	Kaetsu/ 鹿悅	
Grissini	✕✕✕	Tiffin/ 茶園	
One Harbour Road/ 港灣壹號	✕✕✕		

酒店紮根於灣仔區二十年以上而大堂極具三十年代的經典風格。相比之下，客房設計更具現代特色，裝潢流暢簡潔，豪華房間提供更大空間，更寬廣觀景。奢華浴室用大量雲石及花崗岩打造而成。酒店設有十四間靜水沁園日式房間，直接通往水療設施。

■ ADDRESS/地址
TEL. 2588 1234
FAX. 2802 0677
1 Harbour Road, Wan Chai
灣仔港灣道1號
www.hongkong.grand.hyatt.com

■ ROOMS AND SUITES/客房及套房
Rooms/客房 = 536
Suites/套房 = 13

■ PRICE/價錢

👤	$ 2,900-5,600
👥	$ 2,900-5,600
Suites/套房	$ 8,500-55,000
☕	$ 260

Harbour Grand Hong Kong
港島海逸君綽

This L-shaped hotel at the heart of Hong Kong Island offers unique views of the harbour, while its striking lobby, dominated by a vast Swarovski crystal chandelier, underlines its grandeur. All rooms are contemporarily but warmly decorated; seven rooms even come with private patios and Jacuzzis. Dining facilities are numerous and include what is claimed as the longest buffet in Hong Kong. An easy 5-minute walk from the Fortress Hill MTR station.

RESTAURANTS/ 餐廳

Recommended/推薦

Kwan Cheuk Heen/ 君綽軒   XXX
Le 188°   XXX

Also/其他

Harbour Grand Café
Lobby Lounge/ 大堂酒吧
Nagomi/ 和

這棟位處港島中心地帶的L型酒店讓我們欣賞到獨一無二的維港景致。引人注目的酒店大堂以巨型施華洛世奇水晶吊燈作裝飾，富麗堂皇，氣派不凡。所有房間都具備舒適的裝潢更帶有現代風格，當中7間客房甚至擁有私人露台，附設暖水按摩浴池。這裡有各式各樣的餐廳，提供世界各地美食，包括號稱全港最大型的自助餐。酒店位置方便，從港鐵炮台山站只需步行5分鐘。

■ ADDRESS/地址
TEL. 2121 2688
FAX. 2121 2699
23 Oil Street, North Point
北角油街23號
www.harbour-grand.com/hongkong

■ ROOMS AND SUITES/客房及套房
Rooms/客房 ＝742
Suites/套房 ＝86

■ PRICE/價錢
 ♥ $ 1,180-5,000
 ♥♥ $ 1,180-5,000
Suites/套房 $ 3,000-24,000
☕ $ 195

Harbour Grand Kowloon
九龍海逸君綽

First impressions do not disappoint here. This shimmering glass structure is right on the waterfront, offering superb views across Victoria Harbour, and there's a spectacular lobby with an impressive white marble staircase. The bedrooms are bright, comfortable and well-equipped, if sober by comparison to other areas. Make the most of the dramatic rooftop pool with its glass-sided walls, as well as the top floor fitness centre and steam bath.

RESTAURANTS/ 餐廳

Recommended/推薦		Also/其他
Harbour Grill	✗✗✗	Robatayaki/ 炉端燒
Hoi Yat Heen/ 海逸軒	✗✗✗	The Promenade
		Waterfront Bar & Terrace/
		水雲間

這裡的第一印象絕對不會令你失望。這座閃閃發亮的玻璃建築毗鄰維港，金碧輝煌的大堂設有白色雲石階梯。房間開揚舒適，設備齊全，相比酒店其他設施或較樸實。住客可盡情享受天台設有玻璃幕牆的游泳池、頂樓健身中心和蒸氣浴。

■ ADDRESS/地址
TEL. 2621 3188
FAX. 2621 3311
20 Tak Fung Street, Whampoa
Garden, Hung Hom, Kowloon
九龍紅磡黃埔花園德豐街20號
www.harbour-grand.com/kowloon

■ ROOMS AND SUITES/客房及套房
Rooms/客房 ＝506
Suites/套房 ＝48

■ PRICE/價錢

👤	$ 2,900-3,700
👥	$ 3,100-5,800
Suites/套房	$ 6,800-35,000
☕	$ 140

Harbour Plaza 8 Degrees
8度海逸

An eight degree incline is this tall and contemporary hotel's unique selling point, from the lobby ceiling and walls to the glasses in the restaurant. Bedrooms may be quite compact but they are thoughtfully laid out and come in warm colours; the higher the floor, the brighter the room. The swimming pool is pleasant, even if it's surrounded by walls. The hotel should benefit from the huge development project that's upgrading the local area.

RESTAURANTS/ 餐廳

Recommended/推薦	Also/其他
	8 Degrees Café/ 8度餐廳

傾斜8度是這家高聳而現代的酒店的獨特賣點,從大堂天花到牆身以至餐廳玻璃,都是傾斜的。睡房可能比較小巧,但經過精心佈置,以暖色裝潢。樓層越高,房間越開揚。泳池雖然四面被牆圍繞,但環境依然宜人。酒店應可從該區的大型提升環境發展計劃得益。

■ ADDRESS/地址

TEL. 2126 1988
FAX. 2126 1900
199 Kowloon City Road, To Kwa Wan, Kowloon
九龍土瓜灣九龍城道199號
www.harbour-plaza.com/hp8d

■ ROOMS AND SUITES/客房及套房
Rooms/客房 =678
Suites/套房 =24

■ PRICE/價錢

🧍	$ 1,800-2,800
🧍🧍	$ 1,900-3,000
Suites/套房	$ 3,200-4,300
☕	$ 110

Harbour Plaza North Point
北角海逸

Those doing business in North Point or Quarry Bay will find this hotel a useful address for a short stay. Spread over 32 floors, everything feels contemporary, right from when you enter the lobby with its unusual water feature. Bedrooms here are a fair size and have good soundproofing - most only have a shower so if you require a bath ask when booking. There are 180 serviced suites designed for long-stay clients (a minimum of one month).

RESTAURANTS/ 餐廳

Recommended/推薦	Also/其他
	Green/ 綠怡廳
	Hoi Yat Heen/ 海逸軒

北角海逸酒店位置優越，對在北角或鰂魚涌洽談商務的人士來說，是短暫停留的好去處。樓高32層的北角海逸酒店擁有富時代感的裝飾，從大堂的水池即可見一斑。客房寬敞而寧靜：大部分房間只有淋浴設備，如需浸浴，緊記在訂房時事先詢問。酒店另設有180間為長期住客而設的服務式套房（租期最短為1個月）。

■ ADDRESS/地址

TEL. 2187 8888
FAX. 2187 8899
665 King's Road, North Point
北角英皇道665號
www.harbour-plaza.com

■ ROOMS AND SUITES/客房及套房
Rooms/客房 ＝489

■ PRICE/價錢

🧍	$1,950-2,050
🧍🧍	$2,150-2,650
☕	$135

Hullett House

The jewel in the 1881 Heritage complex, once the headquarters of the Marine Police, is Hullett House. This handsome colonial building was restored in 2009 and blends together history, culture and modern day comfort. The strength of the operation certainly lies with the bedrooms – each of the ten very large rooms is individually themed, ranging from art deco or pop art to dynasty and red Chinese. There's a choice of five restaurants.

RESTAURANTS/ 餐廳

Recommended/推薦		Also/其他
Loong Toh Yuen/ 隆濤院	XX	Mariners' rest
St. George	✿ XXX	Stables Grill
		The Parlour

Hullett House堪稱1881年建造的前水警總部內的寶石。這棟富有殖民地色彩的美麗建築物在2009年翻新,將歷史、文化與現代的舒適自在共冶一爐。這文物級酒店的強項絕對是他們的房間,十個極為寬敞的房間各按不同主題裝飾,由裝飾藝術或普普藝術到古典中式風格,一應俱全。這裡亦設有五家餐廳可供選擇。

■ ADDRESS/地址
TEL. 3988 0000
FAX. 2368 2325
2A Canton Road, Tsim Sha Tsui, Kowloon
九龍尖沙咀廣東道2A
www.hulletthouse.com

■ ROOMS AND SUITES/客房及套房
Rooms/客房 = 10
■ PRICE/價錢
👤 $9,000-12,000
👥 $9,000-12,000

Hyatt Regency Sha Tin
沙田凱悅

Opened in 2009, this hotel is just a two minute walk from University station (adjacent to the Chinese University). It is styled in a contemporary way, making clever use of neutral colours and natural materials like stone and wood to create a soothing ambience. The 26 floor building includes well-equipped bedrooms with either harbour or mountain views. Facilities include a smart spa and fitness centre.

RESTAURANTS/ 餐廳

Recommended/推薦	Also/其他
	Café/ 咖啡廳
	Sha Tin 18/ 沙田18

沙田凱悅於2009年開幕，從港鐵大學站（毗鄰香港中文大學）前往僅需步行兩分鐘。酒店設計現代，巧妙運用中性色彩及天然物料如石材及木材製造柔和融洽的感覺。樓高二十六層的酒店擁有設備齊全的海景或山景客房，酒店更配備完善水療設備及健身中心。

■ ADDRESS/地址
TEL. 3723 1234
FAX. 3723 1235
18 Chak Cheung Street, University,
Sha Tin, New Territories
新界沙田大學站澤祥街18號
www.hongkong.shatin.hyatt.com

■ ROOMS AND SUITES/客房及套房
Rooms/客房 ＝434
Suites/套房 ＝133

■ PRICE/價錢

👤	$ 3,000-3,750
👥	$ 3,000-3,750
Suites/套房	$ 4,400-16,800
☕	$ 218

Hyatt Regency Tsim Sha Tsui
尖沙咀凱悅

Occupying floors 3 to 24 of the impressive K11 skyscraper, and connected to the K11 Art Mall, means that the bedrooms here at the Hyatt Regency benefit from impressive views of the city or the harbour. The rooms are decorated in a crisp, modern style; those choosing the Regency Club level have access to the private lounge. There are dining options galore and an impressive selection of whiskies available in the Chin Chin Bar.

RESTAURANTS/ 餐廳

Recommended/推薦		Also/其他
Hugo's/ 希戈	⚔⚔	Café/ 咖啡廳
The Chinese Restaurant/ 凱悅軒	⚔⚔⚔	

尖沙咀凱悅佔據令人印象深刻的K11摩天大樓的3至24層，並與K11購物藝術館相連，代表酒店房間都能看到令人響往的城市繁華景色，又或者是令人迷醉的維港景致。房間風格俐落摩登，選擇嘉賓軒樓層的住客更可享受專用酒廊的服務。酒店提供多個餐飲選擇，值得一提的是請請吧內威士忌種類之多令人目不暇給。

■ ADDRESS/地址
TEL. 2311 1234
FAX. 3721 1235
18 Hanoi Road, Tsim Sha Tsui,
Kowloon
九龍尖沙咀河內道18號
www.hongkong.tsimshatsui.hyatt.com

■ ROOMS AND SUITES/客房及套房
Rooms/客房 ＝348
Suites/套房 ＝33

■ PRICE/價錢
👤	$ 1,800-2,900
👥	$ 1,800-2,900
Suites/套房	$ 3,550-19,800
☕	$ 208

Icon NEW
唯港薈

A team of celebrated designers, including Rocco Yim, Sir Terence Conran and William Lim, were brought together to create this most chic of hotels, which is owned and run by the Hong Kong Polytechnic University. The hotel's style credentials are obvious, from the sweeping modern staircase and the 'vertical garden' to the coolly contemporary bedrooms with floor to ceiling windows. The students provide enthusiastic and courteous service.

RESTAURANTS/ 餐廳

Recommended/推薦	Also/其他
Above & Beyond/ 天外天　　ⅩⅩⅩ	Green The Market

匯聚著名設計師，包括嚴迅奇、泰倫斯·康藍爵士（Sir Terence Conran）和林偉而等，攜手打造出這間由香港理工大學營運、最新最潮的酒店。她的設計風格，令人驚嘆的現代化樓梯和垂直花園，到設計型格時尚、內有全幅落地玻璃窗的客房，都極其鮮明。酒店的服務由學生負責，十分殷勤有禮。

■ ADDRESS/地址
TEL. 3400 1000
FAX. 3400 1001
17 Science Museum Road,
East Tsim Sha Tsui
九龍尖東科學館道17號
www.hotel-icon.com

■ ROOMS AND SUITES/客房及套房
Rooms/客房 ＝236
Suites/套房 ＝26

■ PRICE/價錢

👤	$ 2,200-4,100
👥	$ 2,200-4,100
Suites/套房	$ 3,000-5,100

Intercontinental
洲際

Deceptively unremarkable from the outside, but decidedly impressive once you're in the grand lobby with its magnificent harbour views. All bedrooms are spacious, well-appointed in neutral tones and have large marble bathrooms. Relax in either the attractive swimming pool or the spa pool or take a massage in an outside cabana. Options for dining are particularly good (see separate entries) and the service is meticulous.

RESTAURANTS/ 餐廳

Recommended/推薦			Also/其他
Nobu		✕✕	Harbourside
Spoon by Alain Ducasse	✿✿	✕✕✕	
The Steak House		✕✕✕	
Yan Toh Heen/ 欣圖軒	✿	✕✕✕	

酒店平凡的外表也許會讓人認為不外如是，但踏入富麗堂皇的酒店
大堂，望著一流海景，絕對會令你留下深刻印象。所有客房都非常
寬敞，淺色調的裝潢亦讓人感覺安靜，更設有寬闊的大理石浴室。
你可以在優雅的游泳池或水療池鬆弛身心，或在戶外的池邊小室享
受一下按摩服務。酒店內的餐飲服務非常出色（請參照其他有關的
介紹），而且服務水準一流。

■ ADDRESS/地址
TEL. 2721 1211
FAX. 2739 4546
18 Salisbury Road, Tsim Sha Tsui,
Kowloon
九龍尖沙咀梳士巴利道18號
www.intercontinental.com

■ ROOMS AND SUITES/客房及套房
Rooms/客房 =470
Suites/套房 =25

■ PRICE/價錢

👤	$5,100-8,200
👥	$5,100-8,200
Suites/套房	$9,900-97,000
☕	$280

Intercontinental Grand Stanford
海景嘉福

Although originally built in 1981, this sizeable 18-storey waterfront property has been drastically upgraded over the last few years but still retains its unusual zigzag frontage. The best bedrooms benefit from excellent views over Victoria Harbour and Hong Kong Island and have charming French Empire-style furniture. A fitness centre and outdoor heated swimming pool are both perched on the roof of the building.

RESTAURANTS/ 餐廳

Recommended/推薦			Also/其他

Hoi King Heen/ 海景軒   ✿   ✗✗✗

Café on M
The Mistral/ 海風餐廳

雖然這幢18層的龐大臨海建築物建於1981年，但在過去幾年已大幅升級，並保留了獨特的曲折正門。酒店內最佳的寢室坐擁維港及港島美景，並採用了迷人的法國帝王式傢具。酒店頂層設有健身室及戶外溫水泳池。

■ ADDRESS/地址
TEL. 2721 5161
FAX. 2732 2233
70 Mody Road, East Tsim Sha Tsui,
Kowloon
九龍尖東慶地道70號
www.hongkong.intercontinental.com

■ ROOMS AND SUITES/客房及套房
Rooms/客房 ＝556
Suites/套房 ＝23

■ PRICE/價錢

👤	$ 1,700-4,500
👥	$ 1,700-4,500
Suites/套房	$ 3,500-12,000
☕	$ 228

Island Shangri-La
港島香格里拉

The intricate beauty of possibly the world's largest Chinese silk painting towers over the glamorous atrium and rises up all of 16 storeys. More sparkle is provided by the dazzling array of chandeliers placed around the hotel. Up above, the accommodation is classic and sumptuously appointed, especially those rooms on the Horizon Club floors (52nd to 55th) which come with access to an elegant lounge and a super rooftop terrace.

RESTAURANTS/ 餐廳

Recommended/推薦			Also/其他
Lobster Bar and Grill/ 龍蝦吧		XX	Café TOO
Petrus/ 珀翠	✿	XXXX	Nadaman/ 灘萬
Summer Palace/ 夏宮	✿	XXX	

屹立在迷人的中庭，高高越過酒店的16層：這幅可能是世上最
大的中國絲綢畫，散發著複雜精細的美。酒店四處掛著的吊燈燈
光，五光十色,令人眼花撩亂。樓上是奢華典雅的客房，尤其是52
至55樓豪華閣樓層的房間，可使用優雅的專屬會客廳和美不勝收
的天台庭園。

■ ADDRESS/地址

TEL. 2877 3838
FAX. 2521 8742
Pacific Place, Supreme Court Road,
Admiralty
中區法院道太古廣場
www.shangri-la.com

■ ROOMS AND SUITES/客房及套房
Rooms/客房 =531
Suites/套房 =34

■ PRICE/價錢

👤	$ 3,400-6,250
👥	$ 3,400-6,250
Suites/套房	$ 7,700-32,700
☕	$ 265

JIA

Jia means 'home' but as the idea of having a Philippe Starck designed house is beyond the reach of most, staying at this hip hotel could be the next best thing. The interior is as modern as you expect, with bold, contemporary pieces contrasting with a white palette. It's located in a fairly vibrant area so asking for a studio or suite on an upper floor is a good idea. Afternoon tea and evening wine are included in the rate.

RESTAURANTS/ 餐廳

Recommended/推薦 　　　　　　　　　Also/其他

Jia代表「家」，但對大多數人來説，擁有由知名創意設計大師Philippe Starck（菲利浦史塔克）設計的家是遙不可及的；在這家潮流精品酒店住宿，大概是最好的次選了。內部裝潢一如所想，極富現代特色，強烈的當代作品與純白的調色板相映成趣。酒店位於繁華地段，因此選擇較高樓層的房間會是個好主意。房間價錢已包括歐陸早餐、下午茶及黃昏美酒。

■ ADDRESS/地址
TEL. 3196 9000
FAX. 3196 9001
1-5 Irving Street, Causeway Bay
銅鑼灣伊榮街1-5 號
www.jiaboutiquehotels.com

■ ROOMS AND SUITES/客房及套房
Rooms/客房 ＝26
Suites/套房 ＝28
■ PRICE/價錢

👤	$ 1,500-2800
👥	$ 1,500-2800
Suites/套房	$ 1,900-6,000

JW Marriott
萬豪

This business-oriented hotel boasts 602 rooms spread over 35 storeys and, at its pinnacle, a series of executive floors with their own discreet lounge and meeting rooms. A major renovation in 2009 made the bedrooms more up-to-date and functional. There's a pleasant outdoor swimming pool and a well-equipped fitness centre, as well as a large choice of dining options, from Cantonese to Californian, seafood to wine bar and a tea room.

RESTAURANTS/ 餐廳

Recommended/推薦	Also/其他
	Fish Bar/ 魚吧
	JW's California/ JW's 加州
	Man Ho/ 萬豪殿
	Marriott Café/ 萬豪咖啡室
	The Lounge

以商務住客為主的萬豪酒店樓高三十五層，客房數量達602間。位於頂樓的一列行政套房，更附有設計素雅的休息室和會議室供住客專用。2009年的主要更新是將房間改造得更富現代感、更實用。設有環境宜人的戶外游泳池及設備齊全的健身中心，各地餐飲任君選擇，廣東菜到加州菜應有盡有，海鮮、酒吧、茶室悉隨尊便。

■ ADDRESS/地址

TEL. 2810 8366

FAX. 2845 0737
Pacific Place, 88 Queensway, Admiralty
香港金鐘道88號太古廣場
www.jwmarriotthongkong.com

■ ROOMS AND SUITES/客房及套房
Rooms/客房 ＝577
Suites/套房 ＝25

■ PRICE/價錢

👤	$ 3,700-5,900
👥	$ 4,100-6,200
Suites/套房	$ 8,800-40,000
☕	$ 250

Kowloon Shangri-La
九龍香格里拉

It is not just the grandeur of the lobby, with its marble, sparkling chandeliers and tiered water fountain, which will impress at this business-orientated hotel – the bedrooms, which have all been refurbished, are also a good size when compared to many other similarly priced hotels and service standards are impeccable. The hotel celebrated its 30th anniversary in 2011 and is a popular destination for traditional afternoon tea.

RESTAURANTS/ 餐廳

Recommended/推薦			Also/其他
Angelini		✗✗✗	Café Kool
Shang Palace/ 香宮	✿✿	✗✗✗	Nadaman/ 灘萬
			Tapas Bar

不僅是氣派宏偉的雲石酒店大堂，甚至是閃爍的吊燈與多層噴泉，都令你對這家以商務為主的酒店留下深刻印象。全部客房都經過重新粉飾，跟其他同價酒店比較更見寬敞，而且服務水平更是無庸置疑。2011年是酒店開業30 周年紀念，其傳統英式下午茶一直都備受愛戴。

■ ADDRESS/地址
TEL. 2721 2111
FAX. 2723 8686
64 Mody Road, East Tsim Sha Tsui,
Kowloon
九龍尖東麼地道64號
www.shangri-la.com

■ ROOMS AND SUITES/客房及套房
Rooms/客房 =645
Suites/套房 =43

■ PRICE/價錢

👤	$2,000-4,000
👥	$2,000-4,000
Suites/套房	$3,980-20,000
☕	$235

Langham Place
朗豪

Located in a vibrant, animated neighbourhood, this 42-storey glass tower is filled with every gadget a technophile could ever want and also functions as a wonderful showcase for Chinese modern art - over 1,500 paintings, sculptures and installations are spread around the building. Bedrooms are all crisply contemporary in their style and come in a range from 'Vital' through to 'Prime'. The pool is found on the hotel roof.

RESTAURANTS/ 餐廳

Recommended/推薦			Also/其他
Ming Court/ 明閣	✿✿	✕✕✕✕	The Place
Tokoro		✕✕	

酒店座落於充滿活力的社區內，玻璃塔般的大樓樓高42層，不僅
有每個科技發燒友夢寐以求的電子產品，亦是個空間廣闊的中國
現代美術展覽場。超過1,500 幅畫作、雕塑與裝置藝術品分佈於
整棟大樓之內。客房的設計極富現代感，從「基本」到「全盛」
系列，應有盡有。酒店頂樓設有泳池。

■ ADDRESS/地址
TEL. 3552 3388
FAX. 3552 3322
555 Shanghai Street, Mong Kok, Kowloon
九龍旺角上海街555號
www.hongkong.langhamplacehotels.com

■ ROOMS AND SUITES/客房及套房
Rooms/客房 = 625
Suites/套房 = 40

■ PRICE/價錢

👤	$ 3,000-5,000
👥	$ 3,000-5,000
Suites/套房	$ 5,000-15,000
☕	$ 148

Lan Kwai Fong
蘭桂坊

A stylish mix of Chinese and contemporary furniture, neutral tones and dark wood veneers has been used to create a relaxing environment. Try to secure one of the corner deluxe bedrooms or a suite with a balcony if you need a little more space - rooms from the 21st floor up have the harbour views. The discreet Celebrity Cuisine offers accomplished Cantonese cooking. This is a hotel that genuinely feels part of the local neighbourhood.

RESTAURANTS/ 餐廳

Recommended/推薦	Also/其他

Celebrity Cuisine/ 名人坊 ✿✿ ✕✕

融合了中國傳統與現代的家俱，中性色調及深色木間隔，打造舒
適環境。如果你需要更寬敞空間，建議預訂轉角位置的豪華客房
或附設露臺的套房。由21樓以上的房間可飽覽維港景色。服務周
到的名人坊提供美味的廣東菜。

■ ADDRESS/地址
TEL. 3650 0000
FAX. 3650 0088
3 Kau U Fong, Central
中環九如坊3號
www.lankwaifonghotel.com.hk

■ ROOMS AND SUITES/客房及套房
Rooms/客房 =157
Suites/套房 =5

■ PRICE/價錢

♀	$ 1,400-4,000
♀♀	$ 1,400-4,000
Suites/套房	$ 4,000-7,000
☕	$ 165

Lanson Place

An elegant European-style façade marks Lanson Place out as a stylish boutique hotel, which dovetails effortlessly with its chic location. Classical and contemporary designs interweave to create a calm exclusivity. The interior artwork creates a feeling of warmth and tranquillity. Bedrooms include a small kitchen for long-stay guests, and many look out to HK Stadium. A cool, calm lounge and bar area fit the bill perfectly.

RESTAURANTS/ 餐廳

Recommended/推薦	Also/其他

Lanson Place擁有歐洲風格的優雅外觀，這間型格精品酒店，位處港島時尚區域的一隅。古典和當代設計交織成這裡的獨特氣派，室內的藝術作品，營造溫暖寧靜的感覺。客房內的小廚房，專為長期逗留的客人而設，當中多間房間均能眺望香港大球場。閒靜舒適的休息室與酒吧也是入住期間值得逗留的設施。

■ ADDRESS/地址
TEL. 3477 6888
FAX. 3477 6999
133 Leighton Road, Causeway Bay
銅鑼灣禮頓道133號
www.lansonplace.com

■ ROOMS AND SUITES/客房及套房
Rooms/客房 ＝188
Suites/套房 ＝6

■ PRICE/價錢

🧍	$ 1,800-4,000
🧍🧍	$ 1,800-4,000
Suites/套房	$ 4,800-10,500
☕	$ 120

Le Méridien Cyberport
數碼港艾美

This design-led, corporate hotel with its pleasant sea-front setting is a chic place to stay. Expect up-to-the-minute business facilities and an attractive outside pool. The hip bedrooms, which have rain showers in the bathrooms and internet radios, come in two types: 'Smart' or the larger 'Deluxe Ocean'. Choose from three restaurants, with Japanese, Cantonese or international menus; or just chill out on beanbags in the Podium bar.

RESTAURANTS/ 餐廳

Recommended/推薦	Also/其他
	Nam Fong/ 南方
	Prompt
	Umami

這間以設計作焦點的商務酒店坐擁無敵海景，極度時尚。酒店擁有最先進的商務設施和動人的室外泳池。智能客房或豪華海景客房同樣設計時尚，裝置包括陣雨式淋浴系統和網絡收音機，全都令人讚嘆不已。酒店內有三間餐廳選擇，包括日式、粵式和國際菜式。或者你可坐在平台酒吧的軟墊上小酌一番。

■ ADDRESS/地址
TEL. 2980 7788
FAX. 2980 7888
100 Cyberport Road
數碼港道100號
www.lemeridien.com/hongkong

■ ROOMS AND SUITES/客房及套房
Rooms/客房 =167
Suites/套房 =3

■ PRICE/價錢

👤	$2,300-3,200
👥	$2,700-3,700
Suites/套房	$8,500
☕	$238

LKF
蘭桂坊

Smaller than most hotels in Central, LKF naturally styles itself in the 'boutique' class. Its hub centres round the higher floors: Slash, on the 29th, is a modern and intimate lounge bar and leads up to their restaurant which offers eye-popping city views. Contemporary bedrooms have been thoughtfully designed and come with espresso machines to give you a high, and pristine beds with sumptuous goose down pillows to bring you back down.

RESTAURANTS/ 餐廳

Recommended/推薦	Also/其他
	Azure

相比中環的大型酒店，LKF自然歸入「精品」級酒店之列。其樞紐中心位處較高樓層：29樓的Slash是舒適的現代酒廊；走上30樓的餐廳，客人可將迷人的景觀盡收眼底。寬敞及時尚的客房設有咖啡機讓你提提神，而簡約的睡床放置了豪華的鵝絨枕頭，讓你好好休息。

■ ADDRESS/地址
TEL. 3518 9688
FAX. 3518 9699
33 Wyndham Street, Lan Kwai Fong, Central
中環蘭桂坊雲咸街33號
www.hotel-LKF.com.hk

■ ROOMS AND SUITES/客房及套房
Rooms/客房 ＝86
Suites/套房 ＝9

■ PRICE/價錢

🛉	$ 2,600
🛉🛉	$ 6,000
Suites/套房	$ 7,000-15,000
☕	$ 195

Mandarin Oriental
文華東方

As it approaches its half century, this hotel continues to be successfully updated whilst remaining true to its own celebrated heritage. Bedrooms are divided between Tai Pan style (wood and brown colours) or Veranda style (with brighter décor), but all rooms come with impressive technological gadgetry. The spa is a spiritual haven and the dining and bar options are many and varied, from the chic top-floor M bar to the legendary Captain's Bar.

RESTAURANTS/ 餐廳

Recommended/推薦			Also/其他
Mandarin Grill + Bar/			Café Causette
文華扒房+酒吧	✿	XXXX	Chinnery/ 千日里
Man Wah/ 文華廳	✿	XXX	Clipper Lounge/ 快船廊
Pierre	✿✿	XXXX	The Krug Room

縱然邁向半世紀，酒店在保留優良傳統的同時，依然成功地走在時代之端。客房分為大班樣式（木色及棕色）或外廊樣式（較明亮及附海景），兩者同樣設有先進技術裝置。水療設施令客人彷如置身心靈的天堂，餐飲選擇繁多，從時尚的頂樓酒吧 M bar到享負盛名的Captain's Bar，任君選擇。

■ ADDRESS/地址
TEL. 2522 0111
FAX. 2810 6190
5 Connaught Road, Central
中環干諾道中5號
www.mandarinoriental.com/hongkong

■ ROOMS AND SUITES/客房及套房
Rooms/客房 =436
Suites/套房 =65

■ PRICE/價錢

🧍	$ 3,800-6,000
🧍🧍	$ 3,800-6,000
Suites/套房	$ 6,500-45,000
☕	$ 258

Metropark (Causeway Bay)
銅鑼灣維景

Near to Victoria Park, this 31-storey tower offers good comforts and facilities for business travellers. Most bedrooms are not that large so it's worth asking for one of the bigger executive rooms, many of which have great harbour views. The rooftop swimming pool with its underwater water music is small but appealing and the views from the fitness centre help deal with the pain of exercise. The Café du Parc offers all-day buffet dining.

RESTAURANTS/ 餐廳

Recommended/推薦	Also/其他
	Café Du Parc/ 繽紛維苑餐廳

酒店大樓樓高三十一層，鄰近維多利亞公園，為商務旅客提供舒適環境及設施。多數客房空間不太大，因此要求入住行政套房絕對物有所值，大部分更坐擁無敵海景。小型天台游泳池配備水底音樂，設計別出心裁。健身室的景觀更可令你忘卻運動的勞累。酒店的繽紛維苑餐廳 （Café du Parc）提供全日自助餐。

■ ADDRESS/地址
TEL. 2600 1000
FAX. 2600 1111
148 Tung Lo Wan Road, Causeway Bay
銅鑼灣道148號
www.metroparkhotel.com

■ ROOMS AND SUITES/客房及套房
Rooms/客房 ＝243
Suites/套房 ＝23

■ PRICE/價錢
👤	$ 1,200-3,800
👥	$ 2,500-3,800
Suites/套房	$ 6,800
☕	$ 120

Nikko NEW
日航

Comprehensive banqueting and conference facilities are not the only feature of Hotel Nikko – guests are also provided with a choice of six restaurants, offering a host of different cuisines, to discourage them from leaving the building. Factor in a harbour-front location and smart bedrooms offering up-to-the-minute comforts and you have another worthy competitor in the roll-call of international hotels on this strip of prime real estate.

RESTAURANTS/ 餐廳

Recommended/推薦	Also/其他
	Les Célébrités/ 名仕餐廳
	Sagano/ 嵯峨野
	Toh Lee/ 桃李

完善的宴會及會議設施並非日航酒店的唯一特色，還應算上
其六間菜式各有不同的餐廳，為賓客提供多種選擇，令他們
樂在其中；加上優越海濱地段，以及現代化舒適享受的智能
客房，均令它躋身國際級酒店之列。

■ ADDRESS/地址

TEL. 2739 1111

FAX. 2311 3122
72 Mody Road, East Tsim Sha Tsui,
Kowloon
九龍尖東麼地道72號
www.hotelnikko.com.hk

■ ROOMS AND SUITES/客房及套房
Rooms/客房 ＝445
Suites/套房 ＝18

■ PRICE/價錢

👤	$ 2,500-3,500
👥	$ 2,500-3,500
Suites/套房	$ 7,000-15,000
☕	$ 215

Panorama
麗景

This nicely located hotel offers the latest in contemporary design, with its 324 rooms slotting into 3 different bedroom types: silver, gold and platinum. The higher you go, the better the view but the best rooms are on corner sites where you can even enjoy the stunning harbour vista while relaxing in the bathtub. On the 38th floor is the AVA restaurant that offers a broad range of European dishes in a very modern setting.

RESTAURANTS/ 餐廳

Recommended/推薦	Also/其他
	AVA

位置方便的麗景有324間客房均以當代最新穎的款式,設計出三種不同的房間類型,包括銀賓客房、黃金客房和白金客房。要從更佳位置俯瞰景色,便要更上一層樓;而酒店的最佳客房則位於角位,客人更可以一邊享受浸浴,一邊欣賞迷人的維港景致。位於38樓的AVA餐廳佈置時尚,教人心動,各式各樣的歐陸佳餚正待君細嚐。

■ ADDRESS/地址
TEL. 3550 0388
FAX. 3550 0288
8A Hart Avenue, Tsim Sha Tsui,
Kowloon
九龍尖沙咀赫德道8A號
www.hotelpanorama.com.hk

■ ROOMS AND SUITES/客房及套房
Rooms/客房 =312
Suites/套房 =12

■ PRICE/價錢

🧍	$ 3,000-6,000
🧍🧍	$ 3,000-6,000
Suites/套房	$ 8,000-10,000
☕	$ 198

Royal Plaza
帝京

The Royal Plaza's impressive marble lobby creates a
rather grand ambience for arriving guests. Bedrooms are
designed in a range of styles: from sober, classic elegance,
via early 19th century French Empire, to the contemporary
'Executive Club' on the top two floors. Whatever your choice,
all have city views. There's an outdoor pool with an unexpected
Roman décor complete with columns; the solarium area has a
particularly relaxing atmosphere.

RESTAURANTS/ 餐廳

Recommended/推薦	Also/其他
	La Scala/ 花月庭
	Di King Heen/ 帝京軒

帝京酒店的雲石大堂格調相當華麗，造成一種堂皇的格調迎接來賓。客房的風格琳琳總總，包括十九世紀法國帝國的沉實古雅設計、最高兩層「行政樓層」的當代設計等，各適其式，所有客房都可享受「繁華城市景」。酒店的露天羅馬式泳池以圓柱作裝飾，設計風格令人驚喜；而日光浴地區的氣氛則特別輕鬆惬意。

■ ADDRESS/地址

TEL. 2928 8822
FAX. 2606 0088
193 Prince Edward Road West,
Kowloon
九龍太子道西193號
www.royalplaza.com.hk

■ ROOMS AND SUITES/客房及套房
Rooms/客房 =659
Suites/套房 =34

■ PRICE/價錢

👤	$ 2,600-4,100
👥	$ 3,000-4,500
Suites/套房	$ 5,800-33,800
☕	$ 148

Sheraton
喜來登

One of Hong Kong's biggest hotels is located on the mainland but is a short walk from the Star Ferry Pier, which adds up to great views of Victoria Harbour. These can be best appreciated from the Health Club's rooftop pool, over a plate of oysters in the wine bar, or from a swish sea-facing executive room on the 16th and 17th floors. More down-to-earth but thoroughly pleasant are a cigar room, a wine shop and an international café.

RESTAURANTS/ 餐廳

Recommended/推薦	Also/其他
Celestial Court/ 天寶閣 ✕✕	Morton's of Chicago Oyster & Wine Bar The Café Unkai/雲海

這是香港最大的酒店之一，位於九龍半島，只需短短的步行距離便到天星碼頭。客人可盡覽維多利亞港的壯麗景色，最佳位置包括Health Club的天台游泳池、16樓及17樓的高級面海行政室，在蠔酒吧吃蠔時亦可享受美景。較為沉實但完全舒適的有雪茄廊、酒舖和國際咖啡廳。

■ ADDRESS/地址
TEL. 2369 1111
FAX. 2739 8707
20 Nathan Road, Tsim Sha Tsui, Kowloon
九龍尖沙咀彌敦道20號
www.sheraton.com/hongkong

■ ROOMS AND SUITES/客房及套房
Rooms/客房 ＝691
Suites/套房 ＝91

■ PRICE/價錢

🧍	$ 3,200-5,000
🧍🧍	$ 3,300-5,200
Suites/套房	$ 5,500-13,500
☕	$ 220

The Fleming NEW
芬名

It is the attractive, contemporary lobby – one of The Fleming's most appealing features – which draws you into this centrally located Wan Chai hotel. Bedrooms offer decent dimensions for such an urban environment, with standard rooms measuring 20 square metres. The hotel also acknowledges its varied clientele by offering 'Her space' or 'His Space' rooms with differing amenities. A small restaurant, Cubix, offers international cuisine.

RESTAURANTS/ 餐廳

Recommended/推薦	Also/其他
	Cubix

極具吸引力的當代設計大堂，是芬名酒店其中一項最有魅力的特色，引領你走進這間位處灣仔中心地點的酒店。在這個市區環境中，其客房仍可提供偌大的空間，標準客房面積達20平方米。酒店更為照顧不同客人提供「男士」及「女士」專用客房，附設各具特色的配套品。精巧的餐廳Cubix更可為客人提供多國美食。

■ ADDRESS/地址
TEL. 3607 2288
FAX. 3607 2299
41 Fleming Road, Wan Chai
灣仔菲林明道41號
www.thefleming.com

■ ROOMS AND SUITES/客房及套房
Rooms/客房 = 66
■ PRICE/價錢

♦	$ 1,200-3,680
♦♦	$ 1,200-3,680
☕	$ 98

The Landmark Mandarin Oriental
置地文華東方

   ♿ ☞ ⚙ 🏃 🖼 🅢🅟🅐 ⛷

From the personal airport pickup to the endless spa choices, this is the hotel for those after a little pampering. Not only are the cool and smartly designed bedrooms big on luxury and size (ranging from 450 to 600sq.ft) but they also all have very stylish and impressively laid out bathrooms attached, which all feature either a sunken or a circular bath. MO is the cool ground floor bar for all day dining or night time cocktails.

RESTAURANTS/ 餐廳

Recommended/推薦	Also/其他
Amber ❀❀ ✕✕✕✕	MO Bar

從私人機場迎接服務到應有盡有的水療服務，置地文華東方可讓你盡享尊貴服務。令人讚嘆的不衹是客房面積寬敞（由450呎至600呎），設計型格獨特，還有客房內豪華時尚的浴室設備，包括巨型下沉式或圓形浴缸。地下的MO Bar不論日夜，均是品嘗雞尾酒的好地方。

■ ADDRESS/地址

TEL. 2132 0188

FAX. 2132 0199
15 Queen's Road, Central
中環皇后大道中15號
www.mandarinoriental.com/landmark

■ ROOMS AND SUITES/客房及套房
Rooms/客房 ＝101
Suites/套房 ＝12

■ PRICE/價錢

🛉	$ 3,500-6,800
🛉🛉	$ 3,500-6,800
Suites/套房	$ 9,300-45,000
☕	$ 288

The Langham
朗廷

The clamour of Peking Road is left behind as you enter the hushed surroundings of this elegant establishment. Its impressive lobby, furnished in a classical European style, is luxurious and features some impressive contemporary art and sculptures. Bedrooms are a mix of classic luxury and more attractive contemporary Chinese styling in the Grand rooms. All this charm is underpinned by modern facilities and attentive service.

RESTAURANTS/ 餐廳

Recommended/推薦			Also/其他
T'ang Court/ 唐閣	❀	✕✕✕✕	L'Eclipse
The Bostonian/ 美岸海鮮廳		✕✕	Main St. Deli

進入這棟優雅建築物，讓你立刻忘卻北京道熙來攘往的煩囂。設計奪目的大堂以傳統歐洲風格裝潢，極盡奢華，更以出色當代藝術品及雕塑點綴。豪華客房融合經典奢華風格及相當吸引的當代中國裝潢。一切迷人之處，更見於現代設施及細心服務。

■ ADDRESS/地址

TEL. 2375 1133
FAX. 2375 6611
8 Peking Road, Tsim Sha Tsui,
Kowloon
九龍尖沙咀北京道8號
www.hongkong.langhamhotels.com

■ ROOMS AND SUITES/客房及套房
Rooms/客房 ＝469
Suites/套房 ＝26

■ PRICE/價錢

👤	$ 2,550-4,000
👥	$ 2,550-4,000
Suites/套房	$ 3,000-5,000
☕	$ 218

The Luxe Manor
帝樂文娜公館

Leaving the outside world behind, you enter a stylish jewel box that somehow manages to jumble up oriental influences with Surrealist furnishings to create plenty of quirky charm. The dramatically lit red and black lobby flings together gilt-edged thrones, scallop-shaped banquettes and baroque armchairs upholstered in cartoon characters. Bedrooms are quite compact, apart from the studio rooms and six individually themed suites.

RESTAURANTS/ 餐廳

Recommended/推薦	Also/其他
	Finds
	Ge

踏入珠寶盒般的時尚酒店，彷如脫離現實世界進入了世外桃源。帝樂文娜揉合了東方元素和超現實設計，營造迷人的虛幻氣氛。紅黑色的大堂燈光璀璨，照亮鍍金邊的寶座、印有扇貝圖案的走廊，以及裝上卡通人物坐墊的巴洛克風格扶手椅。除了尊尚豪華客房及六間獨立主題套房外，大部分客房都是精緻小巧。

■ ADDRESS/地址
TEL. 3763 8888
FAX. 3763 8899
39 Kimberley Road,
Tsim Sha Tsui, Kowloon
九龍尖沙咀金巴利道39號
www.theluxemanor.com

■ ROOMS AND SUITES/客房及套房
Rooms/客房 = 153
Suites/套房 = 6

■ PRICE/價錢

👤	$2,600
👥	$3,200
Suites/套房	$9,800
☕	$138

The Mercer   NEW
尚圜

Those who want the convenience of a Central location but also need a little space should consider The Mercer, which opened in 2011. The narrow 31-storey building houses just 15 standard bedrooms but 40 one-bedroom suites. Ubiquitous tones of beige add to the up-to-date feel and bedrooms come with large desks and a host of complimentary services, such as free local calls and minibars. The suites come with warmer colours and velvet sofas.

RESTAURANTS/ 餐廳

Recommended/推薦	Also/其他

如果你既愛中環的便利，又需要寬裕的空間，剛於2011年開業的尚圜酒店絕對值得考慮。建築外型修長，樓高31層，只有15間標準客房，卻有達40間單睡房套間。統一的米白色調營造出時尚感覺，房間更設有大型書桌和附送多項免費服務，包括免費本地電話和迷你吧。套間採用暖色設計，配以絲絨梳化。

■ ADDRESS/地址
TEL. 2922 9900
FAX. 2922 9920
29 Jervois Street, Sheung Wan
上環蘇杭街29號
www.themercer.com.hk

■ ROOMS AND SUITES/客房及套房
Rooms/客房 ＝15
Suites/套房 ＝40

■ PRICE/價錢

👤	$ 1,980-4,000
👤👤	$ 1,980-4,000
Suites/套房	$ 3,000-6,000

The Mira

Give every room an Arne Jacobsen 'Egg chair'; add a cool, urban aesthetic and all the hi-tech extras you'll ever need, and you have The Mira – an eye-catchingly stylish and vibrant modern hotel. What the rooms may lack in size, they more than make up in design and it's worth asking for one facing Kowloon Park; bathrooms are equally impressive and suites are even more spectacular. The sumptuous spa is another great feature.

RESTAURANTS/ 餐廳

Recommended/推薦	Also/其他

Cuisine Cuisine at The Mira/

國金軒 (The Mira)　　❀　🍴🍴🍴

Whisk　　🍴🍴

Yamm

每個房間都放置一張Arne Jacobsen設計的 "蛋椅" ，配合型格、富現代感的設計，再加上所有你需要的高科技產品，你得到的就是The Mira - 一家極為時尚、充滿活力的摩登酒店。這裡的房間面積可能略小，但設計細節可彌補不足，浴室同樣非常現代化。訂房時值得多花時間要求一個面向九龍公園的客房，套房則更加豪華。舒適豪華的水療設施也值得一讚。

■ ADDRESS/地址

TEL. 2368　1111

FAX. 2369 1788

118 Nathan Road, Tsim Sha Tsui, Kowloon

九龍尖沙咀彌敦道118號

www.themirahotel.com

■ ROOMS AND SUITES/客房及套房

Rooms/客房　=446

Suites/套房　=46

■ PRICE/價錢

🧍	$ 3,200-4,500
🧍🧍	$ 3,200-4,500
Suites/套房	$ 5,000-48,000
☕	$ 208

The Peninsula
半島

Opened in 1928, this is the grandee of Hong Kong hotels. Testimony to its niche position is the fleet of Rolls-Royces and the two helipads. The iconic lobby is the place for afternoon tea and the Salon De Ning for intimate cocktails. The superb spa boasts a Roman style pool and a swish terrace. Rooms blend Victorian English with delicate Asian touches; the sumptuous corner suites make the most of their harbour vistas.

RESTAURANTS/ 餐廳

Recommended/推薦		Also/其他	
Chesa/ 瑞樵閣	✗✗	Imasa/ 今佐	
Felix	✗✗	The Lobby/ 大堂茶座	
Gaddi's/ 吉地士	✗✗✗✗	Verandah/ 露台餐廳	
Spring Moon/ 嘉麟樓	✗✗✗		

開幕於1928年的半島酒店是本港酒店業老大哥，一列列的勞斯萊斯和兩個直昇機坪，印證其特殊地位。有代表性的酒店大堂是享用下午茶的好地方，而玲瓏酒廊也是享受雞尾酒的不二之選。一流的水療設施包括羅馬式游泳池和時尚陽台。客房揉合了英國維多利亞風格及雅緻的亞洲風情，位處轉角位的的豪華套房可將廣闊維港景色盡收眼底。

■ ADDRESS/地址
TEL. 2920 2888
FAX. 2722 4170
Salisbury Road, Tsim Sha Tsui, Kowloon
九龍尖沙咀梳士巴利道
www.peninsula.com

■ ROOMS AND SUITES/客房及套房
Rooms/客房 ＝246
Suites/套房 ＝54

■ PRICE/價錢

👤	$5,000-7,000
👥	$5,000-7,000
Suites/套房	$8,200-82,000
☕	$250

The Ritz Carlton　NEW
麗思卡爾頓

Just knowing that this is the highest hotel in the world, occupying the top 16 floors of Hong Kong's tallest building, will leave some feeling decidedly vertiginous. They probably won't wish to know that its cool Ozone bar, on the 118th floor, has an outside terrace or that the swimming pool on the top floor is 500m above sea level. The large, contemporary bedrooms come with telescopes so guests can keep an eye on what's happening down on earth.

RESTAURANTS/ 餐廳

Recommended/推薦			Also/其他
Tin Lung Heen/ 天龍軒	✿	XXX	The Chocolate Library
Tosca		XXX	Ozone

據知這家是全球最高酒店，佔據了香港最高建築物頂部的十六層，部分人置身其中可能會感到暈眩。看來他們亦未必想知道，其位於118層的Ozone酒吧更設有戶外露台，而游泳池也設於海拔500米高處。酒店客房空間偌大，設有望遠鏡，讓賓客能夠細看人間何事。

■ ADDRESS/地址
TEL. 2263 2263
FAX. 2263 2260
International Commerce Centre,
1 Austin Road West, Kowloon
九龍柯士甸道西1號環球貿易廣場
www.ritzcarlton.com/hongkong

■ ROOMS AND SUITES/客房及套房
Rooms/客房 =232
Suites/套房 =80

■ PRICE/價錢

🛉	$6,000-7,800
🛉🛉	$6,000-7,800
Suites/套房	$8,000-100,000
☕	$250

The Royal Garden
帝苑

In a prized position close to Victoria Harbour, the Royal Garden exudes cool class. Its most notable feature is a 110 foot atrium that brims with daylight - its foliage-strewn presence is ubiquitous, as guestrooms are accessible through corridors that overlook it. Those bedrooms have now all been refurbished to a good standard and boast an impressive array of modern facilities. On the roof is a welcoming surprise: a pleasant swimming pool.

RESTAURANTS/ 餐廳

Recommended/推薦	Also/其他
Dong Lai Shun/ 東來順 ⊕ XX	Le Soleil
Inagiku (Tsim Sha Tsui)/ 稻菊 (尖沙咀) XX	Sabatini
	The Greenery/ 雅苑座
	The Royal Garden/ 帝苑軒

帝苑酒店毗鄰維多利亞港，地理位置優越，別樹一格。最具特色的是它110呎高的中庭在充沛的陽光下，令人豁然開朗。酒店以葉飾作點綴，從通往客房的走廊向下望，舉目皆是。喜愛現代設計概念的客人訂房時謹記選擇已重新裝潢的房間。頂層設有一個舒適的露天泳池，為住客帶來意想不到的驚喜。

■ ADDRESS/地址

TEL. 2721 5215
FAX. 2369 9976
69 Mody Road, East Tsim Sha Tsui, Kowloon
九龍尖東麼地道69號
www.rghk.com.hk

■ ROOMS AND SUITES/客房及套房
Rooms/客房 =369
Suites/套房 =48

■ PRICE/價錢

👤	$ 3,400-3,800
👥	$ 3,400-3,800
Suites/套房	$ 16,100
☕	$ 250

The Upper House
奕居

Already on the wish-list of fashionistas everywhere, The Upper House is a discreet and stylishly understated hotel. Art, sculptures and natural materials are used to great effect and help create the feeling of being in a private residence, albeit one with a pervading sense of calm and luxury. Bedrooms are airy and uncluttered but also offer plenty of concealed hi-tech extras; they even have yoga mats! The large bathrooms also come with views.

RESTAURANTS/ 餐廳

Recommended/推薦	Also/其他
Café Gray Deluxe 🍴🍴	

奕居早已成為潮流人士趨之若鶩的住宿熱點。這裏是一家經過精心
設計,細緻豪華的時尚酒店。藝術品、雕塑和天然物料帶來非凡效
果,更營造出私人居所的感覺,瀰漫著平和氣息。房間開揚而秩序
井然,隱藏著不少高科技用品。他們甚至提供瑜珈墊!其大型浴室
更可觀賞美妙景色。

■ ADDRESS/地址

TEL. 2918 1838
FAX. 3968 1200
Pacific Place, 88 Queensway,
Admiralty
香港金鐘道88號太古廣場
www.upperhouse.com

■ ROOMS AND SUITES/客房及套房
Rooms/客房 ＝96
Suites/套房 ＝21

■ PRICE/價錢
👤	$ 3,700-6,500
👥	$ 3,700-6,500
Suites/套房	$ 5,500-12,000
☕	$ 268

W

With room categories like 'Wonderful' and 'Fabulous' one can probably guess that the W hotel is a little unconventional. On top of Elements shopping mall, it offers stylish, modern design at every turn, from the bathroom's rainforest showers to the surround sound in every bedroom. It has an outdoor pool in an impressive elevated position, 76th floors up: the 'wet', along with a gym 'sweat' and a spa 'bliss'. Perhaps 'fab far east' sums it up.

RESTAURANTS/ 餐廳

Recommended/推薦	Also/其他
	Kitchen
	Sing Yin/ 星宴

從「奇妙客房」到「絕佳客房」等客房分類，已可感受到W酒店與別不同。W位於圓方購物商場，從浴室的熱帶雨林花灑以致每間臥房的環迴立體聲，每個角落均設計得時尚而現代。它擁有全球最高樓層的室外泳池--- 76樓：'wet'、健身室 'sweat' 及水療設備 'bliss'。也許 'fab far east' 是最為貼切的形容方式。

■ ADDRESS/地址
TEL. 3717 2222
FAX. 3717 2888
1 Austin Road West, Kowloon Station, Kowloon
九龍柯士甸道西1號九龍站
www.whotels.com/hongkong

■ ROOMS AND SUITES/客房及套房
Rooms/客房 ＝351
Suites/套房 ＝42

■ PRICE/價錢

👤	＄2,500-3,700
👥	＄2,500-3,700
Suites/套房	＄8,000-45,000
☕	＄230

MACAU
澳門

RESTAURANTS
餐廳

STARRED RESTAURANTS

Within this selection, we have highlighted a number of restaurants for their particularly good cooking. When awarding one, two or three Michelin Stars there are a number of factors we consider: the quality and compatibility of the ingredients, the technical skill and flair that goes into their preparation, the clarity and combination of flavours, the value for money and above all, the taste. Equally important is the ability to produce excellent cooking not once but time and time again. Our inspectors make as many visits as necessary, so that you can be sure of the quality and consistency.

A two or three star restaurant has to offer something very special that separates it from the rest. Three stars – our highest award – are given to the very best.

Cuisines in any style of restaurant and of any nationality are eligible for a star. The decoration, service and comfort levels have no bearing on the award.

星級餐廳

在這系列的選擇裡，我們特意指出菜式上佳的餐廳。給予一、二或三粒米芝蓮星時，我們考慮到以下因素：材料的質素和相容性、烹調技巧和特色、氣味濃度和組合、價錢是否相宜，以及味道。同樣重要的是能夠持續提供美食。我們的評審員會因應需要而多次到訪，所以讀者可肯定食物品質和一致性。

二或三星餐廳必有獨特之處，比其他餐廳更出眾。最高評級 -三星- 只會給予最好的餐廳。

不論餐廳的風格如何，供應哪個國家的菜式，都可獲星級。餐廳陳設、服務及舒適程度亦不會影響評級。

Exceptional cuisine, worth a special journey.
出類拔萃的菜餚，值得專程到訪。

One always eats here extremely well, sometimes superbly. Distinctive dishes are precisely executed, using superlative ingredients.

食客可在這裡享用美味的菜餚，有時令人更讚不絕口。獨特的菜式以最高級的材料精密地烹調。

Robuchon a Galera 法國餐廳		XxxX	French contemporary 時尚法式	438

Excellent cuisine, worth a detour.
傑出美食，值得繞道前往。

Skilfully and carefully crafted dishes of outstanding quality.

有技巧地精心烹調菜餚，品質優秀。

The Eight 8餐廳		XxxX	Chinese 中式	442
Wing Lei 永利軒	🍃	XxxX	Cantonese 粵菜	445
Zi Yat Heen 紫逸軒		XxX	Cantonese 粵菜	448

A very good restaurant in its category.
同類別中出眾的餐廳。

A place offering cuisine prepared to a consistently high standard.

持續高水準菜式的地方。

Golden Flower 京花軒	🍃	XxX	Chinese 中式	425
Lei Garden 利苑酒家		XX	Cantonese 粵菜	429
Tim's Kitchen 桃花源小廚		XxX	Cantonese 粵菜	443

EXPERIENCE MACAU !

Macau is a charming city with a unique culture.
See a different Macau, a living museum enchanted by
the rich cultural heritage around the city.

MACAU GOVERNMENT TOURIST OFFICE
www.macautourism.gov.mo

BIB GOURMAND

This symbol indicates our inspectors' favourites for good value. These restaurants offer quality cooking for $ 300 or less (price of a 3 course meal excluding drinks).

這標誌表示評審員認為價錢合理而美味的餐廳。300 元或以下便可享用優質美食（三道菜式的價錢，不包括飲料）。

Lou Kei (Fai Chi Kei) 老記 (筷子基)	NEW	🍴	Cantonese 粵菜	431
Luk Kei Noodle 六記粥麵		🍴	Noodles and Congee 粥麵	432
Noodle & Congee Corner 粥麵莊		🍴	Noodles and Congee 粥麵	435
Oja Sopa De Fita Cheong Kei 祥記		🍴	Noodles and Congee 粥麵	436
Square Eight 食・八方		🍴	Chinese 中式	440

NEW : New entry in the guide/ 新增推介
💱 : Restaurant promoted to a Bib Gourmand or Star/ 評級有所晉升的餐廳

RESTAURANTS BY AREA
餐廳 — 以地區分類

Macau/澳門

NEW : New entry in the guide/ 新增推介

⤻ : Restaurant promoted to a Bib Gourmand or Star/ 評級有所晉升的餐廳

RESTAURANTS BY CUISINE TYPE
餐廳 — 以菜式分類

Cantonese/粵菜

Canton 喜粵		✗✗✗	Taipa/氹仔	421
Chan Kuong Kei (Rua do Dr. Pedro Jose Lobo) 陳光記(羅保博士街)		🍴	Macau/澳門	422
Imperial Court 金殿堂		✗✗✗	Macau/澳門	427
Lei Garden 利苑酒家	✿	✗✗	Taipa/氹仔	429
Lou Kei (Fai Chi Kei) 老記 (筷子基)	NEW 🥠 🍴		Macau/澳門	431
Lung Wah Tea House 龍華茶樓		🍴	Macau/澳門	433
San Tou Tou 新陶陶		✗	Taipa/氹仔	439
Tim's Kitchen 桃花源小廚	✿	✗✗✗	Macau/澳門	443
Tou Tou Koi 陶陶居		✗	Macau/澳門	444
Wing Lei 永利軒	🍃 ✿✿	✗✗✗✗	Macau/澳門	445
Ying 帝影樓		✗✗✗	Taipa/氹仔	447
Zi Yat Heen 紫逸軒	✿✿	✗✗✗	Taipa/氹仔	448

Chinese/中式

Beijing Kitchen 滿堂彩		✗✗	Taipa/氹仔	418
Golden Flower 京花軒 🍃	✿	✗✗✗	Macau/澳門	425
Square Eight 食·八方	🥠	✗	Macau/澳門	440
The Eight 8餐廳	✿✿	✗✗✗	Macau/澳門	442

French/法式

Aux Beaux Arts 寶雅座		✗✗	Macau/澳門	416

French contemporary/時尚法式

Robuchon a Galera 法國餐廳	✿✿✿	✗✗✗	Macau/澳門	438

NEW : New entry in the guide/ 新增推介

🍃 : Restaurant promoted to a Bib Gourmand or Star/ 評級有所晉升的餐廳

International/國際菜

Italian/意式

Japanese/日式

Macanese/澳門菜

Noodles and Congee/粥麵

Portuguese/葡式

Spanish/西班牙菜

PARTICULARLY PLEASANT RESTAURANTS
上佳的餐廳

NEW : New entry in the guide/ 新增推介
❀ : Restaurant promoted to a Bib Gourmand or Star/ 評級有所晉升的餐廳

Antonio
安東尼奧

You really feel you're in Portugal when you're in cosy little Antonio's, with its dark wood floor, Portuguese inspired paintings and crisp blue and white tiles. Ask Antonio for his menu recommendations: not only will he tell you his specials, which include gratinated goat's cheese with honey and olive oil as a starter, and monkfish, rice and prawns as a main course; he'll also happily give you the lowdown on how he got from Portugal to Macau.

置身於舒適的安東尼奧餐廳，感覺就像身處葡萄牙一樣：深色木地板、葡式油畫，以及典型的藍白色瓷磚，裝潢甚具風味。安東尼奧的推介相當不錯，他不但會向你推薦他的拿手菜式，包括蜜糖橄欖油烤山羊芝士作前菜，以及鮟鱇魚鮮蝦飯作主菜；同時亦很樂於細說他從葡萄牙來到澳門的故事。

■ ADDRESS/地址
TEL. 2899 9998
3 Rua dos Negociantes, Taipa
氹仔客商街3號
www.antoniomacau.com

■ OPENING HOURS, LAST ORDER
　營業時間，最後點菜時間
Lunch/午膳 12:00-15:00 (L.O.)
Dinner/晚膳 18:00-22:30 (L.O.)

■ PRICE/價錢
à la carte/點菜　　　　　MOP290-1,100

A Petisqueria
葡國美食天地

Step through the door and you'll instantly feel as though you've been transported to a cosy little restaurant in the Portuguese countryside. A small bar at the entrance leads you into a simple, rustic dining room where the focus is on classic Portuguese cuisine served in a friendly, unpretentious atmosphere. Authentic dishes include bacalhau prepared in five different ways, and fried clams; look out too for the daily specials.

不要因餐廳外觀不吸引而卻步，踏入大門你便會感受到這裡舒適的葡國風情。餐廳入口設有小酒吧，而餐室本身設計簡樸，菜式亦毫不花巧，以親切友善的服務奉上經典的葡國美食。正宗的菜式包括以五種不同方法烹調的馬介休、炒蜆，以及六至七款是日精選。

■ ADDRESS/地址

TEL. 2882 5354
15 Rua S. Joao, Taipa
氹仔生央街15號

■ ANNUAL AND WEEKLY CLOSING
　　休息日期
Closed Monday
週一休息

■ OPENING HOURS, LAST ORDER
　　營業時間，最後點菜時間
Lunch/午膳 12:30-14:15 (L.O.)
Dinner/晚膳 18:45-22:00 (L.O.)

■ PRICE/價錢
à la carte/點菜　　　　　MOP175-430

Aux Beaux Arts
寶雅座

This elegant Parisian-style brasserie has a true Belle Epoque feel with classic 1930s bubble-glass chandeliers and original French paintings from that period, on loan from a Shanghai museum. There's a beautiful glass-enclosed cellar for private parties, the Russian Room for caviar, and the Ice Bar for champagne. Authentic French classics include 'les cocottes': casserole specialities.

這家巴黎風格的餐廳配置著三十年代的經典氣泡玻璃吊燈，與從上海博物館借回來的法國原畫，交織成美麗時期（Belle Epoque)的優雅品味和純正氣質。漂亮的玻璃牆場地適合舉辦私人派對。魚子屋供應魚子醬，香檳庫則提供香檳，美饌佳釀各適其適。經典法國菜式原汁原味，包括公認為砂鍋美食的各種烤肉（les cocottes)。

■ ADDRESS/地址
TEL. 8802 3888
GF, MGM Grand Hotel,
Avenida Dr Sun Yat Sen , Nape
外港新填海區孫逸仙大馬路
美高梅金殿酒店地下
www.mgmgrandmacau.com

■ ANNUAL AND WEEKLY CLOSING
　休息日期
Closed Monday
週一休息

■ OPENING HOURS, LAST ORDER
　營業時間，最後點菜時間
Dinner/晚膳 14:00-24:00 L.O.22:30

■ PRICE/價錢
Dinner/晚膳　set/套餐　　MOP588
　　　　　à la carte/點菜 MOP360-700

Banza
百姓

The Portuguese owner, whose nickname is Banza, visits local markets each morning to decide on the chef's frequently changing daily specials; fish dishes tend to be the most popular choice among his many regulars. The restaurant lies in the shadow of a huge apartment complex. Inside comes in tones of green and white, with large paintings and a cosy mezzanine seating about six. Banza can also give you advice on his selection of Portuguese wines.

「Banza」原是葡萄牙店主的別名，他熱愛每天早上前往本地市場，為經常變出新煮意的每日精選作出決定。眾多佳餚美食之中則以魚類最受食客歡迎。餐廳座落於氹仔，在澳門較寧靜的一區，隱藏於大型住宅屋苑之中。內部裝潢以白、綠為主色，掛有大型畫作。洋溢溫暖氣氛的閣樓約有六個座位。Banza更會向你介紹他精選的葡萄牙美酒。

■ ADDRESS/地址

TEL. 2882 1519
Avenida de Kwong Tung, n°s 154A e 154B, Edf. Nam San Garden, Bl. 5, r/c "G" e "H", Taipa
氹仔廣東大馬路154A及154B號
南新花園第5座地下G,H座

■ ANNUAL AND WEEKLY CLOSING
　休息日期
Closed Monday
週一休息

■ OPENING HOURS, LAST ORDER
　營業時間，最後點菜時間
Lunch/午膳　12:00-15:00 (L.O.)
Dinner/晚膳　18:30-23:00 (L.O.)

■ PRICE/價錢
à la carte/點菜　　　　　MOP200-400

Beijing Kitchen
滿堂彩

'Dinner and a show' at Beijing Kitchen means one and the same, as the cooking is divided between four lively show kitchens which will hold your attention. There's a dim sum and noodle area; a duck section with two applewood-fired ovens; a wok station and a dessert counter whose bounty is well worth leaving room for. Northern China provides many of the specialities. Ask for one of the tables under the bird-cages suspended from the ceiling.

在滿堂彩，你將能見識「晚餐與表演」如何融合為一體，因為這裡的菜式分別在四個開放式「現場直播」之廚房烹調，絕對能吸引你的視線。開放式廚房分為點心與粉麵區；設兩座掛爐式烤鴨磚爐，以棗木為燒製材料的烤鴨區；另外還有鐵鑊區與讓人垂涎三尺的甜品區。這裡大部分的招牌菜都是北方菜。建議選擇有鳥籠飾於天花上的座位。

■ ADDRESS/地址
TEL. 8868 1930
GF, Grand Hyatt Hotel,
Estrado do Istmo, Cotai
路氹連貫公路君悅酒店地下
www.macau.grand.hyatt.com

■ OPENING HOURS, LAST ORDER
營業時間，最後點菜時間
10:30-24:00

■ PRICE/價錢
Lunch/午膳　à la carte/點菜 MOP150-600
Dinner/晚膳　à la carte/點菜 MOP250-600

Belcançāo
鳴詩

Belcançāo is a casual dining restaurant offering a buffet and is ideal for those who can't decide on what to eat. Warm, natural colours of brown and beige decorate the room, while chefs from different countries man the open kitchens. There are stations offering Portuguese, Chinese, Indian and international cuisines and a wide variety of mostly French pastries is also available. Brunch at weekends is from 12:00 - 3pm.

鳴詩是一家提供自助餐的餐廳，氣氛輕鬆，最適合為選菜而苦惱的人。房間以溫暖、自然的棕色和米白色裝飾，來自不同國家的廚師則掌管各個開放式廚房。不同站點提供葡萄牙，國際，中國及印度美食，更有一系列著名法國糕點。周末早午併餐時間為中午十二時至下午三時。

■ ADDRESS/地址
TEL. 2881 8888
GF, Four Seasons Hotel, Estrada da Baia de N. Senhora de Esperanca, s/n, The Cotai Strip, Taipa
氹仔路氹金光大道-望德聖母灣大馬路
四季酒店地下
www.fourseasons.com/macau/

■ OPENING HOURS, LAST ORDER
　　營業時間，最後點菜時間
Lunch/午膳　12:00-14:30 (L.O.)
Dinner/晚膳　18:00-22:30 (L.O.)
■ PRICE/價錢
Lunch/午膳　set/套餐　　MOP288
Dinner/晚膳　set/套餐　　MOP388

Café Encore
咖啡廷

Café Encore is an elegant restaurant on the ground floor of the Encore hotel. The look is that of a classic European café but one with a strong Italian accent. The menu offers a combination of Macanese and Portuguese cuisine, along with a separate menu of Cantonese dishes. But it is the Macanese specialities where the kitchen particularly excels, in such dishes as curried crab and baked African chicken.

咖啡廷位於萬利酒店地下，格調優雅。餐廳的設計以傳統歐洲餐館為藍本，並滲入大量意大利藝術的元素。菜單包括澳門菜與葡國菜，另設粵菜菜單。不過這裡最出色的還是地道澳門菜，例如咖喱蟹與非洲雞。

■ ADDRESS/地址
TEL. 2888 9966
GF, Encore Hotel,
Rua Cicade de Sintra, Nape
外港新填海區仙德麗街萬利酒店地下
www.wynnmacau.com

■ OPENING HOURS, LAST ORDER
營業時間，最後點菜時間
06:30-24:00
■ PRICE/價錢
à la carte/點菜 MOP150-500

Canton
喜粵

Located in a corner of the world's biggest indoor gaming floor, Canton is a smart restaurant with a chic smoked glass facade and elegant walkway that has a glass floor and classic English Georgian-style plaster ceiling. The dining room is a deep sensual red in colour, and very modern in design. A Kouan-Chiau (gastronomic) version of Cantonese cooking prevails, though Shanghai steamed dumplings have their own section.

座落於世上最大室內娛樂場的一角，喜粵擁有時尚的煙霧玻璃外觀，配備玻璃地板的高貴走廊，以及英國喬治風格的經典灰泥天花板，設計別出心裁！餐室呈誘人的深紅色，設計甚具現代感。喜粵的菜單以廣州粵菜為主，亦有提供一系列的餃子。

■ ADDRESS/地址
TEL. 8118 9930
Shop 1018, Casino level, The Venetian Resort, Estrada da Baia de N. Senhora de Esperanca, s/n, The Cotai Strip, Taipa
氹仔路氹金光大道-望德聖母灣大馬路威尼斯人酒店娛樂場地下1018號舖
www.venetianmacao.com

■ OPENING HOURS, LAST ORDER
營業時間，最後點菜時間
Lunch/午膳 11:00-15:00 L.O.14:45
Dinner/晚膳 18:00-23:00 L.O.22:45

■ PRICE/價錢
à la carte/點菜 　　　　　MOP300-700

Chan Kuong Kei (Rua do Dr. Pedro Jose Lobo)
陳光記(羅保博士街)

Red and yellow are the colours of this very clean shop, as well as the uniforms worn by the efficient team of well-organised ladies who run it. Their barbecue meats and noodles attract an eclectic mix of customer, ensuring that it is always crowded and full of life. The roast goose and the barbecue pork are two of the most popular choices but it is also worth trying the double or triple rice plates.

此店非常整潔，主色是紅色和黃色，就連勤快的女店員身上的制服也不例外。這裡的燒味與粉麵吸引了各式各樣的客人，店裡經常客似雲來，充滿生命力。這裡的燒鵝和叉燒最受歡迎，雙拼與三拼飯同樣值得一試。

■ ADDRESS/地址
TEL. 2831 4116
19 Rua do Dr. Pedro Jose Lobo, Centro
澳門羅保博士街19號

■ ANNUAL AND WEEKLY CLOSING
休息日期
Closed 3 days Lunar New Year
農曆新年休息3天

■ OPENING HOURS, LAST ORDER
營業時間，最後點菜時間
10:30-21:30 (L.O.)

■ PRICE/價錢
à la carte/點菜   MOP25-180

Clube Militar de Macau
澳門陸軍俱樂部

                                                  XX

& ⊟ 32 ℃

Built in 1870 for the benefit of army officers, this striking pink-hued building was renovated in 1995 when its restaurant was opened to the public; sadly the delightful sitting room and bar are only available to its club members. The room has a charming colonial feel, thanks largely to the echoing teak floorboards, netted windows and ceiling fans. The kitchen focuses on traditional Portuguese flavours and offers a popular lunchtime buffet.

建於1870年，這座最初為澳門陸軍軍官而設的粉紅色建築物，於1995年完成翻新，並將餐廳對外開放，惟俱樂部內的雅致大廳及酒吧則只限會員使用。大廳內的柚木地板，配上窗紗的大窗及天花板上的風扇，予人濃厚的殖民地色彩。俱樂部供應傳統的葡萄牙菜式，其午間自助餐更廣受食客歡迎。

■ ADDRESS/地址

TEL. 2871 4000
975 Avenida da Praia Grande
南灣大馬路975號
www.clubemilitardemacau.net

■ OPENING HOURS, LAST ORDER
   營業時間, 最後點菜時間
Lunch/午膳 12:00-15:00 L.O. 14:45
Dinner/晚膳 19:00-23:00 L.O. 22:45

■ PRICE/價錢
set/套餐   MOP128
à la carte/點菜   MOP250-400

Don Alfonso
當奧豐素

This opulent dining room features dozens of red Murano chandeliers and a huge fresco of the Italian coast divided into five parts. The somewhat dated feel and bright lights can detract from the experience but the Italian cuisine uses well-selected ingredients, and flavours are clean and sharp. Service can be almost overly attentive. If you're lucky, you'll be here during one of the owner's quarterly visits when he prepares his tasting menu.

豪華的餐室設有許多紅色的穆拉諾穆玻璃吊燈，以及一幅把意大利海岸分為五部分的巨型壁畫，盡顯其獨特之處。古老的風格和明亮的燈光可能令人分心，不過這裡的意大利菜式選材不俗，清新味美，服務更幾乎是太過周到。如果你運氣不錯，還有機會一試店主每年一季的特備餐單。

■ ADDRESS/地址

TEL. 8803 7722

3F, Grand Lisboa Hotel,
Avenida de Lisboa
葡京路新葡京酒店3樓
www.grandlisboa.com

■ OPENING HOURS, LAST ORDER
　　營業時間，最後點菜時間
Lunch/午膳　12:00-14:30 (L.O.)
Dinner/晚膳　18:30-22:30 (L.O.)

■ PRICE/價錢
Lunch/午膳　set/套餐　　　MOP280-480
　　　　　　à la carte/點菜 MOP780-1,650
Dinner/晚膳　set/套餐　　　MOP680-1,590
　　　　　　à la carte/點菜 MOP780-1,650

Golden Flower
京花軒

Adorned with the colours of gold and orange, this is an elegant and sophisticated restaurant within the Encore hotel. The white leather circular booths are the prized seats but wherever you sit you'll receive charming service from the strikingly attired ladies, including the 'tea sommelier'. The kitchen is noted for its dextrous preparation of three different cuisines: the Sichuan, Lu and Tan specialities are all created using superb ingredients.

京花軒座落於澳門萬利酒店內，以金色和橙色裝潢，既典雅又獨特。設有白色皮質圓形卡位，不管安坐何處，都能享受衣著端莊的女侍應為你提供的悉心服務，包括「調茶師」。廚房最出色之處是能俐落地烹調出三種不同菜系的菜式：川菜、魯菜和譚家菜，採用優質材料自不在話下。

■ ADDRESS/地址

TEL. 8986 3689

GF, Encore Hotel,
Rua Cicade de Sintra, Nape
外港新填海區仙德麗街萬利酒店地下
www.wynnmacau.com

■ ANNUAL AND WEEKLY CLOSING
　　休息日期
Closed Monday
週一休息

■ OPENING HOURS, LAST ORDER
　　營業時間，最後點菜時間
Dinner/晚膳　18:00-23:00　L.O.22:30

■ PRICE/價錢
à la carte/點菜　　　　　MOP450-1,200

Il Teatro
帝雅廷

To recommend a restaurant for something other than its food may seem odd, but at Il Teatro it appears most diners turn up primarily to watch the stunning fountains; these are in a lake and are musically choreographed to change colour and appearance every few minutes. Ask for a table with a view and don't wear sneakers, or you won't get in. The cuisine? Straightforward Italian fare, such as seafood risotto or pasta, served with style and élan.

推薦一家餐廳的菜餚以外的物品聽上來有點奇怪，不過大部分到帝雅廷的食客似乎主要是為了觀賞噴泉美景。餐廳七成以上的座位是面向表演湖噴池，每數分鐘音樂水柱交替、激光穿梭的震撼，在帝雅廷可盡收眼簾。記得預訂面向噴泉的座位！不過要記住穿著波鞋是不准進入的。至於菜餚方面，餐廳提供簡單的意大利菜，例如海鮮意大利飯或意大利粉，菜式風格獨特，服務殷勤周到。

■ ADDRESS/地址
TEL. 8986 3663
GF, Wynn Hotel,
Rua Cidade de Sintra, Nape
外港填海區仙德麗街永利酒店地下
www.wynnmacau.com

■ ANNUAL AND WEEKLY CLOSING
  休息日期
Closed Monday
週一休息

■ OPENING HOURS, LAST ORDER
  營業時間，最後點菜時間
Dinner/晚膳 17:30-23:30 (L.O.)

■ PRICE/價錢
à la carte/點菜   MOP400-800

Imperial Court
金殿堂

This is an elegant and contemporary restaurant, found on the same floor as the VIP lobby. The Grand Imperial Court upstairs has a more classical and comfortable setting. The focus of attention in the main room is its massive marble pillar with a carved dragon. The kitchen prepares Cantonese cuisine, served by attentive staff. However, if you just want a quick bite then simply visit the Noodle House.

與貴賓大堂位於同一樓層的金殿堂，集優雅與現代感於一身。上層的金殿堂貴賓廳設計更見經典舒適。主餐廳最吸引人的地方要算是雕龍大型雲石柱。餐廳主要供應廣東菜，職員服務細心。但如你只想趕快吃飽，大可直接到「麵店」。

■ ADDRESS/地址

TEL. 8802 3888
GF, MGM Grand Hotel,
Avenida Dr. Sun Yat Sen, Nape
外港新填海區孫逸仙大馬路
美高梅金殿酒店地下
www.mgmgrandmacau.com

■ OPENING HOURS, LAST ORDER
營業時間，最後點菜時間
Lunch/午膳 11:00-15:00 L.O. 14:00
Dinner/晚膳 18:00-23:00 L.O. 22:30

■ PRICE/價錢
Lunch/午膳　à la carte/點菜 MOP300-1,000
Dinner/晚膳　à la carte/點菜 MOP500-1,000

La Paloma
芭朗瑪

Secluded like hidden treasure from the rest of the city, La Paloma is a very appealing restaurant and bar, enhanced by a charming terrace, floor-to-ceiling glass and stone walls which are part of the original 17th century fortress foundations. A bold nouveau riche style of furniture lends it a casual chic; it's wonderfully intimate and romantic at night. The refined Spanish cuisine offers a great assortment of tapas and exquisite paellas.

芭朗瑪餐廳及酒吧，位於一座十七世紀舊城堡改建而成的酒店，遠離城市的煩囂。迷人的露台、落地玻璃和古堡原來的石牆，構成芭朗瑪的獨特風采。傢具陳設高尚優雅，氣派舒適時尚，晚上更是浪漫醉人。餐廳的西班牙菜精緻優雅，涵蓋多種西班牙前菜（tapas）及精美的西班牙海鮮飯（paella）。

■ ADDRESS/地址

TEL. 2837 8111

2F, Pousada de São Tiago Hotel,
Avenida da República, Fortaleza
de São Tiago da Barra
西灣民國大馬路聖地牙哥古堡酒店2樓
www.saotiago.com.ma

■ OPENING HOURS, LAST ORDER
   營業時間，最後點菜時間
Lunch/午膳 12:00-14:30 (L.O.)
Dinner/晚膳 18:30-22:30 (L.O.)

■ PRICE/價錢
Lunch/午膳 set/套餐   MOP198-258
          à la carte/點菜 MOP330-730
Dinner/晚膳 set/套餐   MOP690
          à la carte/點菜 MOP330-730

Lei Garden
利苑酒家

Smart restaurant set amongst the canals of this vast hotel's third floor - arrive on a gondola if you wish...Venetian guests predominate here; gamblers mostly give it a miss as it's too far from the gaming tables. Walls of marble provide the backdrop to a comprehensive range of traditional Cantonese dishes which are delivered by an efficient and well-organised team of servers. The best place to be seated is in one of the cosy booths.

餐廳設於三樓，佔據此巨型酒店的運河旁位置，雄據地利。有興趣不妨乘坐貢朵拉前往餐廳。這裡的顧客以酒店住客為主；因為離博彩桌太遠，娛樂場玩家通常會選擇其他餐廳。雲石的牆壁與清一色的傳統廣東菜配合得天衣無縫。侍應生服務速度簡直快如閃電，極有效率！這裡最好的座位是靠近前門的舒適卡位。

■ ADDRESS/地址
TEL. 2882 8689
Shop 2130, 3F Grand Canal Shoppes, The Venetian Resort, Estrada da Baia de N. Senhora de Esperança, Taipa
氹仔路望德聖母灣大馬路威尼斯人酒店大運河購物中心3樓2130號舖
www.venetianmacao.com

■ ANNUAL AND WEEKLY CLOSING
　休息日期
Closed 3 days Lunar New Year
農曆新年休息3天

■ OPENING HOURS, LAST ORDER
　營業時間，最後點菜時間
Lunch/午膳 11:30-15:00 L.O. 14:30
Dinner/晚膳 18:00-23:00 L.O. 22:15

■ PRICE/價錢
à la carte/點菜　　　　　　　MOP130-1,150

Litoral
海灣餐廳

⏲120

The neat and tidy façade of Litoral compensates for the charmless street in which it's located. The small exterior is deceiving: the interior goes over two floors and 250 diners can be accommodated – though this can prove a bit of a challenge to the waiting staff. The rustic atmosphere is courtesy of Portuguese nuance, which also influences the menus, along with local dishes. Try the curry shrimp with crabmeat and baked Portuguese chicken.

雖然餐廳所處的街道稍欠魅力，但整潔的正門令人留下好印象。看似狹窄的外觀頗有誤導成份：內裡共分為兩層，可以容納約250位顧客—不過這對餐廳員工來說可能是個挑戰！樸素的氣氛極具葡萄牙特色，這亦反映在餐廳菜式及本地菜式中。特別推介咖喱蟹肉蝦及焗葡國雞。

■ ADDRESS/地址

TEL. 2896 7878

261A Rua do Almirante Sérgio
河邊新街261A舖
http://restaurante-litoral.com

■ ANNUAL AND WEEKLY CLOSING
　休息日期
Closed 3 days Lunar New Year
農曆新年休息3天

■ OPENING HOURS, LAST ORDER
　營業時間，最後點菜時間
Lunch/午膳 12:00-15:00 (L.O.)
Dinner/晚膳 17:30-22:30 (L.O.)

■ PRICE/價錢
à la carte/點菜　　　　MOP250-450

Lou Kei (Fai Chi Kei)　NEW
老記 (筷子基)

If you're looking for a simple, good value supper then Lou Kei may well fit the bill. Granted, it may not be in the centre of town, but every cab driver knows this lively place, which has been renowned for over 20 years for its sizeable selection of tasty noodles, congee and Cantonese dishes; frogs' legs in a clay pot and sea crab congee are both highly recommended. The interior is bright and neat while the service is polite and attentive.

若然您想品嚐價廉物美的美食，老記必定是不二之選。儘管餐廳位於市中心外，但是所有的士司機皆知這間馳名食府的所在地。老記二十多年來提供美味粥品麵食及廣東菜式，其田雞腿煲及水蟹粥更備受食客推崇，店內光猛潔淨，侍應親切有禮。

■ ADDRESS/地址
TEL. 2856 9494
Avenida Da Concórdia N, 12R/C
E S/L Loja H
和樂大馬路12號宏基大廈第4座H及M舖

■ OPENING HOURS, LAST ORDER
營業時間，最後點菜時間
17:30-05:00 (L.O.)

■ PRICE/價錢
à la carte/點菜　　　MOP50-250

Luk Kei Noodle
六記粥麵

The second generation owner-chef insists on making his very popular noodles the traditional way: with a bamboo stick. This is a very clean and popular shop, found on a lively street. The small menu provides photos of the specialities which include noodles with dried prawn roe; crunchy deep-fried wontons; crispy fish balls with soft centres served with either oyster or soy sauce; and the filling congee with crab.

第二代店主兼大廚堅持以傳統手法，炮製極受歡迎的"竹昇麵"。此店既清潔又受歡迎，座落在充滿活力的街道上。小小的餐牌上附有特色食品的照片，包括蝦子撈麵、炸鴛鴦（炸雲吞及米通綾魚球），還有水蟹粥。

■ ADDRESS/地址

TEL. 2855 9627

1-D Travessa da Saudade
沙梨頭仁慕巷 1 號 D

■ ANNUAL AND WEEKLY CLOSING
　休息日期
Closed 4 days Lunar New Year
農曆新年 4 天休息

■ OPENING HOURS, LAST ORDER
　營業時間，最後點菜時間
Dinner/晚膳 18:30-02:30 (L.O.)

■ PRICE/價錢
à la carte/點菜   MOP40-70

Lung Wah Tea House
龍華茶樓

Little has changed from when this old-style Cantonese tea house, up a flight of stairs, opened in the 1960s: the large clock still works, the boss still uses an abacus to add the bill and you still have to refill your own pot of tea at the boiler. The owner buys fresh produce, including their popular chicken dish, from the market across the road. Their stir-fried noodles with beef is another speciality. Get here early for the fresh dim sum.

這家有一列樓梯的傳統廣東茶樓自一九六零年代開業以來，變化不大——古老大鐘依然不停擺動，老闆依然用算盤算帳單，你依然要自行到熱水器沖茶。店主從對面街市選購新鮮食材，包括茶樓名菜油雞。此外，此處的干炒牛河亦是一絕。建議預早前來享用新鮮點心。

■ ADDRESS/地址

TEL. 2857 4456

3 Rua Norte do Mercado Aim-Lacerda
提督市北街3號

■ ANNUAL AND WEEKLY CLOSING
　　休息日期
Closed 4 days Lunar New Year,
4 days May and 4 days October
農曆新年、五月及十月各休息4天

■ OPENING HOURS, LAST ORDER
　　營業時間，最後點菜時間
07:00-14:00 (L.O.)

■ PRICE/價錢
à la carte/點菜　　　　　　MOP25-140

Ngao Kei Ka Lei Chon
牛記咖喱美食

Set at the corner of a main road and a narrow street full of industrious little shops; with regulars popping in and out throughout the day. The broken neon lights outside may make it seem less appealing but this is a friendly, well-run and well-staffed little noodle shop. Bestsellers are the crab noodles and the crab congee but it's also worth trying the clear soup with beef flank and the spicy chicken or beef curry with noodles.

此店位於大街的一角的小巷內，座落其中的都是客似雲來的小店，常客每天往來不絕。店外破落的霓虹燈看似減弱了餐廳的吸引力，但無損這家小麵店職員的態度友善、管理有序，服務令人滿意。最暢銷的美食要算是水蟹、蟹黃炆伊麵和蟹粥，清湯牛腩和椰汁咖哩雞、牛跟麵也值得一試。

■ ADDRESS/地址

TEL. 2895 6129
GF, 1 Rua de Cinco de Outubro
十月初五街1號地下

■ OPENING HOURS, LAST ORDER
　　營業時間，最後點菜時間
08:00-02:00 (L.O.)

■ PRICE/價錢
à la carte/點菜　　　　　MOP60-160

Noodle & Congee Corner
粥麵莊

This simple, good value eatery is located – incongruously – on a gallery that opens onto the casino. It's really a cafeteria, or even 'tea-eria', as one wall is full of teapots. What's special for diners is the view they have of chefs from different parts of the country preparing a noodle speciality from their home region using fresh, tasty produce. These can be combined with various soups and ingredients: the menus, handily, include photos.

這家簡樸的餐廳提供價錢合宜的美食，位於娛樂場上層樓上，彼此風格迥然不同。粥麵莊的確是一家餐館，而其中一道牆更放滿茶壺，洋溢著「茶檔」的感覺。特別的是食客更可在晚餐時觀賞來自五湖四海的廚師，採用新鮮味美的食材，分別炮製出家鄉的特色麵食的烹飪過程！餐廳亦提供不同款式的湯類和其他菜式；菜單附有圖片，便於瀏覽。

■ ADDRESS/地址

TEL. 8803 7755
1F, Grand Lisboa Hotel,
Avenida de Lisboa
葡京路新葡京酒店1樓
www.grandlisboa.com

■ OPENING HOURS, LAST ORDER
    營業時間，最後點菜時間
Open 24 hours
24小時營業

■ PRICE/價錢
à la carte/點菜   MOP50-200

Oja Sopa De Fita Cheong Kei
祥記

Although handily placed on Rua da Felicidade, you'll need to weave round shoppers and stalls to get to Cheong Kei. A family business since the '70s, this tiny noodle shop sticks to its roots and their thin, fine noodles are pressed by bamboo shoots in their own little factory nearby. Their soup uses dried prawns and bonito and is cooked for 8 hours. The wontons with noodles are clearly a must but also try the dried prawn roe with stewed noodles.

雖然祥記位於福隆新街，選址便利，但還是得花一番功夫繞過購物的人潮及攤販。這家小麵店是七十年代開業的家族生意，鄰近自設小型廠房製造幼細竹昇面。麵湯以蝦乾和柴魚熬製八小時，雲吞麵當然不能缺少，蝦籽撈麵亦不容錯過。

- **ADDRESS/地址**
TEL. 2857 4310
68 Rua de Felicidade
福隆新街68號

- **ANNUAL AND WEEKLY CLOSING**
  休息日期
Closed 4 days each month
每月休息4天

- **OPENING HOURS, LAST ORDER**
  營業時間，最後點菜時間
12:00-01:00 (L.O.)

- **PRICE/價錢**
à la carte/點菜   MOP18-50

436

Okada
岡田

🦽 👆 🍽16 🛎

Situated alongside the casino, there are no prizes for guessing the clientele of this attractive restaurant whose pale, dry-stone walls are its most appealing feature, its garden views obscured by a wall of bamboo. Apart from the main room, there's a sushi counter and grill bar. The menu delivers a large Japanese menu – sushi, sashimi, tempura, teppanyaki, grilled fish – but authenticity can be sacrificed in the desire to 'refuel' gamblers.

這間日式料理毗鄰娛樂場,不用猜想都知食客固然也是娛樂場的顧客。餐廳的淺色石牆魅力獨特,十分迷人;而竹林的排列則使園林景致若隱若現。餐廳設有主餐室、壽司吧和燒烤吧。菜單涵蓋大量日本菜式,包括壽司、天婦羅、鐵板燒、烤魚等等。味道可能不夠正宗,不過可以為食客「充 電」,然後繼續到娛樂場大展身手。

■ ADDRESS/地址

TEL. 8986 3663
GF, Wynn Hotel,
Rua Cidade de Sintra, Nape
外港新填海區仙德麗街永利酒店地下
www.wynnmacau.com

■ ANNUAL AND WEEKLY CLOSING
　休息日期
Closed Tuesday
週二休息

■ OPENING HOURS, LAST ORDER
　營業時間,最後點菜時間
Dinner/晚膳　17:30-23:30 (L.O.)

■ PRICE/價錢
à la carte/點菜　　　MOP300-1,300

Robuchon a Galera
法國餐廳

♿ 🍽26 ☏🍽 ⛄

Joël Robuchon's restaurant is a lavishly adorned and stylish location in which to dine. The early 19th century ambience has a warm, soft feel, accentuated by elegant and expensive fabrics. Excellent fresh ingredients underpin the contemporary Gallic cuisine and it's well worth leaving room for the impressive selection of homemade pastries on the dessert trolley. The wine list is equally superb, with over 7,800 wines from around the world.

Joël Robuchon的餐廳裝潢非常奢華時尚，供食客享受美食。溫暖柔和的感覺營造自十九世紀早期的氣氛，再飾以昂貴的布料，更顯感覺高雅。用優質新鮮的食材炮製出一道道當代法國菜，甜品車上的家鄉酥餅充滿魅力，值得留肚品嚐。酒牌亦不遑多讓，提供超過7800款來自全球的美酒。

■ ADDRESS/地址

TEL. 2888 3888

3F, Hotel Lisboa,
2-4 Avenida de Lisboa
葡京路2-4號葡京酒店3樓
www.hotelisboa.com

■ OPENING HOURS, LAST ORDER
營業時間，最後點菜時間
Lunch/午膳 12:00-14:30 (L.O.)
Dinner/晚膳 18:30-22:30 (L.O.)

■ PRICE/價錢

Lunch/午膳	set/套餐	MOP400-638
	à la carte/點菜	MOP1,100-2,100
Dinner/晚膳	set/套餐	MOP1,588-2,288
	à la carte/點菜	MOP1,100-2,100

San Tou Tou
新陶陶

Found on a narrow street in the centre of Taipa is this Cantonese restaurant, run by the same family for three generations and now supervised by two brothers. The cooking is very traditional and the chicken soup served in very hot clay pots is what attracts so many. But there are plenty of other, more affordable, specialities. The restaurant is spread over two floors and the air conditioning is most efficient!

此廣東菜餐廳位於冰仔中心的小巷上，家族經營了三代，現時由兩兄弟主理。煮法非常傳統，這裡的燉雞湯是用砂煲盛載，吸引大量食客。除此之外，這裡也提供很多其他價錢相宜的選擇。餐廳雖分為兩層，但並不影響其冷氣系統的流通！

■ ADDRESS/地址

TEL. 2882 7065
26 Rua Correia da Silva, Taipa
冰仔告利雅施利華街26號

■ ANNUAL AND WEEKLY CLOSING
　　休息日期
Closed 1 week Lunar New Year, 2 days early May and 2 days early October
農曆新年7天、五月初及十月初各休息2天

■ OPENING HOURS, LAST ORDER
　　營業時間，最後點菜時間
Lunch/午膳 11:30-15:00 (L.O.)
Dinner/晚膳 17:30-22:00 (L.O.)

■ PRICE/價錢
Lunch/午膳　à la carte/點菜 MOP100-300
Dinner/晚膳　à la carte/點菜 MOP300-600

Square Eight
食・八方

Square Eight is a large, informal, western-style eatery that never closes its doors. It's vibrant and busy, and its cuisine covers large swathes of Asia, from China to Thailand to Korea. You're given a large sheet of paper with all the dishes, and you just tick the ones you'd like. Service is fast and furious, but staff are engaging and attentive. A long, open-plan kitchen adds to the hustle and bustle of the place.

食・八方二十四小時開放，地方寬敞，環境輕鬆時尚。餐廳人氣旺盛，生氣勃勃，美食超越中西界限，涵蓋中菜、泰國菜、韓國菜等。點菜單上羅列出全部菜式，食客可以自行打剔點選。環境時而喧鬧，不過服務快捷周到。長形的開放式廚房為餐廳更添一份忙碌氣氛。

■ ADDRESS/地址

TEL. 8802 3888

GF, MGM Grand Hotel,
Avenida Dr. Sun Yat Sen, Nape
外港新填海區孫逸仙大馬路
美高梅金殿酒店地下
www.mgmgrandmacau.com

■ OPENING HOURS, LAST ORDER
  營業時間，最後點菜時間
Open 24 hours
24小時營業

■ PRICE/價錢
à la carte/點菜   MOP60-250

Tenmasa
天政

An utterly charming restaurant named after the original Tenmasa, which opened in Tokyo in 1937 and is still going strong. Taipa's version boasts a sushi bar, a tempura counter, tatami floor and decked walkways leading across golden pebble ponds to private rooms. Here you can sit and watch the chef at work, admiring his precise light frying of superb ingredients and wonderfully well-balanced dishes. Attentive waitresses wear smart kimonos.

譽滿東京的天政早於1937年開業，至今仍廣受歡迎，更把料理帶到澳門新濠鋒。澳門的天政設有壽司吧、榻榻米地板、鋪板走廊、金石水池、私人餐室，以及天婦羅檯。食客可安坐在天婦羅檯，觀看廚師大顯身手，將優質食材炮製成美味菜式。服務員穿著整潔的和服，服務周到。

■ ADDRESS/地址
TEL. 8803 6611
11F, Altira Hotel,
Avenida de Kwong Tung, Taipa
氹仔廣東大馬路新濠鋒酒店11樓
www.altiramacau.com

■ OPENING HOURS, LAST ORDER
營業時間，最後點菜時間
Lunch/午膳 12:00-14:30 (L.O.)
Dinner/晚膳 18:00-22:30 (L.O.)

■ PRICE/價錢
Lunch/午膳　set/套餐　　　MOP180-900
　　　　　　à la carte/點菜 MOP400-1,200
Dinner/晚膳 set/套餐　　　MOP400-2,100
　　　　　　à la carte/點菜 MOP400-1,200

The Eight
8餐廳

The Eight's stylish appearance can't fail to impress: water cascades down walls, images are projected onto the floor... and that's just the entrance corridor. Even the goldfish on the walls inside the restaurant are hand-sewn. The menu includes some very innovative Cantonese dishes which includes dim sum like deep-fried abalone puff stuffed with black mushroom and asparagus and the baked tartelette with crabmeat in curry sauce.

8餐廳的時尚設計令人印象深刻：流水沿著牆壁潺潺而下，地板上更投射著粼粼影像…這只是入口走廊而已！餐廳牆上的金魚也都是人手繡成的!餐牌包括部分非常創新的廣東菜，點心類如特式鮑魚酥及葡香焗蟹撻。

■ ADDRESS/地址

TEL. 8803 7788
2F, Grand Lisboa Hotel,
Avenida de Lisboa
葡京路新葡京酒店2樓
www.grandlisboahotel.com

■ OPENING HOURS, LAST ORDER
營業時間，最後點菜時間
Lunch/午膳 12:00-14:30 (L.O.)
Dinner/晚膳 18:30-22:30 (L.O.)

■ PRICE/價錢
Lunch/午膳　à la carte/點菜 MOP160-1,000
Dinner/晚膳　à la carte/點菜 MOP400-1,000

Tim's Kitchen
桃花源小廚

⬚30 ◐🍴 ⬡

One for the connoisseurs – Hong Kong foodies make special pilgrimages here. This restaurant is filled with opera photos and costumes. The Cantonese dishes may look simple, but they are well prepared. These may include steamed pork slices with eggplant & preserved vegetables and sweet & sour pork ribs. Make sure you try the crystal prawn; while in winter there is always the snake ragout - a joy for the taste buds!

桃花源是行家的必然之選，香港食家也少不免到此朝聖。餐廳放滿歌劇照片和戲服裝飾。粵菜餐牌看似簡單，其實經過精心炮製。菜式包括梅菜肉片蒸茄瓜及京都骨。萬勿錯過玻璃蝦球，冬天的重頭戲則離不開蛇羹。實在能「感動味蕾」！

■ ADDRESS/地址
TEL. 8803 3682
Shop F25, GF, Hotel Lisboa,
East Wing, 2-4 Avenida de Lisboa
葡京路2-4號葡京酒店東翼地下F25號鋪
www.hotelisboa.com

■ OPENING HOURS, LAST ORDER
營業時間，最後點菜時間
Lunch/午膳 12:00-15:00 L.O. 14:30
Dinner/晚膳 18:30-23:00 L.O. 22:00

■ PRICE/價錢
Lunch/午膳　à la carte/點菜 MOP200-700
Dinner/晚膳　à la carte/點菜 MOP400-1,300

Tou Tou Koi
陶陶居

⊡ 24 🔲

As this 80 year old restaurant is simply always packed, it's vital to make reservations; you can then also pre-order the duck. It's dim sum during the day and Cantonese cuisine at night and among the favourites are deep-fried crab, chicken soup and fish from the tank in the dining room. Service is sufficiently swift to accommodate the non-stop flow of customers. A refurbishment has left the restaurant looking much more contemporary.

有80多年歷史的陶陶居總是賓客如雲，必須訂座，你亦可順道預訂八寶鴨。日間以點心為主，晚上則提供粵菜，受歡迎菜式包括金錢蟹盒和古法雞煲，以及新鮮烹調的海魚。服務非常具效率，以應付絡繹不絕的人流。酒家翻新後裝潢更見時尚。

■ ADDRESS/地址

TEL. 2857 2629
6-8 Travessa do Mastro
爐石塘巷6-8號

■ OPENING HOURS, LAST ORDER
營業時間，最後點菜時間
Lunch/午膳 09:00-15:00 (L.O.)
Dinner/晚膳 17:00-24:00 L.O. 23:30

■ PRICE/價錢
Lunch/午膳　à la carte/點菜 MOP90-150
Dinner/晚膳　à la carte/點菜 MOP200-400

Wing Lei
永利軒

✿✿   ✗✗✗✗

☞ 🅿 🖵12 ☎⍾

An opulent restaurant in vibrant red, characterised by vast lanterns at the entrance and a superb three-dimensional dragon made of ninety thousand pieces of crystal; the comfy red dining chairs add to a feeling of well-being. As befits such sumptuous surroundings, the service is both courteous and attentive. Gamblers and a large number of families create a noisy ambience as they tuck into a big menu of classic Cantonese dishes.

這家紅噹噹的餐廳入口掛著一些大型燈籠，襯托一條以九萬片水晶製成的立體龍，盡展豪華氣派；而舒適的紅色座椅讓人更添好感。餐廳的裝潢實屬一流，服務也親切周到。食客多是一家大小或娛樂場玩家，環境熱鬧非常。餐廳供應傳統粵菜，菜式選擇良多。

■ ADDRESS/地址

TEL. 8986 3663
GF, Wynn Hotel,
Rua Cidade de Sintra, Nape
外港新填海區仙德麗街永利酒店地下
www.wynnmacau.com

■ OPENING HOURS, LAST ORDER
  營業時間，最後點菜時間
Lunch/午膳 11:30-15:00 (L.O.)
Dinner/晚膳 18:00-23:00 (L.O.)

■ PRICE/價錢
à la carte/點菜   MOP300-1,700

Yamazato NEW
山里

The restaurant on the second floor of the Hotel Okura combines traditional Japanese customs with a modern aesthetic. It comes divided into a number of areas, including a sushi bar and private rooms overlooking a garden, but the most striking feature is the paper pod tea ceremony room for those wanting a very special experience. The authentic cuisine includes a daily changing kaiseki, sushi and special grilled dishes.

這家揉合日本傳統及現代美學的日本料理位於澳門大倉酒店二樓。店內分為數個區域,包括壽司吧及可觀賞日式庭園的獨立廂房。最獨特之處是食客可在圓球形的和紙茶道室內體驗日本茶道。餐廳提供每天轉換的懷石料理、壽司及特色燒物。

■ ADDRESS/地址

TEL. 8883 8883

Level 2, Hotel Okura, Galaxy Macau,
Avenida Marginal Flor de Lotus, Cotai
路氹城蓮花海濱大馬路
澳門銀河渡假城大倉酒店2樓
www.hotelokuramacau.com

■ OPENING HOURS, LAST ORDER
   營業時間,最後點菜時間
12:00-23:00 (L.O.)

■ PRICE/價錢

Lunch/午膳 set/套餐		MOP220-400
	à la carte/點菜	MOP450-1,700
Dinner/晚膳 set/套餐		MOP450-1,880
à la carte/點菜		MOP450-1,700

Ying
帝影樓

This is a terrific restaurant with breathtaking views looking north to Macau. The beautifully styled interior has been designed with taste and verve; even the beaded curtains – featuring gold cranes and crystal trees – are striking. The Cantonese dishes on offer are prepared with contemporary twists and great flair, and are served by charmingly professional staff. This is the place to come to celebrate that special occasion.

帝影樓坐擁澳門北部的壯麗景致，扣人心弦。餐廳內部設計品味獨特，風格絢麗；甚至珠簾亦配有金鶴和水晶樹，使裝潢更添神采。餐廳的粵菜融入了當代元素，烹調技藝精湛。服務專業，態度令人賓至如歸。這裡的一些粵菜菜式可謂冠絕全城。

■ ADDRESS/地址

TEL. 8803 6600

11F, Altira Hotel,
Avenida de Kwong Tung, Taipa
氹仔廣東大馬路新濠鋒酒店11樓
www.altiramacau.com

■ OPENING HOURS, LAST ORDER
　營業時間，最後點菜時間
Lunch/午膳 11:00-14:30 (L.O.)
Dinner/晚膳 18:00-22:30 (L.O.)

■ PRICE/價錢
à la carte/點菜　　　　　MOP160-1,760

Zi Yat Heen
紫逸軒

Conveniently located on the 1st floor of the Four Seasons Hotel Macau, Zi Yat Heen is an elegant and spacious restaurant, with a large glass-encased wine cellar at its centre. Chef Ho has created a traditional Cantonese menu but with a lighter, fresher taste by using premium ingredients and minimal seasonings. Interesting creations include the baked lamb chops with coffee sauce, while a more authentic choice would be the pigeon with Yunnan ham.

紫逸軒位於澳門四季酒店一樓，格調高雅，地方寬敞，正中位置更有大型玻璃櫃餐酒庫。大廚何先生烹製傳統粵菜時採用最新鮮的食材與最少的調味料，帶來更鮮味清新的粵菜。有趣創作菜式包括咖啡汁焗羊排，而更傳統的選擇有酥香雲腿伴鴿脯。

■ ADDRESS/地址

TEL. 2881 8888

GF, Four Seasons Hotel, Estrada da Baia de N. Senhora de Esperanca, s/n, The Cotai Strip, Taipa
氹仔路氹金光大道-望德聖母灣大馬路四季酒店地下
www.fourseasons.com/macau

■ OPENING HOURS, LAST ORDER
　營業時間，最後點菜時間
Lunch/午膳 12:00-14:30 (L.O.)
Dinner/晚膳 18:30-22:30 (L.O.)

■ PRICE/價錢

set/套餐	MOP2,010
à la carte/點菜	MOP400-1,500

HOTELS
酒店

HOTELS BY ORDER OF COMFORT
酒店 — 以舒適程度分類

Altira
新濠鋒

High quality design, a serene atmosphere and wondrous peninsula views produce something quite spectacular here. Guests arrive at the stylish lobby on the 38th floor and the luxury penthouse feel is enhanced by a superb lounge and terrace on the same level. Bedrooms, all on an upper floor, face the sea and merge tranquil tones with sheer contemporary style. As if this weren't enough, there's also a sumptuous spa boasting a pool-with-a-view.

RESTAURANTS/ 餐廳

Recommended/推薦		Also/其他
Tenmasa/ 天政	✗✗	Aurora/ 奧羅拉
Ying/ 帝影樓	✗✗✗	Kira/ 吉良

新濠鋒酒店設計獨特，舒適典雅，位處優越地段，讓澳門半島的環
迴美景盡入眼簾，令人讚嘆不已。時尚尊貴的大堂位於38樓，同
層的「天宮」酒廊備有室內酒廊及露天陽台高雅舒適，散發著豪華
瑰麗的味道。客房位於其他較高樓層，海景一望無際，寧靜感覺和
現代設計相互交織，氣派超凡。此外，酒店設有豪華的水療設施，
享用服務的同時更可飽覽美景。

■ ADDRESS/地址
TEL. 2886 8888
FAX. 2886 8666
Avenida de Kwong Tung, Taipa
氹仔廣東大馬路
www.altiramacau.com

■ ROOMS AND SUITES/客房及套房
Rooms/客房 ＝184
Suites/套房 ＝32
■ PRICE/價錢

👤	MOP1,800-3,300
👥	MOP1,800-3,300
Suites/套房	MOP3,300-70,000
☕	MOP180

Banyan Tree NEW
悅榕莊

Forming part of Galaxy Macau, this luxurious resort in Cotai City, not far from Macau International Airport, comprises 246 suites plus 10 villas which have their own private gardens and swimming pools. The very comfortable bedrooms all have large baths set by the window, while other facilities include an impressive state-of-the art spa – the biggest in the group – and four restaurants. Guests also enjoy full access to all of Galaxy's facilities.

RESTAURANTS/ 餐廳

<table>
<tr><td>Recommended/推薦</td><td>Also/其他</td></tr>
<tr><td></td><td>Banyan Lounge/ 悦榕吧
Belon/ 貝隆</td></tr>
</table>

作為路氹城澳門銀河綜合渡假城的一部分及毗鄰澳門國際機場，
澳門悦榕莊共有246間套房和10間擁有私人花園和泳池的別墅。
所有的寬敞套房內均設有私人悦心池，其他設施包括集團最大及
最頂級的水療中心及4間餐廳，住客更可享用銀河綜合渡假城內
的所有設施。

■ ADDRESS/地址
TEL. 8883 8833
FAX. 8883 6108
Galaxy, Avenida Marginal Flor de Lotus,
Cotai
路氹城蓮花海濱大馬路澳門銀河渡假城
www.banyantree.com/en/macau/

■ ROOMS AND SUITES/客房及套房
Suites/套房 ＝246
Villas/別墅 ＝10

■ PRICE/價錢
Suites/套房 MOP2,880-63,800
Villas/別墅 MOP23,600-35,100
☕ MOP220

Encore
萬利

For VIPs who want an even more exclusive resort experience than the Wynn, there is Encore – their luxury brand. The word 'standard' certainly does not apply here as the choice is between a suite or a villa, all of which are lavishly decorated in reds and golds. You also get an exceptional spa which offers bespoke treatments and Bar Cristal, as small as a jewel box and just as precious. Even the casino is largely made up of VIP game rooms.

RESTAURANTS/ 餐廳

Recommended/推薦		Also/其他

| Café Encore/ 咖啡廷 | ✕✕ | 99 Noodles/ 99 麵 |
| Golden Flower/ 京花軒 | ✿ ✕✕✕ | |

尊貴如你，如欲享受比永利更獨特尊貴的度假體驗，大可選擇萬利——永利旗下的帝皇級品牌。「標準」一詞絕對不適用於萬利，你可選擇入住萬利豪華套房或尊貴豪華套房，兩者均以紅色與金色裝潢，更顯富麗堂皇。你亦可於貴賓級水療中心盡情享受度身訂造的療程，酒店內的Bar Cristal酒吧更一如其名——如珠寶盒一般嬌小而高貴。附設賭場內，絕大部分均為貴賓遊樂房。

■ ADDRESS/地址
TEL. 2888 9966
FAX. 2832 9966
Rua Cidade de Sintra, Nape
外港新填海區仙德麗街
www.wynnmacau.com

■ ROOMS AND SUITES/客房及套房
Suites/套房 ＝414
■ PRICE/價錢
Suites/套房　MOP9,000-16,000
☕　　　　　MOP110

Four Seasons
四季

Opened in the summer of 2008, Four Seasons fuses East and West by blending together Colonial Portuguese and Chinese traditions. The lobby functions like a living room, with its fireplace, Portuguese lanterns and Chinese lacquer screens. The hotel also has a luxury shopping mall and connects to The Venetian and gaming at the Plaza Casino. If you want respite from the buzz and the glitz, then escape to the spa or relax by one of five pools.

RESTAURANTS/ 餐廳

Recommended/推薦			Also/其他
Belcanção/ 鳴詩		✗✗	Splash/ 撲滿
Zi Yat Heen/ 紫逸軒	❀ ❀	✗✗✗	Windows

2008年夏季開幕的四季融合了東方和西方元素，將殖民地時代葡萄牙與中國傳統元素融為一體。大堂有如客廳，設有壁爐、葡國燈籠和中國雕漆屏風。酒店亦設有豪華購物商場，直通威尼斯人酒店及百利沙娛樂場。如果你想從五光十色中喘息一下，可享用水療設備和五個泳池的池畔酒吧。

■ ADDRESS/地址

TEL. 2881 8888
FAX. 2881 8899
Estrada da Baia de N. Senhora de
Esperanca, s/n, The Cotai Strip, Taipa
氹仔路氹金光大道-望德聖母灣大馬路
www.fourseasons.com/macau

■ ROOMS AND SUITES/客房及套房
Rooms/客房 ＝276
Suites/套房 ＝84

■ PRICE/價錢
👤	MOP2,700-4,600
👥	MOP2,700-4,600
Suites/套房	MOP5,100-40,000
☕	MOP210

Grand Hyatt
君悅

The hotel forms part of the 'City of Dreams' urban resort, which includes a casino, shopping mall and a number of restaurants and hotels, and shares the same 'water' theme. The lobby sets the tone, with its striking 22m ceiling and fabulous artwork, with drops appearing to fall from a cloud. The stylish, contemporary bedrooms are split between the two towers. Mezza9 opens onto a terrace and offers nine different dining options.

RESTAURANTS/ 餐廳

Recommended/推薦		Also/其他
Beijing Kitchen/ 滿堂彩	ⅩⅩ	Mezza9

君悅酒店是「新濠天地」城市度假村的一部份，度假村內設有賭場、商場及一系列餐廳與酒店，以「水」為共同主題。大堂已可見酒店格調——足有22米高的天花與出色的藝術品，配搭彷似要從天上雲層落下的水點。富當代時尚感的房間分布於兩棟大樓中。延伸成室外庭園的Mezza9為顧客提供九種不同餐點，任君選擇。

■ ADDRESS/地址
TEL. 8868 1234
FAX. 8867 1234
City of Dreams,
Estrada do Istmo, Cotai
路氹連貫公路
www.macau.grand.hyatt.com

■ ROOMS AND SUITES/客房及套房
Rooms/客房 =503
Suites/套房 =288

■ PRICE/價錢

🛉	MOP1,300-3,200
🛉🛉	MOP1,300-3,200
Suites/套房	MOP2,300-13,000
☕	MOP220

Grand Lisboa
新葡京

Impossible to miss, the Grand Lisboa, opened in December 2008, can be seen from miles away with its eye-popping, brightly-lit lotus design atop a shining diamond. Opulent soundproofed bedrooms typically feature brown walls, red armchairs and Asian paintings, and offer grand sea or city vistas. If you have a corner room or a suite, you'll get the added bonus of a sauna; if you have neither, you can at least make use of a sumptuous spa.

RESTAURANTS/ 餐廳

Recommended/推薦

Don Alfonso/ 當奧豐素

Noodle & Congee Corner/ 粥麵莊

The Eight/ 8餐廳

Also/其他

The Kitchen/ 大厨

2008年12月開幕的新葡京外形像一片耀目的黃蓮葉，座落於一顆閃爍的鑽石之上，遠處可見，實在不容錯過！客房非常隔音，擁有典型的棕色牆壁、紅色扶手椅和亞洲油畫，並坐擁豪華海景或澳門的秀麗風光。角位客房及套房更設有桑拿設施，其他客房亦可享用豪華的水療設施。

■ ADDRESS/地址

TEL.2828 3838
FAX. 2888 2828
Avenida de Lisboa
葡京路
www.grandlisboahotel.com

■ ROOMS AND SUITES/客房及套房

Rooms/客房 =381
Suites/套房 =50

■ PRICE/價錢

🚹	MOP3,800-5,700
🚹🚹	MOP3,800-5,700
Suites/套房	MOP7,800-48,000
☕	MOP150

Lisboa
葡京

The Lisboa is one of the city's more 'traditional' hotels with its 1970s style façade providing a stark contrast to the brand new Grand Lisboa. There are 10 types of guestroom available; ask for a Tower room, as these are more luxurious and larger in size than the rooms in the east wing. 2011 saw the addition of an indoor swimming pool, so guests no longer have to nip over the Grand Lisboa to use theirs.

RESTAURANTS/ 餐廳

Recommended/推薦	Also/其他

Robuchon a Galera/
法國餐廳 ✿✿✿ ✖✖✖

Tim's Kitchen/ 桃花源小廚 ✿ ✖✖✖

New Furusato/ 新故鄉

Portas do Sol/ 葡京日麗

葡京酒店是澳門的「傳統」酒店之一，保留著七十年代的外觀，
與新落成的相映成趣。酒店共有十種客房，尊尚客房比東翼的客
房更大更豪華，物有所值。她更於2011年新增了室內游泳池，
想游泳的客人不用再前往新葡京酒店，更見方便。

■ ADDRESS/地址
TEL. 2888 3888
FAX. 2888 3838
2-4 Avenida de Lisboa
葡京路2-4號
www.hotelisboa.com

■ ROOMS AND SUITES/客房及套房
Rooms/客房 ＝876
Suites/套房 ＝50

■ PRICE/價錢

👤	MOP1,850-3,400
👥	MOP1,850-3,400
Suites/套房	MOP4,400-18,000
☕	MOP140

Mandarin Oriental NEW
文華東方

Being a non-gaming hotel is not the only reason the Mandarin Oriental stands out – the hotel, which opened in 2010, is also a model of taste and discretion. Local artists' work adds a sense of locale to the bedrooms which come in muted, contemporary tones and offer great views – even from the bathtub! Those in search of further relaxation can choose between a very serene spa and a slick bar. As expected, standards of service are very strong.

RESTAURANTS/ 餐廳

Recommended/推薦	Also/其他
	Vida Rica

於2010年開業的澳門文華東方酒店，出眾之處不但在於不經營賭場，更是品味的典範。本地藝術家的創作，為色調柔和時尚的客房更添韻味，而且即使從浴室也能欣賞醉人景觀。想進一步放鬆身心，更可到幽靜的水療中心或雅緻的酒吧。一如所料，服務質素保持極高水準。

■ ADDRESS/地址

TEL. 8805 8888
FAX. 8805 8899
Avenida Dr. Sun Yat Sen, Nape
外港新填海區孫逸仙大馬路
www.mandarinoriental.com/macau

■ ROOMS AND SUITES/客房及套房
Rooms/客房 ＝186
Suites/套房 ＝27

■ PRICE/價錢

👤	MOP3,500-4,300
👥	MOP3,500-4,300
Suites/套房	MOP6,200-6,900
☕	MOP228

MGM Grand
美高梅金殿

Its iconic wave-like exterior makes MGM Grand one of Macau's most instantly recognisable hotels. The interior is pretty eye-catching too: topped by a vast glass ceiling, the Grande Praça covers over 1,000 square metres and is where you'll find an assortment of bars and restaurants. If the sheer scale is too much then just head for the spa. Spread over 35 floors, bedrooms are suitably luxurious and come with good views and glass-walled bathrooms.

RESTAURANTS/ 餐廳

Recommended/推薦			Also/其他
Aux Beaux Arts/ 寶雅座		XX	Rossio/ 盛事
Imperial Court/ 金殿堂		XXX	
Square Eight/ 食 · 八方	☺	X	

標誌性的波浪形建築設計讓MGM Grand成為澳門最令人矚目的酒店之一。室內設計同樣出眾，在巨型玻璃天幕下，Grande Praça佔地逾1000平方米，設有多間酒吧和餐廳。如果看膩了這絕頂繁華，不妨前往恬靜的水療中心。分佔35層，客房華麗得恰到好處，而且景觀優美，浴室採用玻璃間隔。

■ ADDRESS/地址

TEL. 8802 8888

FAX. 8802 3333

Avenida Dr. Sun Yat Sen, Nape

外港新填海區孫逸仙大馬路

www.mgmgrandmacau.com

■ ROOMS AND SUITES/客房及套房

Rooms/客房 =468

Suites/套房 =125

■ PRICE/價錢

🚹	MOP3,200-3,800
🚹🚹	MOP3,200-3,800
Suites/套房	MOP7,800-9,800
☕	MOP150

Okura NEW
大倉

Providing sanctuary from the outside world is this tastefully decorated, discreet and elegant hotel, which forms part of Galaxy Macau resort. Its charming staff wear kimonos and provide attentive service. Bedrooms are spacious and up-to-the-minute and dining options include assorted Japanese cuisines and international fare. The Sakazuki bar serves 50 different varieties of sake and the stylish Crystal Piano bar on the top floor has stunning views.

RESTAURANTS/ 餐廳

Recommended/推薦		Also/其他
Yamazato/ 山里	✕✕✕	The Terrace/ 和庭

讓賓客遠離煩囂，正是澳門銀河渡假城內裝修典雅與品味並重的
大倉酒店。身穿日本和服的服務員為賓客提供親切貼心的服務，
設計時尚的酒店客房寬敞舒適，酒店設有提供日式及世界美食的
餐廳，其「清酒盃」酒吧提供５０多種清酒供賓客享用，而位於
酒店頂層的「水晶鋼琴」更讓賓客飽覽壯麗的景致。

■ ADDRESS/地址
TEL. 8883 8883
FAX. 8883 2345
Galaxy, Avenida Marginal Flor de Lotus,
Cotai
路氹城蓮花海濱大馬路澳門銀河渡假城
www.hotelokuramacau.com

■ ROOMS AND SUITES/客房及套房
Rooms/客房 ＝429
Suites/套房 ＝59

■ PRICE/價錢

🧍	MOP2,200-5,600
🧍🧍	MOP2,200-5,600
Suites/套房	MOP3,000-20,000
☕	MOP180

Pousada de Mong-Há
望廈迎賓館

Exquisite boutique hotel, built into the hillside on the foundations of a 17ᵗʰ century fort alongside traditional Portuguese villas. Atmospheric old steps lead from the entrance up to reception. By contrast, the interior is modern, chic and very stylish, with subdued taste the key. Guestrooms boast cool marble floors and rich colours and fabrics; all look onto the Straits of Macau. Discover the pool amongst charming little hillside terraces.

RESTAURANTS/ 餐廳

Recommended/推薦

Also/其他

IFT Educational Restaurant/
旅遊學院教學餐廳

這家超值的賓館由旅遊學院營運，位處寧靜的望廈山半山腰，
遠離娛樂場的煩囂，確是與眾不同。賓館被一個可愛的花園環繞
著，而接待處的學院學生則隨時為你服務。客房地方不大，尤其
是單人房，不過環境寧靜，並擁有亞洲設計風格。賓館的餐廳是
體驗澳門菜的好去處。

■ ADDRESS/地址
TEL. 2851 5222
FAX. 2855 6925
Colina de Mong-Há,
Rampe do Forte de Mong-Há
望廈山
www.iftedu.mo

■ ROOMS AND SUITES/客房及套房
Rooms/客房 ＝16
Suites/套房 ＝4
■ PRICE/價錢
♟   MOP600-1,100
♟♟   MOP600-1,100
Suites/套房 MOP1,100-1,500
☕   MOP120

Pousada de São Tiago
聖地牙哥古堡

Exquisite boutique hotel, built into the hillside on the foundations of a 17th century fort alongside traditional Portuguese villas. Atmospheric old steps lead from the entrance up to reception. By contrast, the interior is modern, chic and very stylish, with subdued taste the key. Guestrooms boast cool marble floors and rich colours and fabrics; all look onto the Straits of Macau. Discover the pool amongst charming little hillside terraces.

RESTAURANTS/ 餐廳

Recommended/推薦	Also/其他
La Paloma/ 芭朗瑪　　　✗✗	

這家座落於山腰的精品酒店，精緻優雅。由一座十七世紀的舊城堡改建而成，毗鄰傳統的葡式住宅。古樸的石階別具風情，拾級而上便可由入口到達接待處。酒店內部與外觀形成鮮明的對比，設計十分現代時尚，獨樹一格，卻不浮誇造作。客房採用大理石地板、鮮明的顏色和布質材料，品味非凡；所有客房都坐擁澳門內港的醉人景色。迷人的山腰陽台設有一個戶外泳池。

■ ADDRESS/地址
TEL. 2837 8111
FAX. 2855 2170
Avenida da República,
Fortaleza de São Tiago da Barra
西灣民國大馬路聖地牙哥大炮台
www.saotiago.com

■ ROOMS AND SUITES/客房及套房
Suites/套房 ＝12

■ PRICE/價錢
Suites/套房　MOP3,000-4,000
⛾　　　　　MOP121

Rocks
萊斯

Being part of the Fisherman's Wharf, this interesting seaside hotel's ambience is inspired by the Victorian era and has a lobby full of Victorian-style décor and furnishings including a fireplace, paintings and a large white marble staircase. A cosy terrace overlooks the bay, while relaxing bedrooms have a balcony and sea views. Of particular note...unlike most hotels, there's no casino here – just right for those who prefer the quieter side of Macau.

RESTAURANTS/ 餐廳

Recommended/推薦

Also/其他

Vic's Café/ 怡景

萊斯酒店座落於澳門漁人碼頭，海邊的醉人環境靈感來自維多利亞時期。酒店大堂佈滿富維多利亞風格的裝飾及傢俱，包括火爐、掛畫及大型白色雲石樓梯。舒適怡人的花園可盡收海灣醉人景致，設有海景露臺的臥室可讓你盡情放鬆身心。注意，和大部分酒店不同，這裡不設賭場，專為嚮往澳門寧靜一面的人士而設。

■ ADDRESS/地址

TEL. 2878 2782

FAX. 2870 8800

Macau Fisherman's Wharf

澳門漁人碼頭

www.rockshotel.com.mo

■ ROOMS AND SUITES/客房及套房

Rooms/客房 =66

Suites/套房 =6

■ PRICE/價錢

🚹	MOP1,880-2,880
🚹🚹	MOP1,880-2,880
Suites/套房	MOP4,080-6,660
☕	MOP130

Sands
金沙

This huge, bright gold building has a vast 'Sands' logo –
prime Las Vegas real estate relocated in Asia. The hotel,
with its own entrance and areas, is separate from the
casino, though dining on the mezzanine, overlooking three
vast gaming areas, resembles peering down onto a stock
exchange trading floor. The spacious lobby is of western
style, as are the bedrooms, which are all large and luxurious
suites; each has a sea or city view.

RESTAURANTS/ 餐廳

Recommended/推薦	Also/其他
	Copa/ 高雅
	Golden Court/ 金沙閣
	Perola/ 金帆船

這家龐大的金沙酒店，金色外牆閃閃發亮，並擁有巨型的「金沙」霓虹燈招牌，是拉斯維加斯博彩業鉅頭於亞洲營運的娛樂場酒店。酒店與娛樂場分開，設有獨立的入口和範圍，不過在夾樓用餐時，卻可俯瞰三個大型博彩廳，恰似觀看股交所會場一般！寬敞的大堂和客房均以西式設計，所有客房都是寬闊的豪華套房，更坐擁海景或城市美景。

■ ADDRESS/地址
TEL. 2888 3388
FAX. 2888 3377
203 Largo de Monte Carlo
蒙地卡羅前地203號
www.sands.com.mo

■ ROOMS AND SUITES/客房及套房
Rooms/客房 = 204
Suites/套房 = 34

■ PRICE/價錢
👤	MOP1,598-3,398
👥	MOP1,598-3,398
Suites/套房	MOP2,598-4,398
☕	MOP200

The Venetian
威尼斯人

You need a map to find your way round the largest integrated resort in Asia. It's based on Venice: third floor canals with singing gondoliers! Identikit luxury is assured in a towering bedroom skyscraper that has 3,000 capacious rooms. Opulent fakes are everywhere: frescoes, colonnades, sculptures. It's impossible to stay here without being swept along by hoards of gamblers. The Cirque de Soleil show, ZAIA, will be sure to take your breath away.

RESTAURANTS/ 餐廳

Recommended/推薦		Also/其他

Recommended/推薦			Also/其他
Canton/ 喜粵		✕✕✕	Morton's of Chicago
Lei Garden/ 利苑酒家	✿	✕✕	North/ 北方館
			Portofino

你需要一張地圖才能環遊全亞洲最大型的綜合度假酒店！概念源自威尼斯，三樓運河上的貢多拉船夫更會一邊掌船一邊唱歌！高聳而立的摩天大樓擁有三千間寬敞客房，同樣極盡奢華。壁畫、列柱、雕塑等均仿照原物而製，展露豪華氣派。置身於威尼斯人難免會到娛樂場一展身手。Cirque du Soleil®(太陽劇團™)ZAiA™肯定會讓你屏息。

■ ADDRESS/地址

TEL. 2882 8888

FAX. 2882 8889

Estrada da Baia de N. Senhora de Esperanca, s/n, The Cotai Strip, Taipa
氹仔路氹金光大道-望德聖母灣大馬路
www.venetianmacao.com

■ ROOMS AND SUITES/客房及套房

Rooms/客房 =2900
Suites/套房 =100

■ PRICE/價錢

👤	MOP1,500-2,100
👥	MOP1,500-2,100
Suites/套房	MOP2,500-3,500
🛏	MOP200

Wynn
永利

The Wynn's easy-on-the-eye curving glass façade is enhanced with a lake and dancing fountains, while the classically luxurious interior includes Murano glass chandeliers, plush carpets and ubiquitous marble. An attractively landscaped oasis pool forms the centrepiece to corridors lined with the top retail names. Bedrooms – classical but contemporary – display a considerable degree of taste. The Prosperity tree, meanwhile, is not easily forgotten...

RESTAURANTS/ 餐廳

Recommended/推薦			Also/其他
Il Teatro/ 帝雅廷		XXXX	Café Esplanada/ 咖啡苑
Okada/ 岡田		XX	Red 8/ 紅8
Wing Lei/ 永利軒	✿✿	XXXX	

永利的弧形玻璃外觀十分奪目，更設有表演湖及噴池。至於酒店內部則散發著經典的豪華氣息：穆拉諾穆玻璃吊燈、豪華的地毯，且觸目所及皆是大理石。走廊中心設有一個造形迷人的綠洲池，而兩旁則置滿名店。客房融合了經典和當代的風格設計，盡顯優越品味。此外，永利的吉祥樹更會令你印象深刻。

■ ADDRESS/地址
TEL. 2888 9966
FAX. 2832 9966
Rua Cidade de Sintra, Nape
外港新填海區仙德麗街
www.wynnmacau.com

■ ROOMS AND SUITES/客房及套房
Rooms/客房 ＝460
Suites/套房 ＝140

■ PRICE/價錢
👤	MOP3,500-3,700
👥	MOP3,500-3,700
Suites/套房	MOP7,800-35,000
☕	MOP178

MAPS
地圖

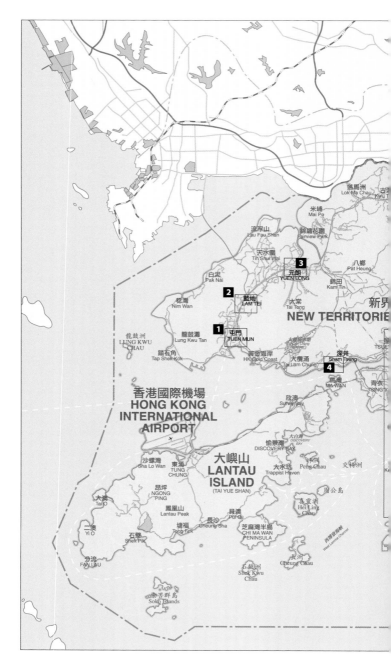

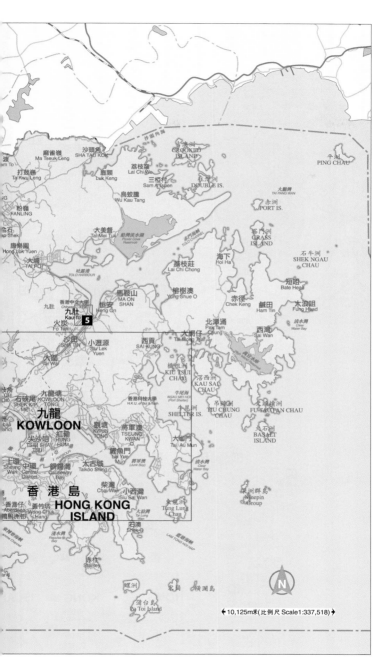

麻雀嶺 Ma Tseuk Leng
沙頭角 SHA TAU KOK
荔枝窩 Lai Chi Wo
鹿頸 Luk Keng
三椏村 Sam A Tsuen
烏蛟騰 Wu Kau Tang
吉澳洲 CROOKED ISLAND
往灣洲 DOUBLE IS.
平洲 PING CHAU
大鵬灣 TAI PANG WAN
赤洲 PORT IS.
茶果洲 GRASS ISLAND
石牛洲 SHEK NGAU CHAU

打鼓嶺 Ta Kwu Leng
粉嶺 FANLING
康樂園 Hong Lok Yuen
大埔 TAI PO
大美督 Tai Mei Tuk
船灣淡水湖 Plover Cove Reservoir
荔枝莊 Lai Chi Chong
海下 Hoi Ha

吐露港 TOLO HARBOUR
馬鞍山 MA ON SHAN
榕樹澳 Yong Shue O
赤徑 Chek Keng
短咀 Bate Head
鹹田 Ham Tin
大浪咀 Fung Head

香港中文大學 Chinese Univ. of HK
九肚 Kau To **5**
火炭 Fo Tan
梅安 Heng On
北潭涌 Pak Tam Chung
西灣 Sai Wan
清水灣 Clear Water Bay

沙田 SHA TIN
小瀝源 Siu Lek Yuen
西貢 SAI KUNG
大網仔 Tai Mong Tsai
大埔 Tai Wa
橋咀洲 KIU TSUI CHAU
滘西洲 KAU SAI CHAU

石硤尾 SHEK KIP MEI
九龍塘 KOWLOON TONG
香港科技大學 H.K.U. of Sci & Tech
牛尾洲 SHELTER IS.
吊鐘洲 JIN CHUNG CHAU
火石洲
伏頭門洲 FU TAU PAN CHAU

九龍 KOWLOON
尖沙咀 TSIM SHA TSUI
紅磡 HUNG HOM
觀塘 KWUN TONG
將軍澳 TSEUNG KWAN O
鯉魚門 Lei Yue Mun
大坳門 Tai Au Mun
火石洲 BASALT ISLAND

上環 Sheung Wan
中環 Central District
銅鑼灣 Causeway Bay
太古城 Taikoo Shing
柴灣 Chai Wan
將軍澳 Junk Bay
小西灣 Siu Sai Wan

香港島 HONG KONG ISLAND
香港仔 Aberdeen
黃竹坑 Wong Chuk Hang
大浪灣 Tung Lung Chau
果洲群島 Ninepin Group

淺水灣 Repulse Bay
赤柱 Stanley
石澳 Shek O

螺洲
家島
橫瀾島
蒲台島 Po Toi Island

←10,125m米(比例尺 Scale 1:337,518)→

N

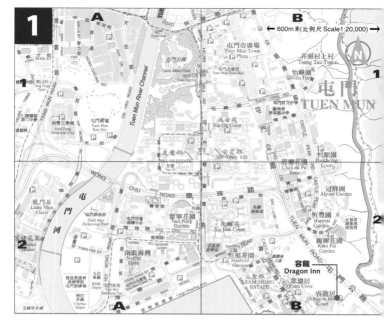

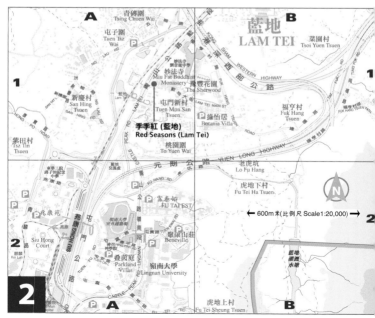

493

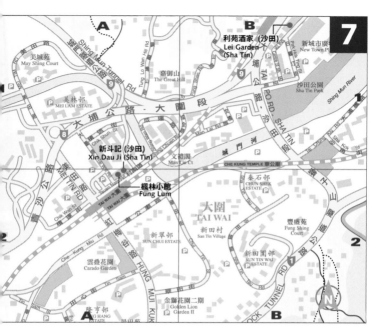

7

利苑酒家 (沙田)
Lei Garden
(Sha Tin)

新城市廣場
New Town Pl

美城苑
May Shing Court

嘉御山
The Great Hill

沙田公園
Sha Tin Park

城門河
Shing Mun River

美林邨
MEI LAM ESTATE

新斗記 (沙田)
Xin Dau Ji (Sha Tin)

文禮閣
Man Lai Ct

車公廟
Che Kung Temple

泰石邨
CHUN SHEK
ESTATE

楓林小館
Fung Lum

大圍
TAI WAI

豐盛苑
Fung Shing
Court

新翠邨
SUN CHUI ESTATE

新田村
San Tin Village

新田圍邨
SUN TIN WAI
ESTATE

雲疊花園
Carado Garden

金獅花園二期
Golden Lion
Garden II

隆亨邨
LUNG HANG
ESTATE

8

樂仁學校
Lok Yan School

首導小學
Good Counsel
Primary School

澤安邨
Chak On Est

南華中學
Nam Wa
Secondary School

蘇屋邨
So Uk Est

大坑東
Tai Hang
Tung

天主教善導小學
SKH Kei Oi
Primary School

李鄭屋游泳池
Lei Cheng Uk
Swimming Pool

坤記竹昇麵
Kwan Kee Bamboo Noodle

元洲邨
UN CHAU
ESTATE

李鄭屋邨
Lei Cheng Uk Estate

深水埗運動場
Sham Shui Po
Sports Ground

← 545m 米(比例尺 Scale 1:18,155) →

幸福邨
FORTUNE
EST

亞洲高球會
Asia Golf Club

嶺南同學會小學
Lingnan Alumni Association
Primary School

石硤尾邨
SHEK KIP
MEI EST

麗閣邨
LAI KOK
ESTATE

怡閣苑
Yee Kok
Court

劉森記麵家 (福榮街)
Lau Sum Kee
(Fuk Wing Street)

泰潮
Thai Chiu

譚仔雲南米線 (深水埗)
Tam's Yunnan Noodles
(Sham Shui Po)

深水埗公園
Sham Shui Po Park
Swimming Pool

麗安邨
LAI ON
ESTATE

容記小菜王
Yung Kee Siu Choi Wong

深水埗公園
Sham Shui Po
Park

添好運 (深水埗)
Tim Ho Wan
(Sham Shui Po)

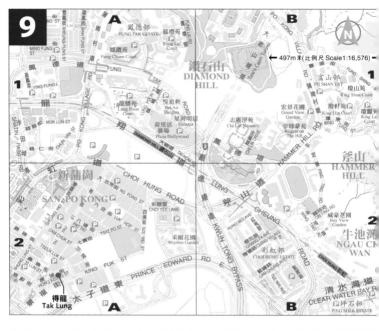

9

A | B

FUNG TAK ESTATE
福德邨
Fung Chuen Court
鳳鑽苑

鳳德邨

鑽石山
DIAMOND HILL

← 497m 米(比例尺 Scale1:16,576) →

富山邨
FU SHAN EST
瓊山苑
King Shan Court

龍蟠苑
Lung Poon Court

悦庭軒
Bel Air Heights
星河明居
Galaxia

宏景花園
Grand View Garden
瓊軒苑
King Hin Court

瓊麗苑
King L
Court

志蓮淨苑
Chi Lin Nunnery

帝峰豪苑
Regent on The Hill

荷里活廣場
Plaza Hollywood

HAMMER HILL
斧山

CHOI HUNG ROAD

新蒲崗
SAN PO KONG

彩頤里
CHOI YEE LANE

采頤花園
Rhythm Garden

彩虹邨
CHOI HUNG ESTATE

威豪花園
Bay View Garden

牛池灣
NGAU C
WAN

KING FUK ST

PRINCE EDWARD RD

太子道東

得龍
Tak Lung

清水灣道
CLEAR WATER BAY

坪石邨
PING SHEK ESTATE

A | **B**

7

彩盈
Choi Ying

九龍灣園泳場
Kowloon Bay Sports Ground

朱石樓中學
Chu Shek Lun Secondary School

KAI LOK RD

KAI SHUN ROAD

啟業街
KAI WAH ST
啟信道

啟祥道 KAI CHEUNG RD

牛頭角
Am
Gard

國際展貿中心
Hong Kong International Trade & Exhibition Centre

HING STREET

九龍巴士公司
九龍灣車廠
KMB Depot

翡翠拉麵小籠包 (九龍灣)
Crystal Jade La Mian Xiao Long Bao (Kowloon Bay)

利苑酒家 (九龍灣)
Lei Garden (Kowloon Bay)

正斗粥麵專家 (九龍灣)
Tasty (Kowloon Bay)

牛頭角
LOWER NGAU
TAU KOK EST

上海小南國 (九龍灣)
Shanghai Xiao Nan Guo (Kowloon Bay)

肇順名滙鮮專門店
Siu Shun Village Cuisine

九龍灣
KOWLOON BAY

德福廣場
Telford PLAZA II

Mega Box

建造業議會訓練學院
九龍灣訓練中心
CITA Kowloon Bay Training Centre

牛頭角
NGAU TAU KOK

← 449m 米(比例尺 Scale1:14,981) →

10

A | **B**

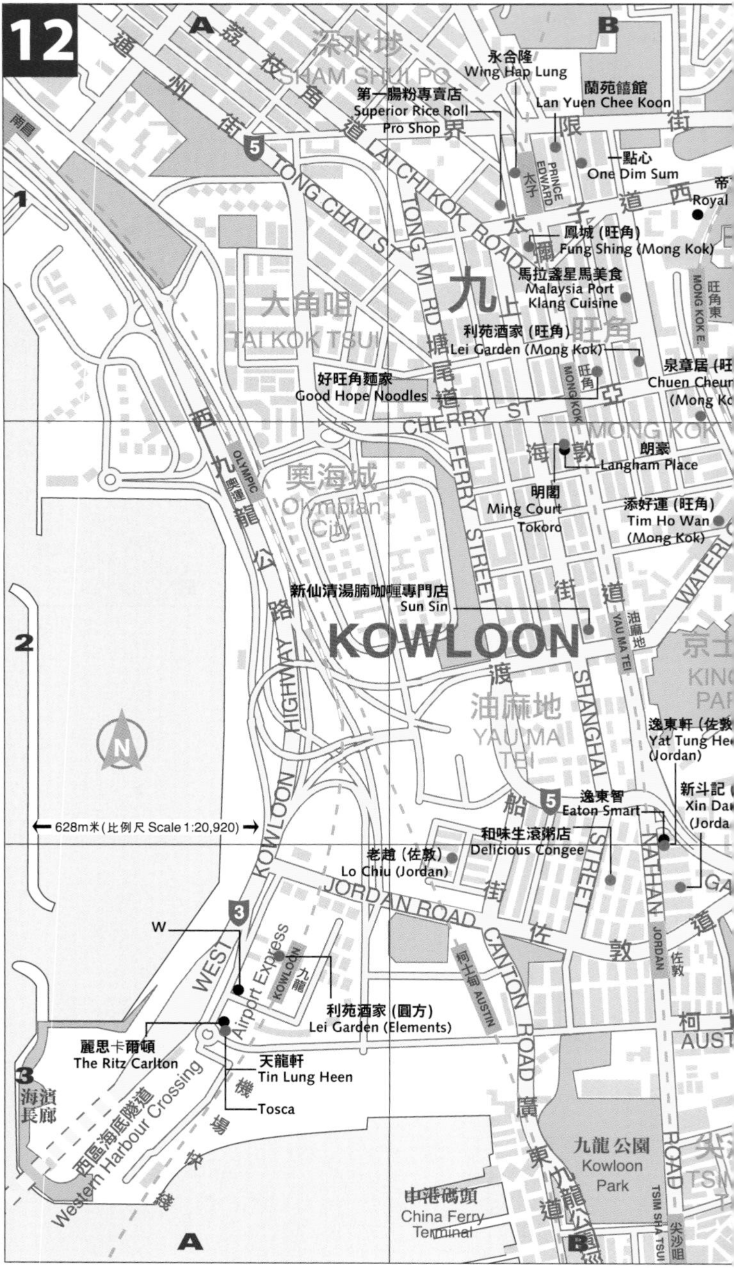

12
A
B
深水埗
SHAM SHUI PO
永合隆
Wing Hap Lung
蘭苑饎館
Lan Yuen Chee Koon
第一腸粉專賣店
Superior Rice Roll Pro Shop
一點心
One Dim Sum
Royal
鳳城 (旺角)
Fung Shing (Mong Kok)
馬拉盞星馬美食
Malaysia Port Klang Cuisine
利苑酒家 (旺角)
Lei Garden (Mong Kok)
泉章居 (旺
Chuen Cheun
(Mong Ko
好旺角麵家
Good Hope Noodles
朗豪
Langham Place
明閣
Ming Court
Tokoro
添好運 (旺角)
Tim Ho Wan (Mong Kok)
新仙清湯腩咖喱專門店
Sun Sin
大角咀
TAI KOK TSUI
奧海城
Olympian City
KOWLOON
油麻地
YAU MA TEI
逸東軒 (佐敦
Yat Tung He
(Jordan)
新斗記
Xin Da
(Jorda
逸東智
Eaton Smart
和味生滾粥店
Delicious Congee
老趙 (佐敦)
Lo Chiu (Jordan)
628m米 (比例尺 Scale 1:20,920)
W
利苑酒家 (圓方)
Lei Garden (Elements)
麗思卡爾頓
The Ritz Carlton
天龍軒
Tin Lung Heen
Tosca
海濱長廊
西區海底隧道
Western Harbour Crossing
Airport Express
九龍公園
Kowloon Park
中港碼頭
China Ferry Terminal
TONG CHAU ST
LAI CHI KOK ROAD
TONG MI RD
CHERRY ST
FERRY STREET
SHANGHAI STREET
NATHAN ROAD
JORDAN ROAD
CANTON ROAD
WEST KOWLOON HIGHWAY
OLYMPIC
PRINCE EDWARD
MONG KOK
MONG KOK E.
YAU MA TEI
JORDAN
AUSTIN
TSIM SHA TSUI

14

A | B

AUSTIN RD W 柯士甸道西

避風塘興記
Hing Kee

港景峯
The Victoria
Towers

港景峯
HK Scout Ctr

尖沙咀警署
Tsim Sha Tsui
Police Station

老趙 (尖沙咀
Lo Chiu
(Tsim Sha T

1

九龍公園
游泳池
Swimming Pool
Sports Centre

富豪 (尖沙咀)
Fu Ho (Tsim Sha Tsui)

新同樂
Sun Tung Lok

國金軒 (The Mira)
Cuisine Cuisine at The Mira

Whisk

The

九龍公園

China Ferry Terminal
中港客運碼頭

Fandango

香港文物探知館
HK Heritage
Discovery Ctr.

KOWLOON PARK

翡翠拉麵小籠包 (尖沙咀)
Crystal Jade La Mian
Xiao Long Bao (TST)

清真寺
Jamia Masjid
Islamic Centre

HAIPHONG RD

爵樂
Gaylord

鼎泰豐 (尖沙咀)
Din Tai Fung (Tsim Sha Tsui)

Silvercord
新港中心

一風堂
Ippudo

2

世界商業中心
World Comm
Centre

亞太中心
ASHLEY RD

國際
廣場
iSquare

新文娛中心
New T&T Centre

利寶太陽廣場
Lippo Sun Plaza

朗廷
The Langham

唐閣
T'ang Court

海岸中心
Ocean
Centre

北京道一號
1 Peking Rd

阿一海景飯店
Ah Yat Harbour

美岸海鮮舫
The Bostonian

南海一號
Nanhai No.1

夜上海 (九龍)
Yè Shanghai (Kowloon)

海運大廈
Ocean Terminal

Hullett House

隆濤院
Loong Toh Yuen

半島
The Peninsula

St. George

Al Molo

芽莊 (尖沙咀)
Nha Trang (Tsim Sha Tsui)

BLT Steak

星光行
Star House

北京樓 (九龍)
Peking Garden
(Kowloon)

瑞樵閣
Chesa

香港太空館
HK Space Museum

香港文化中心
HK Cultural Centre

Felix

吉地士
Gaddi's

旅客諮詢中心
Visitor Info Centre

鐘樓
Clock
Tower

嘉麟樓
Spring Moon

香港藝術
HK Museum

3

往中環
To Central

天星碼頭
Star Ferry Pier

往灣仔
To Wan Chai

九龍公眾碼頭
Kowloon Public Pier

尖沙咀
TSIM SHA TSUI

N

← 250m米 (比例尺 Scale 1:8,333) →

A | B

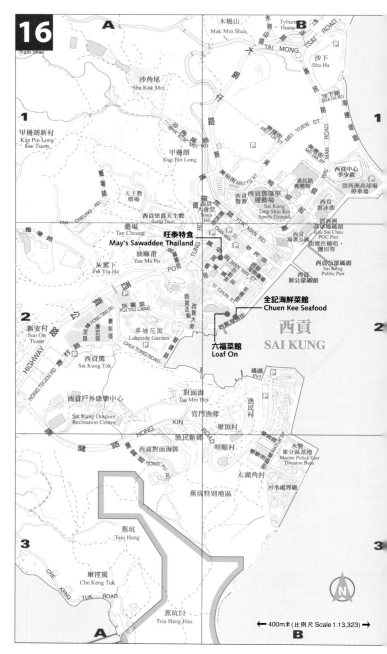

A B

木棉山
Muk Min Shan

Tyburn
House

沙下
Sha Ha

南山
Nam Shan

沙角尾
Sha Kok Mei

甲邊朗新村
Kap Pin Long
San Tsuen

1

甲邊朗
Kap Pin Long

天主教
墳場

西貢崇真天主教
Sung Tsun

灰窰下
Fui Yiu Ha

油麻莆
Yau Ma Po

旺泰特食
May's Sawaddee Thailand

西貢鄧肇堅
運動場
Sai Kung
Tang Shiu Kin
Sports Ground

西貢
游泳池

西貢警署

西貢大會堂
Town Hall

西貢中心
李少欽

沙西洲高球場
停車場

西貢公眾碼頭
滘西洲
蠔涌碼頭福頭
街渡往橋咀，
鹽田等

滘西洲
PGC Pier
西貢公眾碼頭
Sai Keng
Public Pier

西貢
新公眾碼頭

新安村
Sun On
Tsuen

翠塘花園
Lakeside Garden

西貢篤
Sai Kung Tuk

六福菜館
Loaf On

全記海鮮菜館
Chuen Kee Seafood

西貢
SAI KUNG

2

碼頭
Pier

對面海
Tui Min Hoi

官門漁邨

漁民村

水警
東分區基地
Marine Police East
Division Base

西貢戶外康樂中心
Sai Kung Outdoor
Recreation Centre

渻民新邨

明順村

太湖角村

污水處理廠

蕉坑特別地區

蕉坑
Tsiu Hang

3

蕉徑篤
Che Keng Tuk

蕉坑口
Tsiu Hang Hau

N

← 400m米(比例尺 Scale 1:13,323) →

A B

502

礼頓山
Leighton Hill

加路連山
CAROLINE HILL

掃桿埔運動場
SO KON PO
RECREATION GROUND

南華體育會運動場
SOUTH CHINA ATHLETIC
AKSN STADIUM

印度遊樂會

連
道

加
路
連
山
道

東院道
EASTERN
HOSPITAL ROAD

CAROLINE HILL ROAD

LEIGHTON ROAD

樂
善
道

WONG NAI CHUNG ROAD

BROADWOOD RD

HAPPY VIEW TERRACE

聖馬加利教堂
St Margaret's

樂活道

孔聖堂
Confucius
Hall

奧運大樓
Olympic House

比華利山
Beverly Hill

古
道

World
Building

黃
泥
涌
道

聖保祿
天主教

聖保祿
中學

樂翠台
Villa Rocha

香港大球場
HONG KONG
STADIUM

跑馬地
Happy Race Track

HAPPY VALLEY
RECREATION GROUND

St.Paul's
Sec Sch

香港三育
中學

雲地利台

道

掃桿埔
SO KON PO

← 234m/米(比例尺 Scale 1:7,463) →

樂陶苑
Villa Lotto

VENTRIS ROAD

跑馬地
HAPPY VALLEY

BROADWOOD ROAD

譚公廟

養和醫院
I.K. Sanatorium
& Hospital

正斗粥麵專家（跑馬地）
Tasty (Happy Valley)

奕蔭街 YIK YAM ST

景光街

KING KWONG ST

毓秀街

奕蔭街

YUK SAU ST

業平街

HO WO LANE

駿景
台
Valley
View
Terr

BLUE POOL ROAD

永安街

TSUN YUEN ST

山村道

晉源街

SHIN WING KAI

VILLAGE

RD 山村道

TSU MAN ST

譽滿坊
Dim Sum

景平街

成和道

SING WOO ROAD

鳳輝台 FUNG FAI TERR

聚文街

山光苑
Shan Kwong
Towers

猶太墳場
JEWISH
CEMETERY

KWAI FONG ST

跑馬地
警署

藍塘別墅
Villa
Monte Rosa

駿景軒
Golden Valley

VILLAGE TERR

山光道
SHAN KWONG ROAD

東蓮
覺苑

成和道

SING WOO CRESCENT

STUBBS ROAD

司
徒
拔
道

賽馬會
體育綜合大樓

冬青道 HOLLY RD

玫瑰新邨
Villa Monte Rosa

賽馬會會所
Jockey Club
Clubhouse

HAWTHORN RD

箕璉坊
GREEN LANE

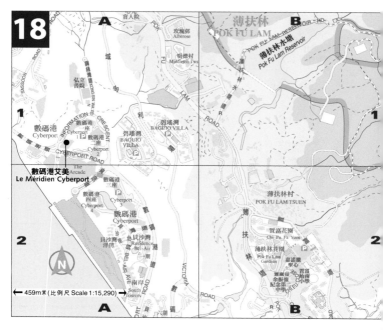

18

首人院

玫瑰邨
Alberose

閩德村
Middleton Tws

薄扶林
POK FU LAM

薄扶林水塘
Pok Fu Lam Reservoir

弘立書院
GONGSUM RD

CRESCENT

INFORMATION

數碼港
Cyberport

數碼港一座
Cyberport 1

數碼港二座
Cyberport 2

利

碧瑤灣
BAGUIO VILLA

CYBERPORT ROAD

The Arcade

數碼港艾美
Le Méridien Cyberport

數碼港三座
Cyberport 3

數碼港四座
Cyberport 4

薄扶林村
POK FU LAM TSUEN

數碼港
Cyberport

貝沙灣
Residence Bel-Air

薄扶林

薄扶林道
VICTORIA ROAD

賢富花園
Chi Fu Fa Yuen

薄扶林花園
Pok Fu Lam Gardens

嘉富麗苑
余服強紀念第
中學

BEL-AIR AVE

South Towers

← 459m米 (比例尺 Scale 1:15,290) →

19

← 230m米 (比例尺 Scale 1:7,692) →

堅尼地城
KENNEDY TOWN

城西道 SHING SAI RD

卑路乍灣公園
Belcher Bay Park

利瑪竇宿
Ricci Hall

堅尼地城新海旁 KENNEDY TOWN NEW PRAYA

堅尼地城海旁
KENNEDY TOWN PRAYA

Bistronomique

吉席街 CATCHICK ST

BELCHER'S ST

TAI PAK ST

士美非路 HAU WO ST

科士街 FORBES ST

ROCK HILL ST 石山街

CADOGAN STREET

DAVIS ST

SMITHFIELD

KWAN NICK ST

NORTH ST

CHING UN TERR

TO LI TERRACE

士美非路
市政大廈

POKFIELD ROAD

堅尼地城
(建築中)
Under Contruction

蒲飛路 P.
POKFIELD P.

薄扶林道
POK FU LAM RD

港大
聖約翰
學院

西環邨
SAI WAN EST

觀龍樓
KWUN LUNG LAU

聖嘉祿
St. Charles

賴廉士
體育中心

何世光夫人
體育中心

504

1號碼頭 Pier 1

Caprice

龍景軒
Lung King Heen

往珀麗灣
To Park Island

2號碼頭
Pier 2

往愉景灣
To Discovery Bay

3號碼頭
Pier 3

4號碼頭
Pier 4

往梅窩
To Mui Wo

5號碼頭
Pier 5

往長洲
To Cheung Chau

6號碼頭
Pier 6

往坪洲
To Peng Chau

往梅窩
To Mui Wo

7號碼頭
Pier 7

往尖沙咀

四季
Four Seasons

Agnès b. Le Pain Grille (Central)

Bettys Kitschen

天星碼頭
Star Ferry Pier

國金軒 (國際金融中心)
Cuisine Cuisine (IFC)

利苑酒家 (國際金融中心)
Lei Garden (IFC)

正斗粥麵專家 (國際金融中心)
Tasty (IFC)

香港站停車場

國際金融中心商場
IFC Mall

國際金融中心一期
Intern'l Finance
Ctr 一期

麥奀記(忠記)麵家（永吉街）
Mak An Kee Noodle
(Wing Kut Street)

國際金融中心二期
Two International
Finance
Centre

中環中心
The Center

Brass'

23

交易廣場
Exchange²
Square

郵政總局
General Post Office

翠玉軒
The Square

文華扒房+酒吧
Mandarin Grill + Bar

文華廳
Man Wah

Pierre

文華東方
Mandarin Oriental

CONNAUGHT RD C

8½ Otto e Mezzo - Bombana

北京樓 (中環)
Peking Garden (Central)

Dot Cod

Zuma

L'Atelier de
Joël Robuchon

CENTRAL

Amber

置地文華東方
The Landmark
Mandarin Oriental

港島廳
Island Tang

終審法院
Court of Final
Appeal

長江集團中心
Cheung Kong
Center

507

A   B

N

← 236m米 (比例尺 Scale 1:7,851) →

1

博覽海濱花園
Expo Promenade

金
Golden Bauh

香港會議展覽中心新翼
HKCEC New Wing
貿易發展局
TDC Business Inf

博覽道中 EXPO DRIVE CE

滿福
Dyn

Grand Hyatt Steakhouse
Grissini
港灣壹號
One Harbour Road

君悅
Grand Hyatt

會議道

分域碼頭
Fenwick Pier

CONVENTIC

香港會議展覽中心
HK Convention &
Exhibition Centre

(往中環入口)

LUNG KING ST.

分域碼頭街

港

中信大廈
Citic Tower

紅十字會
總部
HK Red Cross
Headquarters

香港演藝學院
HK Academy
for Performing Arts

香港
藝術中心
Art Centre

瑞安中心
Shui On Centre

灣仔政府大廈
Wanchai
Tower

灣仔
消防局

港灣
消防局

入境事
務大廈
Immigration
Tower

中
Centr

電訊大廈
Telecom House

稅務大樓
Revenue
Tower

夏慤道

告 士 打 道

2
夏慤花園
Harcourt Garden

堅偉樓
Caine House

美國萬通大廈
Miss Manuel Tower

夏慤大廈
Harcourt House

東亞銀行
港灣中心
Bank of
East Asia

GLO

大
Fin

警政大樓
Arsenal House

警察總部
Police Headquarters

車氏粵菜軒
Che's

留園雅敘
Liu Yuan Pavilion
Uno Más

祥記飯店
Cheung Kee

莎巴
Sabah

警政大樓東翼
Arsenal House
East Wing

熙信
Asian

永華雲吞麵家
Wing Wah

中國海外

灣仔 WAN CHA

QUEENSWAY

囍宴 甜·藝
Xi Yan Sweets

福臨門 (灣仔)
Fook Lam Moon (Wan Chai)

修
Southorn Playground

修頓中心
Southorn
Centre

修頓體育館
Southorn Stadium

蝦麵店
Prawn Noodle Shop

Madam Sixty Ate

Cépage

Bo Innovation

一碗麵 (聖佛蘭士街)
Olala (St. Francis Street)

新九記粥麵
Sun Kau Kee Noodle Shop

洪聖廟

KENNEDY

ROAD

St. Francis' Canossian
嘉諾撒聖方濟各書院

3
寶雲道
Bowen

BOWEN DRIVE

BOWEN ROAD

道

QUEEN'S

和忠大廈
Wu Chung Hse

香港
國藝波
育科

黃泥台 FUNG WONG YERT

A   B

灣仔渡輪碼頭
Wan Chai Ferry Pier

HUNG HING ROAD 鴻興道

MARSH ROAD 馬師道

WAN SPRING ST 永盛街

鳳東軒 (灣仔)
at Tung Heen (Wan Chai)

港灣道
體育館
Wan Chai
Swimming Pool

TONNOCHY ROAD 杜老誌道

灣仔運動場
WAN CHAI
SPORTS GROUND

馬師道

港灣
ROAD

海港中心
Harbour Centre

HARBOUR
CENTRE

HARBOUR ROAD

伊利莎伯大廈
Elizabeth House

香港
會議展覽
中心
HK
Exhibition
Centre

灣景花園

華潤大廈
China Resources
Building

灣仔中心
大廈
Sun Hung
Kai Centre

新鴻基
中心
Sun Hung
Kai Centre

崇光

菲
The Fleming 芬名

HARBOUR DRIVE 港灣徑

ROAD

HARBOUR ROAD 港灣道

告士打道 GLOUCESTER ROAD

軒鯉詩道

ROAD

菲林明道

灣仔警署
Wanchai
Police Station

ROAD

駱克道

謝斐道

編寧中心
AXA Centre

King's 皇子
王子

富聲 (灣仔)
Fu Sing (Wan Chai)

WEST 東美

CANAL ROAD EAST 堅拿道東

再興
Joi Hing

靠得住
Trusty Congee King

HENNESSY ROAD 軒尼詩道

利苑酒家 (灣仔)
Lei Garden (Wan Chai)

強記飯店 (灣仔)
Keung Kee Meat Shop
(Wan Chai)

SHARP ST. W. 霎西街

CANAL 堅拿道

Wooloomooloo Steakhouse
(Wan Chai)

Mirror

伊利
中心

聖雅各褔群會
圖書館

LEIGHTON

BENNINGTON 邊寧頓街

杭州酒家
Hong Zhou

WAN CHAI ROAD 灣仔道

美味廚
Megan's Kitchen

鄧肇堅
維多利亞官立中學

摩理臣山游泳池
Morrison Hill
Swimming Pool

摩理臣山
MORRISON HILL

SPORTS RD

KWAN 教利道

翡翠拉麵小籠包 (灣仔)
Crystal Jade La Mian Xiao
Long Bao (Wan Chai)

CROSS LANE 交加街

WOODAN RD

香港專業
教育學院

摩理臣山
分校

聖公會鄧肇堅中學
SKH Tang Shiu Kin

馬會總部
HKJC
Headquarters

灣仔
WAN CHAI

賽馬會
假道花園

Wan Chai Park 灣仔公園

東院
李陞小學

鄧肇堅醫院
社區健康中心

伊利沙伯
體育館
QE Stadium

皇后大道東 QUEEN'S ROAD EAST

HAU TAK LANE 厚德里

賽馬博物館
Racing Museum

香港足球會球場
HKFC Soccer/Rugby Field

EAST 東
循道衛理
Methodist
Church

KENNEDY RD 堅尼地道

香港華仁書院
Wah Yan Coll, HK

AIA
友邦大廈

入口
Stands

義井入口

高主教書院
小學部

回教墳場
MUSLIM CEMETERY

黃泥涌道

C D

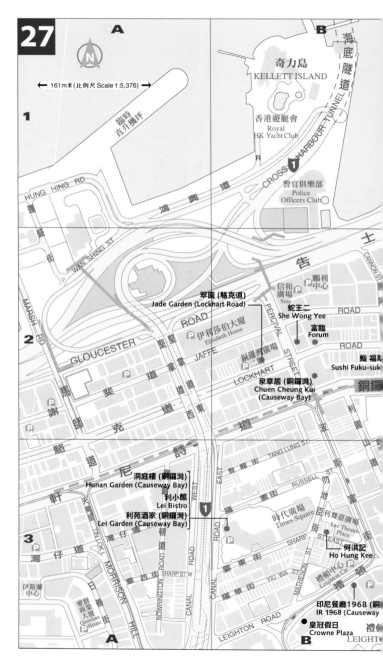

← 161m米 (比例尺 Scale 1:5,376) →

A

B

海底隧道

奇力島
KELLETT ISLAND

臨時直升機坪

香港遊艇會
Royal
HK Yacht Club

HUNG HING RD
鴻興道

蓮臨街

MARSH RD
馬師道

CROSS HARBOUR TUNNEL

警官俱樂部
Police
Officers Club

1

WAN SHING ST

告士

CANNON ST

翠園 (駱克道)
Jade Garden (Lockhart Road)

信和廣場
Sino

鵬利中心

蛇王二
She Wong Yee

GLOUCESTER ROAD
堅拿道

伊利莎伯大廈
Elizabeth House

銅鑼灣廣場

JAFFE
謝斐道

LOCKHART
駱克道

富臨
Forum

ROAD

鮨 福助
Sushi Fuku-suk

2

泉章居 (銅鑼灣)
Chuen Cheung Kui
(Causeway Bay)

銅鑼

PERCIVAL STREET

駱克道

尼詩道

軒尼詩道

MORRISON HILL

洞庭樓 (銅鑼灣)
Hunan Garden (Causeway Bay)

利小館
Lei Bistro

利苑酒家 (銅鑼灣)
Lei Garden (Causeway Bay)

EAST

TANG LUNG ST

RUSSELL ST

登龍街

時代廣場
Times Square

利舞臺廣場
Lee Theatre
Plaza

何洪記
Ho Hung Kee

3

伊斯蘭中心

BOWRINGTON ROAD

灣仔道

CANAL ROAD

SHARP ST W

ST EAST

SHARP

禮頓中心
Leighton Ctr

愛群商業大廈
Guardian House

菲林明道

CANAL ROAD

堅拿道東

YIU WA ST

MATHESON ST

羅素街

利園

印尼餐廳1968 (銅
IR 1968 (Causeway

皇冠假日
Crowne Plaza

禮頓

LEIGHTON ROAD

LEIGHT

A

B

銅鑼灣避風塘
Causeway Bay
Typhoon Shelter

C **D** **28**

VICTORIA PARK ROAD

維多利亞公園
VICTORIA PARK

1

園 4 道

打

士

道

加路連道 HOUSTON
廣播道 ALDEALNO ST

PATERSON ST

KINGSTON STREET

京士頓街

打

士

道

銅 鑼 灣
CAUSEWAY BAY

海南少爺 (銅鑼灣)
Hainan Shaoye
(Causeway Bay)

百德
大廈

三越城新

珠城大廈
Pearl City
Mansion

記利佐治街 GLOUCESTER

GREAT GEORGE ST

皇室大廈
Windsor House

CAUSEWAY BAY

威 道

2

心
ont Ctr

SEWAY BAY

怡 和 街

香港大廈

恒隆
中心
Hang Lung

鼎泰豐 (銅鑼灣)
Din Tai Fung (Causeway Bay)
富榮 (銅鑼灣)
Fu Sing (Causeway Bay)

京業
中心

客家爺爺 (銅鑼灣)
Hakka Yé Yé
(Causeway Bay)

JARDINE'S CRESCENT

YEE WO ST

樂賓
大廈

百德新街
Palibury

富豪金殿
Regal Palace

TUNG LO WAN RD

聖馬利
亞堂

宏利保險大廈

LAN FONG RD

The Drawing
Room

伊榮街 IRVING

敬誠街
PENNINGTON

Jia

Lanson Place 聖保祿學校
St. Paul's Convent
School

何東
中學

KA NING PATH

HYSAN AVE

新寧
大廈

YUN PING RD

LEIGHTON

聖保祿醫院
St Paul's Hospital

COTTON PATH

何東
分校

3

Mist

竹寿司
hi Ta-ke
飯堂
Fan Tang

SUNNING RD

HOI PING RD

禮頓

嘉路

黑園
Farm House
雪園 (銅鑼灣)
Snow Garden (Causeway Bay)

郵政
總局

路政署
港島區

HAVEN ST

連山道

聖保祿修院

紀律人員體育
及康樂會

保良局
Po Leung Kuk

C **D**

A

B

北角
NORTH POINT

← 313米(比例尺 Scale 1:10,417) →

1

北角渡輪碼頭
North Point Ferry Pier

維多利亞港
VICTORIA HARBOUR

阿鴻小吃
Hung's Delicacies

華順越南餐廳
Café Hué

利苑酒家 (北角)
Lei Garden (North Point)

喫Yuè

港島海逸君綽
Harbour Grand Hong Kong

城市花園
City Garden

2

君綽軒
Kwan Cheuk Heen Le 188°

海峰園
Harbour Heights

香港樹仁大學
Shue Yan University

留家廚房
Kin's Kitchen

石記廚房
Shek Kee Kitchen

華姐清湯腩
Sister Wah

3

維多利亞公園
VICTORIA PARK

銅鑼灣維景 ●
Metropark (Causeway Bay)

A

B

北角海逸
Harbour Plaza North Point

嘉頭
Pier

4

東
East

品汽車
輪碼頭

廊
IMMEAMSEMENT

C

嘉華國際
K. Wah
Cen

柯達大廈
Kodak (一期)
House

健康
中
心
大
楼

消防
東街

北角政府
合署
North Point
Gov't Offices

北角雲景暨
警察總署
東區總部

東港中心
Eastern
Harbour
Centre

鰂魚涌公園
(第二期)
Quarry Bay
Park II

HO
CHAK
ST

MAIN HONG CONG

JAVA ROAD

水務署
香港及離島分處

禮中華
中華
NATION ST

樂基
中心
NATION
MUI RD

JAVA

KING'S

健泰村

模範邨
MODEL
HOUSING
EST

MARBLE ROAD

健威花園
Healthy Gardens

港灣城
Tiger Plus

港
丹

健康中街
HEALTHY ST C

北角邮政
北角邮政

新都城
道

P

ROAD

KUN HONG RD

富榮花園
Full Wealth
Gardens

健康中街
HEALTHY ST W

HEALTHY VILLAGE

賽馬台
Braemar Terr

MODEL

北立
官立

華信花園
Wah Shun
Gardens

TANNER

丹拿花園
Tanner Garden

百福花園
Bedford Gardens

K YUEN ST

QUARRY BAY

TEMPLE RD

天后

PAK

FUK

QUARRY BAY

HAU

賽馬山花園
Pacific Palisades

寶馬山

R

壇峰園
Kingsford
Garden

培僑
中學
Pui Kiu
Mid Sch

蕙雅閣
Wilshire
Tws

大潭郊野公園

蘇浙公學
Kiangsu-
Chekiang
College

賽西湖公園
Choi Sai Woo Park

賽西湖大廈

2

Braemar Hill Mansion

寶馬山
BRAEMAR HILL

馬

理

(鰂魚涌擴建部份)

BRAEMAR HILL ROAD

P

RIDE

CECIL

SIR

東
區
自
然

第

段

聖貞德
St. Joan of Arc
Sec Sch

3

C

D

515

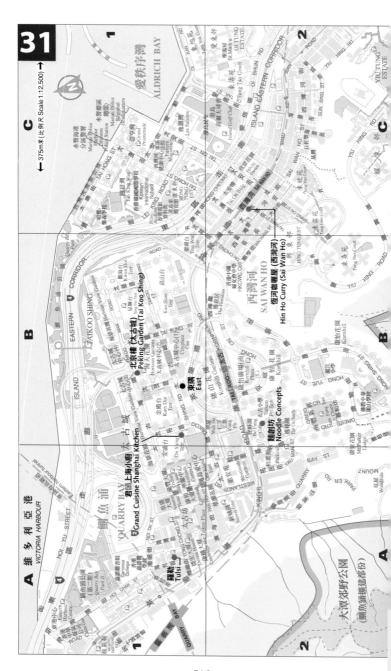

筲箕灣避風塘
Shau Kei Wan Typhoon Shelter

香港海防博物館

魚類批發市場
Fish Wholesale Market

愛秩序灣
ALDRICH BAY

東旭苑
Tung Yuk Court

聖馬可
St.Mark's

愛秩序灣海濱花園

愛秩序灣官立中學

阿公岩
A Kung Ngam

愛東邨
OI TUNG ESTATE

愛蝶灣
Aldrich Garden

安利
On Lee

Idrich Bay Promenade

ALDRICH BAY RD

EASTERN CORRIDOR

恆河咖喱屋 (筲箕灣)
Hin Ho Curry (Shau Kei Wan)

筲箕灣 SHAU KEI WAN

明
華
大
廈

Perfect Mount

愛秩序灣遊樂場

金華街 KAM WA

工廠街 FACTORY ST

筲箕灣中心

工廠街遊樂場

Elsa High Sch Kellett

MING WAH DAI HA

NAM HONG ST

YIU HING RD

耀東邨
IU TUNG ESTATE

東盛苑
Tung Shing Court

民街 NGOI MAN ST

SHAU KEI WAN ROAD

柴灣道 CHAI WAN ROAD

鵬志會梁李秀娛

慈幼 Salesian School

慈幼會修院

聖馬可
St. Mark's

筲箕灣
SHAU KEI WAN

← 242m米 (比例尺 Scale 1:8,064) →

MACAU

澳門

1

關閘邊檢大樓
Border Gate
Frontier Post
關閘
Border
Gate
關運動場

澳門特警總部

馬路北大賽馬路 A. NORTE DO HIPÓDROMO 友誼大賽馬路

馬場
Hipódromo

市場街
常澄公園

RUA CENTRAL DA AREIA PRETA

環宇天下
La Cité

友誼圓形廣場

AVENIDA DA PONTE DA AMIZADE

海名居
La Baie Du
Noble

黑沙環
填海區

廣福女花園
Jardim
Kong Fok On

廣福祥花園
Jardim
Kong Fok
Chéong

RUA DE MAIO

建華大廈
Kin Wa

保利達
Polytec
Garden

保利達花園
Polytec
Garden

2

ISTMO DE FERREIRA DO AMARAL

礪峰廟
孫館

望廈山
市政公園
g Há
ress
ra

望廈迎賓館
usada de Mong-Há
a
on
Tam
mple

Mong Ha

金海山花園
Kam Hoi San

廣華新邨
Kwong Wa

黑
沙
環

RUA NOVA DA AREIA PRETA

海濱花園
Hoi Pan
Garden

南粵新村
San Chun

東華新邨
Tong Wa
San Chun

廣華新邨
Kwong Wa

新谷花園
Jardins Sun
Yick

Mong Ha Sun
Chuen

八達新村
Pat Tat San
Chuen

福海花園

AVENIDA DO CORONEL MESQUITA

普濟禪院
(觀音堂)

望廈新邨
望廈墳場

觀音廟公園

AVENIDA DO OUVIDOR ARRIAGA

AVENIDA DE VENCESLAU

E. MARGINAL DA AREIA PRETA

A. DE MAIO

AVENIDA DO DR. FRANCISCO VIEIRA MACHADO

AVENIDA DA AMIZADE

沙 環
Areia Preta

南華新邨
Nam Wa
San Chun

馬交石
AVENIDA DO DR.

RUA DOS PESCADORES
漁翁街

馬交石炮台斜路

望洋石
炮台斜路

河邊新街

通訊博物館
ESTRADA DE D. MARIA

治安警察廳

友誼大橋 FRIENDSHIP BRIDGE

蘭圜
Lan
Un
an Un
tel

AVENIDA DO

Reservoir
貯 水 塘

3

國父紀念館
Mem. of
Dr. Sun

松山及
松山纜車
Cable
Car

GUIA

AVENIDA DE CAGILHAS

RODRIGUES

看台 GrandPrix Control
Tower
賽車看台

東望洋山
Guia Hill

DE RODRIGUES

新八佰伴

ESTRADA DO

外港客運
碼頭
Macau Ferry
Terminal

東望洋燈塔
Guia
Lighthouse
東望洋聖母雪地殿教堂

東望洋炮台
Guia Fortress

海角馬路

唐城
Tang Dynasty

港澳直昇機坪
Heliport
Platform

澳門綜藝館
Macau Forum

大賽車及
葡萄酒博
物館
Grand
Prix &
Wine
Museum

逸世蓮花
Lotus
Monument

東西匯泉
East Meets
West

火山

外 港
Outer Harbour

東方拱門

新 口 岸
澳門博物館大馬路

35

A   B

RUA DO ALMIRANTE SÉRGIO
PEREIRA MARQUES
RUA DO ALMIRANTE LOURENÇO

何東圖書館
聖若瑟修院

大馬路 A DA PRAIA GRANDE
亞利鴉士大馬路

1

下環

Praia de Manduco

海灣
Litoral

RUA DO

媽閣
Barra

南灣湖
Nam Van Lake

REPÚBLICA
A DA

何

AVENIDA DOUTOR STANLEY HO

A PANORÂMICA DO LAGO NAM VAN

聖地牙哥古堡
Pousada de São Tiago

芭朗瑪
La Paloma

A PANORÂMICA DO LAGO

臣園大馬路

西灣湖
Sai Van Lake

AVENIDA

RUA DO LAGO SAI VAN

士大馬路

孫逸仙

2

西灣湖景大馬路

聖方濟
各書館

時代商業中心

DA PRAIA GRANDE

澳門陸軍俱樂部
Clube Militar de M

何東圖書館

南華商業中心
京都

中央
中華
廣場

A. 大馬路
中央

澳

A. 大馬路
中央

新葡京
Grand Lisboa

聖若瑟修院
(三巴仔修院)
Theatre
五世
劇院

陳光記(羅保博士街)
Chan Kuong Kei
(Rua do Dr. Pedro Jose Lobo)

聖老楞
佐堂

澳氹前地

友邦廣場

亞利鴉士大馬路

AVENIDA DR. MARIO

中國銀行
大廈

AVENIDA D. INFANTE D'HENRIQUE

AVENIDA DE LISBOA

葡京
Lisboa

AVENIDA D

當奧豐素
Don Alfonso

粥麵莊
Noodle & Congee Corner

AVENIDA DOUTOR STANLEY HO

8餐廳
The Eight

高樓斜巷

音樂噴泉
Cybernetic Fountain

A DA PRAIA DO BOM PARTO

南灣湖
Nam Van Lake

法國餐廳
Robuchon a Galera

桃花源小廚
Tim's Kitchen

MACAU-TAIPA BRIDGE
澳氹大橋

永
W

帝雅廷
Il Teatro

岡田
Okada

永利軒
Wing Lei

3

A   B

新 口 岸
Outer Habour
Reclamation Area

鵰鷺碼頭
Legend Wharf

週阿密館

文化中心廣場

仙大橋路

AVENIDA XIAN XING RUA

AVENIDA DR. CARLOS D'ASSUMPCAO

ALAMEDA DR. CARLOS D'ASSUMPCAO

AVENIDA 24 DE JUNHO

南方大廈

1

菜斯
Rocks

港 新 埔
海 NAPE

美高梅金殿
MGM Grand

壹號湖畔
One Central

文華東方
Mandarin Oriental

寶雅座
Aux Beaux Arts
金殿堂
Imperial Court
食·八方
Square Eight

**參考下面
See below**

2

← 469m米 (比例尺 Scale 1:15,625) →

新 口 岸
Outer Habour
Reclamation Area

鳳明街
RUA DE PEQUIM

南方大廈

中華總商會大廈

澳門世貿中心

渔人碼頭
Fisherman's Wharf

金沙
Sands

RUA DE BERLIM

RUA DO GOVERNADOR

RUA DE PARIS

RUA DE BRUXELAS

RUA DE ROMA

RUA DE LONDRES

RUA DE MADRID

皇朝廣場

中珠大廈

博多利大廈

凱旋門
Arc de Triomphe

東南亞商業中心

德華廣場

珠江大廈

澳門回歸賀禮陳列館
Macau Handover Pavilion

文化中心廣場

澳門文化中心
Macao Cultural Centre

澳門藝術博物館
Museum of Art

萬利
Encore

咖啡廷
Café Encore
京花軒
Golden Flower

AVENIDA 24 DE JUNHO

AVENIDA DR. CARLOS D'ASSUMPCAO

AVENIDA SIR ANDERS LJUNGSTEDT

市日大廈

宋玉生廣場

3

NAPE

← 356m米 (比例尺 Scale 1:11,856) →

D

觀音像
Statue of
Kun Iam

← 627m米 (比例尺 Scale 1:20,909) →

Macau-Taipa Bridge
澳氹大橋

Sai Van Bridge
西灣大橋

澳海大馬路

海洋花園本馬路

Est dos Seal Tanques
海洋會所

Nordoette路

Estrada

玫瑰山莊

冰仔炮臺

冰仔雕塑
Taipa Monument

110.8

小潭山

Est Lou Lim Ieok

冰仔雕塑
Taipa Monument

史伯泰海軍

天政
Tenmasa
帝影樓
Ying

觀音岩

冰仔

澳門
University

將軍馬路

新濠鋒
Altira

菩提禪院
Pou Tai Un Monastery

Kwong Tung
百姓
Banza

柯維納馬路
Est Governador Albano Oliveira

澳門賽馬會
Macau Jockey Club

Avenida de

揚廉若

四面佛
Four-Faces Buddha

賽馬場
Macau Jockey Club

Av do Estadio

澳門
運動場
Stadium &
Aquatic Centre

奧林匹克
Stadium &
Aquatic Centre

游泳館

Taipa Village

葡國美食天地
A Petisqueira

安東尼奧
Antonio

新陶陶
San Tou

星光海運大馬路

Avenida dos Jagos da Asia Oriental

悅榕莊
Banyan Tree

大倉
Okura

山里
Yamazato

望德聖母灣大馬路 Estrada da Baia

蓮花海濱大馬路

Avenida de Cotai

西堤馬路 A MARGINAL FLOR DE LOTUS

珠 海 市
ZHU HAI CITY

路

人工濕地

通往珠海市，橫琴
To Zhu Hai City

蓮花大橋
Lotus Bridge

ESTRADA FLOR

PICTURE COPYRIGHT
圖片版權

70-Above & Beyond, 71-Agnès b. Le Pain Grillé (Central), 72-Ah Yat Harbour View, 73-Al Molo, 74-Amber, 75-Angelini, 76-Ba Yi/Michelin, 77-Bettys Kitschen, 78-Bistronomique/Michelin, 79-BLT Steak, 80-Bo Innovation, 81-Bombay Dreams, 82-Brass', 83-Café Gray Deluxe, 84-Michelin, 85-Caprice, 86-Casa Lisboa, 87-Celebrity Cuisine, 88-Celestial Court, 89-Cépage, 90-Chan Kan Kee Chiu Chow, 91-Michelin, 92-Chesa, 93-Michelin, 94-Chilli Fagara, 95-Chiu Chow Garden (Tsuen Wan), 96-Michelin, 97-Chuen Cheung Kui (Mong Kok), 98-Chuen Kee Seafood/Michelin, 99-City Hall Maxim's Palace/Michelin, 100-Crystal Jade La Mian Xiao Long Bao , 101-Crystal Jade La Mian Xiao Long Bao/Michelin, 102-Crystal Jade La Mian Xiao Long Bao , 103-Cuisine Cuisine at The Mira, 104-Cuisine Cuisine (IFC), 105, 106, 107-Michelin, 108-Din Tai Fung (Causeway Bay), 109-Din Tai Fung (Tsim Sha Tsui), 110-Domani, 111-Dong Lai Shun, 112-Dot Cod, 113-Michelin, 114-Dragon King (Kwun Tong), 115-Michelin, 116-Dynasty, 117-Fandango/Michelin, 118-Fan Tang/Michelin, 119-Michelin, 120-Felix, 121-Fofo by el Willy, 122-Fook Lam Moon (Kowloon), 123-Fook Lam Moon (Wan Chai), 124, 125, 126, 127-Michelin, 128-Fu Sing (Causeway Bay)/Michelin, 129-Fu Sing (Wan Chai)/Michelin, 130-Gaddi's, 131-Gaylord, 132-Gold by Harlan Goldstein, 133-Golden Bauhinia, 134-Golden Leaf, 135-Golden Valley, 136, 137-Michelin, 138-Grand Hyatt Steakhouse, 139-Grissini, 140-Hainan Shaoye (Causeway Bay), 141-Hakka Yé Yé (Causeway Bay), 142-Hakka Yé Yé (Central), 143-Harbour Grill, 144, 145, 146, 147, 148-Michelin, 149-Hoi King Heen, 150-Hoi Yat Heen, 151, 152-Michelin, 153-Hugo's, 154-Hunan Garden (Causeway Bay), 155-Hung's Delicacies/Michelin, 156-Inagiku (Tsim Sha Tsui), 157-Ippudo, 158-IR1968 (Causeway Bay), 159-Island Tang, 160-Jade Garden (Lockhart Road), 161, 162-Michelin, 163-Keung Kee Meat Shop (Wan Chai), 164-Kin's Kitchen, 165-Kwan Cheuk Heen/Michelin, 166-Kwan Kee Bamboo Noodle/Michelin, 167-La Marmite, 168-Michelin, 169-L'Atelier de Joël Robuchon, 170-Michelin, 171-Lei Bistro, 172-Lei Garden (Causeway Bay), 173-Lei Garden (Elements), 174-Lei Garden (IFC), 175-Lei Garden (Kowloon Bay), 176-Lei Garden (Kwun Tong), 177-Lei Garden (Mong Kok), 178-Lei Garden (North Point), 179-Lei Garden (Sha Tin), 180-Lei Garden (Tsim Sha Tsui), 181-Lei Garden (Wanchai), 182-Le 188°, 183-Lil' Siam, 184-Linguini Fini, 185, 186, 187, 188-Michelin, 189-Lobster Bar and Grill, 190, 191-Michelin, 192-Loong Toh Yuen, 193-Michelin, 194-Lung King Heen, 195-Madam Sixty Ate, 196, 197, 198-Michelin, 199-Mandarin Grill + Bar, 200-Man Wah, 201-Mask of Sichuen & Beijing/Michelin, 202-Michelin, 203-Megan's Kitchen/Michelin,

204-Mesa 15, 205-Ming Court, 206-Mirror, 207-Mist, 208-Nanhai No.1, 209-Nha Trang (Central), 210-Nha Trang (Tsim Sha Tsui), 211-Nicholini's, 212-Nobu, 213, 214, 215-Michelin, 216-Olé, 217-Michelin, 218-One Harbour Road, 219, 220-Michelin, 221-8½ Otto e Mezzo - Bombana, 222-Peking Garden (Central), 223-Peking Garden (Kowloon), 224-Peking Garden (Tai Koo Shing), 225-Petrus, 226-Pierre, 227, 228-Michelin, 229-Regal Palace, 230, 231, 232-Michelin, 233-Shanghai Garden, 234-Michelin, 235-Shanghai Xiao Nan Guo (Kowloon Bay), 236-Shang Palace, 237-Shek Kee Kitchen, 238, 239, 240, 241-Michelin, 242-Spoon by Alain Ducasse, 243-Spring Moon, 244-Steik World Meats, 245-St. George, 246-Summer Palace, 247, 248-Michelin, 249-Sun Tung Lok, 250, 251, 252-Michelin, 253-Sushi Sase, 254-Sushi Ta-ke, 255, 256-Michelin, 257-Tak Lung, 258-Michelin, 259-T'ang Court, 260-Tasty (Happy Valley), 261-Tasty (Hung Hom), 262-Tasty (IFC), 263-Tasty (Kowloon Bay), 264-Thai Basil, 265-Thai Chiu/Michelin, 266-The Bostonian, 267-EH/Michelin, 268-The Chinese Restaurant, 269-The Drawing Room, 270-Michelin, 271-The Press Room, 272-The Square, 273-The Steak House, 274, 275-Michelin, 276-Tim's Kitchen, 277-Tin Lung Heen, 278-Tokoro, 279-Tosca, 280-Trattoria Doppio Zero, 281, 282, 283, 284-Michelin, 285-Uno Más, 286-Wagyu Kaiseki Den, 287-Michelin, 288-Whisk, 289, 290, 291-Michelin, 292-Wooloomooloo Steakhouse (Wan Chai), 293-Xin Dau Ji (Jordan)/Michelin, 294-Michelin, 295-Xi Yan Sweets, 296-Yan Toh Heen, 297-Yat Tung Heen (Jordan), 298-Yat Tung Heen (Wan Chai), 299-Yellow Door Kitchen, 300-Yè Shanghai (Admiralty), 301-Yè Shanghai (Kowloon), 302-Yuè, 303-Michelin, 304-Yung Kee, 305-Michelin, 306-Zuma, 312-City Garden, 314-Conrad, 316-Crowne Plaza, 318-De Edge, 320-East, 322-Eaton Smart, 324-Four Seasons, 326-Grand Hyatt, 328-Harbour Grand Hong Kong, 330-Harbour Grand Kowloon, 332-Harbour Plaza 8 Degrees, 334-Harbour Plaza North Point, 336-Hullett House, 338-Hyatt Regency Sha Tin, 340-Hyatt Regency Tsim Sha Tsui, 342-Icon, 344-Intercontinental, 346-Intercontinental Grand Stanford, 348-Island Shangri-La, 350-JIA, 352-JW Marriott, 354-Kowloon Shangri-La, 356-Langham Place, 358-Lan Kwai Fong, 360-Lanson Place/Michelin, 362-Le Meridien Cyberport, 364-LKF, 366-Mandarin Oriental, 368-Metropark (Causeway Bay), 370-Nikko, 372-Panorama, 374-Royal Plaza, 376-Sheraton, 378-The Fleming, 380-The Landmark Mandarin Oriental, 382-The Langham, 384-The Luxe Manor, 386-The Mercer, 388-The Mira, 390-The Peninsula, 392-The Ritz Carlton, 394-The Royal Garden, 396-The Upper House, 398-W, 414, 415-Michelin, 416-Aux Beaux Arts, 417-Michelin, 418-Beijing Kitchen, 419-Belcanção, 420-Café Encore, 421-Canton, 422, 423-Michelin, 424-Don Alfonso, 425-Golden Flower, 426-Il Teatro, 427-Imperial Court, 428-La Paloma, 429-Lei Garden, 430-Litoral, 431, 432, 433, 434-Michelin, 435-Noodle & Congee Corner, 436-Michelin, 437-Okada, 438-Robuchon a Galera, 439-Michelin, 440-Square Eight, 441-Tenmasa, 442-The Eight, 443-Tim's Kitchen, 444-Michelin, 445-Wing Lei, 446-Yamazato, 447-Ying, 448-Zi Yat Heen, 454-Altira, 456-Banyan Tree, 458-Encore, 460-Four Seasons, 462-Grand Hyatt, 464-Grand Lisboa/Michelin, 466-Lisboa/Michelin, 468-Mandarin Oriental, 470-MGM Grand, 472-Okura, 474-Pousada de Mong-Há , 476-Pousada de São Tiago, 478-Michelin, 480-Sands, 482-The Venetian, 484-Wynn.

NOTES
備註

Manufacture française des pneumatiques Michelin
Société en commandite par actions au capital de 504 000 004 EUR
Place des Carmes-Déchaux – 63000 Clermont-Ferrand (France)
R.C.S. Clermont-Fd B 855 200 507

© **Michelin et Cie, Propriétaires-éditeurs**
Dépot légal Novembre 2011

Made in Japan

Published in 2011

E-mail : michelinguide.hongkong-macau@cn.michelin.com

Maps : (C) 2011 Cartographic data Universal Publications, Ltd / Michelin
Design : Akita Design Kan Inc. Tokyo, Japan
Printing and Binding: Toppan, Tokyo, Japan